LAFAYETTE

LAFAYETTE

HERO OF THE
AMERICAN REVOLUTION

GONZAGUE SAINT BRIS

Translated by George Holoch

PEGASUS BOOKS
NEW YORK

LAFAYETTE

Pegasus Books LLC
80 Broad Street, 5th Floor
New York, NY 10004

First Pegasus Books edition May 2010

Interior design by Maria Fernandez

Library of Congress Cataloging-in-Publication Data is available.

ISBN: 978-1-60598-087-4

10 9 8 7 6 5 4 3 2 1

Printed in the United States of America
Distributed by W. W. Norton & Company

LAFAYETTE

FOREWORD

I pity anyone who has not given
half his heart to Lafayette.
—JOSEPH DELTEIL

ECENT FRANCO-AMERICAN RELATIONS HAVE BEEN
afflicted with mutual misunderstanding. As happens
whenever warm feelings are succeeded by a dawning
sense of estrangement, the gap created by differences of opinion,
magnified by unequal status and disparity of circumstances, has
appeared unbridgeable. At the time of the invasion of Iraq,
Americans considered the French cowardly and ungrateful, while
the French saw the Americans as warmongers heading in the
wrong direction and destroying everything in their path.

Everything was different in the century of the Enlightenment,
when Lafayette embodied the highest qualities: the spirit of perfection allied to the spirit of progress, real courage and passion
in harmony with the sincere desire to promote both political and
philosophical progress. Both sides of the ocean experienced the
finest version of our exchange: the insurgents displayed the

bravery of pioneers in building a new world, while the kingdom of France was represented by the boldness and spirit of a young libertarian marquis notably lacking in caste prejudice and eager to do battle for the shared ideal proclaimed in Philadelphia, the ideal of brotherly love. It was the happy time of the Hero of Two Worlds, the go-between, when America looked toward Europe, when freedom and enterprise came together, under a combination of influences, in the formulation of an unprecedented model of democracy that for the first time proclaimed as a goal the pursuit of happiness. Since then, the old friendship has been shaken and the two-hundred-year alliance deeply troubled. While the two world wars had brought the countries together in shared sacrifice, recent events in the Middle East seemed for a time to threaten a definitive end to the alliance. But the realization seems to have been growing that a divorce would be futile between cousins estranged by the turmoil of immediate events or brothers temporarily divided by different interpretations of history. We have much to contribute to each other: lessons from a society founded on diversity and free enterprise where everyone has a chance to succeed, and those from an old nation that has remained young because it has never stopped believing in the reality and the future of its dream of liberty, equality, fraternity. With such powerful common and deeply intertwined roots, France and America are congenitally united.

Because of the incredible breadth of his career, Lafayette still embodies the spirit of freedom. His reputation is secure in the United States: forty cities, seven counties, and even a mountain bear his name. And in France, ever since the celebration of the bicentenary of the Revolution, he has enjoyed increasing favor in public opinion.

In a 2006 survey, he was rated favorably by 57 percent of respondents. In answer to the question: "Among the figures of the period of the French Revolution, which are those you view most favorably?" Lafayette came ahead of all the heroes of the period, even widely distancing Napoleon Bonaparte. A later survey confirmed his privileged position. Not only did Lafayette remain in first place, but he left far behind him, in a veritable rout, Danton and Saint-Just at 21 percent, followed by Mirabeau at 17, Louis XVI at 15, and Marat dead last at 8. Moreover, Lafayette drew only 6 percent of negative opinions, whereas Danton and Robespierre had twice as many enemies as friends.

Indeed, the principles of the Revolution appear to be the founding myth of national consciousness—70 percent of the French consider it a positive event in the long run—while the violence that ensued has been deeply rejected by our contemporaries. The leaders of the Committee of Public Safety are no longer admired. The very idea of terror as a means of government traumatized the French people. Lafayette is admired among all age groups and all political tendencies as much for what he excludes as for what he represents. In him, the French salute the hero of American independence, the champion of the rights of man, and a symbol of national union and freedom, along with an enemy of violence and intolerance. In the survey, the French condemned the shedding of blood; the national consensus has formed around the year 1 of the Revolution and not the excesses of the Jacobin period. At the time of the 1989 celebrations, domestic opinion came into agreement with international opinion, which had always taken 1789, not 1793, as the reference point for the French Revolution.

Two hundred fifty years after his birth is an appropriate occasion to present Lafayette as he was and to display the brilliance of his modernity, because he was in every way a man ahead of his time. It is not accidental that he enjoys such a favorable opinion today; it echoes the prodigious popularity and extraordinary acclaim he experienced in his lifetime. He was a champion of the rights of man who stood up for Indians and blacks in America and Protestants and Jews in France, and also fought for the Italians, the Irish, the Poles, the Belgians, and the Dutch. With the awakening of the nations, he showed his devotion to the idea of Europe. He anticipated a new political prototype, a man who synthesizes. Neither an extreme leftist nor a benighted conservative, he was an open-minded liberal and a dynamic centrist. The precocity he showed as major-general in the army of the United States at the age of nineteen marked his entire career.

Like a figure out of legend, Lafayette was a hero from the age of seven to seventy-seven; his celebrity was matched by the length of his active career. A media figure before the media existed, Lafayette handled crowds like a great communicator. For his entire life, he preferred popularity to power. He chose what he called "the delicious sensation of the smile of the multitude." This aspect of his personality has not always been understood or explained, and yet he constantly acted as a public relations agent for the cause of freedom. My aim is to do justice to this great man whose role has unaccountably been glossed over by history. Why has Lafayette been generally misunderstood, widely underestimated, and perpetually criticized? This man between two shores, two regimes, two worlds, was an extraordinary bridging figure whose value has been lost sight of, even though the great figures of his time eagerly testified to the major importance of his activities. He was of the generation that gave birth to a new world. When Voltaire presented Benjamin Franklin and John Adams to the Académie Française, he called them "the precursors in Europe of the Star of Liberty rising in America." It is fitting that the voice of a woman, Mme de Staël, was raised in defense of the hero of two worlds. When he was taxed with naïveté, she declared: "If this is how you incur the reproach of foolishness, may our men of intelligence for once deserve it!"

Surrounding the subject of this biography, I have attempted to paint the multicolored portraits of a galaxy of figures whose unique and fascinating personalities animated the two revolutions. An astonishing century seemed to be coming into being between the eighteenth and nineteenth, the century of Lafayette and his contemporaries in all their vivid contrasts. In this connection, it is worth considering Benjamin Franklin's description of Louis XVI: "He is the man I have known whose appearance merits Shakespeare's expression 'the milk of human kindness.'" In an unparalleled cast of historic figures, one can glimpse the paradoxes lying beneath the polished surface of history. While the principal figure is fascinating, I have been unable, as I have retraced his life—five kings, two revolutions, two republics, and an empire—to shake off the impression that I was witnessing the extraordinary spectacle of an age.

CHAPTER ONE

ENDGAME:
A TROUBLESOME CORPSE

A T THE CHÂTEAU DE VERSAILLES, ON MAY 10, 1774, AT 3:30 in the afternoon, a valet dressed in blue approached a candle that had been burning on the ledge of a balcony looking out on the Cour de Marbre since that morning and blew out the flame.

It was more than a signal, it was a message. Hundreds of watchful eyes had seen it and transmitted it throughout the palace and to the capital. By evening, all Paris was informed: one of the longest reigns in the history of France, fifty-nine years, had just come to an end with the death of Louis XV. It was a terrible death. On April 27, he was in the Petit Trianon, his palace of pleasures, with his favorite Madame du Barry, and a few courtiers, when he felt the first signs of a discomfort that continued to increase. There was talk of indigestion and fever, but until May 3, the king was told nothing about the real nature of his disease. The surgeon La Martinière had, however, recognized its seriousness by April 28, since he had not been afraid to declare with a bluntness that would have been unthinkable in any other circumstances: "Sire, you have to be in Versailles when you are ill!"

In Versailles implied in surroundings worthy of harboring the death throes of the most important monarch in Europe. In Versailles, death itself would be imbued with majesty. In the Petit Trianon it would be shameful and hidden. There was a time and place for everything, and the king understood that. The time for symbols had come. They would now be more important than realities and even more so than feelings. The favorite was immediately dismissed. Du Barry, who had represented in the public eye all the king's weaknesses, no longer had a place at Versailles. Vice left and virtue entered the room where the king would experience the degrading ordeals that smallpox inflicted on its victims. Virtue was represented by his daughters: Madame Adélaïde, Madame Victoire, and Madame Sophie, foul-tempered and conspiratorial old maids; the youngest, Madame Louise, who was in a convent, joined them. They watched over their father's last days with such devotion that they fell ill themselves after the king was buried. The Dauphin, the Dauphine, and the princes and princesses were kept away because of the risk of infection. The king wanted to have an edifying Christian end. He confessed his sins and publicly repented through the voice of Cardinal de la Roche-Aymon, head chaplain of Versailles, for having "scandalized his people," for which "he was heartily sorry." For the two final days, his body was covered with scabs and gave off an increasingly fetid odor that grew shocking, horrible, unbearable.

Fortunately, the intolerable odor did not reach Paris and the most delicate nose in France. Its owner grew up in a sunny southern province so aromatic that it was known as "the perfumed wench." He was born in Provence, surrounded by orange, lemon, and bergamot trees, and raised in the perfume town of Grasse. He was alert, witty, and passionate, a plump and high-spirited man. His refined nose breathed sensuality and took in all these aromas as invitations to happiness. He had breathed in the odor of paint in the studios of Boucher and Chardin and then the aromas of the royal court. He had traveled through the frivolous and sensual delights of society, and found happiness in the fragrances of pastoral masquerades and erotic encounters. This delicate, bold, and sensuous nose was joined to an acute painter's vision in the person of Jean-Honoré Fragonard.

Fragonard was born in Grasse, the luminous capital of perfume, and its light was a constant inspiration for his art. When he was six, his merchant father took the family to Paris. At thirteen, he was placed as a notary's clerk, where he spent more time drawing than copying documents. Recognizing this promising talent, his parents were acute enough to send him to the master of still-life, Jean-Siméon Chardin. He soon moved into the orbit of the celebrated and fashionable painter François Boucher, who suggested that he enter the competition for the Prix de Rome. He was accepted at his first attempt in 1752, with *Jeroboam Sacrificing to the Idols*. With the support of his new patron, Carle van Loo, head of the École Royale, he traveled to Rome, where he set up his easel. He examined the works of Michelangelo and glanced at those of Raphael, but he preferred the baroque masters Tiepolo and Pietro di Cortone to the giants of the Renaissance. His traveling companion through the cities of Italy was the young painter Hubert Robert, his fellow student at the academy. They drew views of the Roman countryside, and then moved on to Bologna, Venice, and Genoa. They shared a gentle passion for the delicate and gilded, the pink and blue of love and libertinage, creating masterly images of moments of beauty. When Fragonard returned to France in 1761 the Paris public saluted his talent, although his acceptance piece was transformed, by royal command, into a Gobelins tapestry. France was living through a refined decadence that recalled the Regency but was even more excessive. How better to react to the collapse of the banking system and the threat of instant ruin than by the pursuit of pleasure? Words mirrored the boldness of behavior and contemporary thought—the libertine spirit had found its champions: Crébillon, Restif de la Bretonne, and Duclos. Voluptuousness was everywhere, but it found sovereign expression in the paintings of Fragonard, ruling with subtlety and an air of freedom. Fêtes galantes, laughing masks, games of blind man's buff, furtive embraces in shady groves, and licentious conversations in secret rooms all seemed to anticipate *Les Liaisons dangereuses*. The bedroom became the theater of this society that turned the aesthetic of pleasure into high art. In *The Adoration of the Shepherds*, Fragonard depicted raw nature as a pastoral backdrop for the ballet of desire. As a poet of the erotic, he had no equal in transforming a natural setting into a theater of sensuality. The pinnacle of this earthly paradise was clearly *The Lock*, poised between reality and fantasy, the forbidden and the permitted. Is the door being bolted before or opened after the pleasures of love? Fragonard created a sequence of paintings for the last of the favorites of Louis XV, the Countess du Barry, intended to decorate her pavilion at Louveciennes, four panels of intense eroticism: *The Pursuit, The Meeting, Love Letters*, and *The Lover Crowned*, collectively known as *The Progress of Love*. It might be seen as his farewell to fleeting pleasures, a final embrace before the storm that would sweep away everything in its path, including the golden-haired royal mistress.

In the year of the king's death, Fragonard began to paint *The Fair at Saint-Cloud*, a commission from the Duke of Penthièvre, the legitimate son of Louis XIV and Mme de Montespan. This was the period of his most tender, domestic canvases, a period when he still knew nothing but happiness.

All of France was intoxicated with perfume. Ninon de Lenclos, Mme de Pompadour, and Mme du Barry covered themselves with scent, women adored violet and rose, and Jean-Jacques Rousseau consecrated the craze in a striking pronouncement: "The sense of smell is the sense of the imagination." The family trees of the great court dynasties were graced with marvelously aromatic flowers. The great families turned the court into a sweet-smelling bouquet. The intoxication with aromas was so powerful that Marie Antoinette, who loved violet and rose, capriciously imposed the use of scents on the men of the court. The men joined in, even the clergy, in a kind of high mass of aromas, powder, and lavender water. Powder for wigs, floral extracts, oils, pomades, creams, and soaps were all the rage. Scents seemed to make free-spirited women lose their heads; the wildest of them took baths of strawberry and raspberry, and washed with sponges soaked in milk. While the folly of perfumes ran its course, history was preparing its revenge: in the midst of the Revolution a perfume appeared insolently named "Elixir of guillotine."

Fragonard, too far from Versailles to have sensed the death of Louis XV—whose odor was so overpowering that the candles in the palace were said to have gone out by themselves—did however encounter the Revolution through his senses. His past companions, laughing dancers, flighty princes, and bold women, had disappeared. Many of his friends had been or were about to be guillotined. His clients belonged to a world that had literally been decapitated. Even his charming friend Hubert Robert was behind bars. Fragonard, now gray, survived and continued to paint, but he was out of fashion. Only the protection of David kept him alive and provided him lodging in the Louvre. His artistic career was at an end. A year before the Revolution, misfortune had struck like a warning. His daughter, Rosalie, a gifted painter who gave promise of a brilliant career, died at the age of eighteen. Fragonard was devastated and fell ill with acute gastroenteritis. When people spoke to him of his former appetite for life, he lifted his nose in the air, the nose that had taken in the morning mists and the perfumed twilight, and said: "Get by any way you can, nature told me when she pushed me into existence." The Revolution had shattered forms and revolutionized colors. The Goncourt brothers wrote: "Sunlight and smoke were mingled together; the temple was smoldering; day turned into night; the sun sank into the shadows emitting showers of flame. The emanations of a sulfurous fire illuminated the faces of the crowd. Clouds and fabrics swirled, horror showed in the way people stood and on their faces, and an immense cry seemed to arise from this entire temple. This cry, so new for the eighteenth century, was passion. The romance of Callirhoe traces the origin of art to Euripides; it showed a way forward for French painting: pathos."

Fragonard heard this cry from the window in the Louvre from which he gazed on December 8, 1793. The pathos his painting had anticipated had become an everyday reality in Paris toward the end of that terrible year. Every morning two or three tumbrils left the state's prisons to feed the bloodthirsty guillotine, and that day the neck of a pretty woman that had been covered with kisses by Louis XV had just been severed. The shedding of Mme du Barry's blood struck Fragonard with great force. He knew that the joy of life had ended when the infernal machine severed the head of his former patroness. Her decapitation, after she had begged the executioner for "just one more minute of life," signaled the end of a century that had been dedicated to delicacy and charm. At his window in the Louvre, Fragonard recoiled, attempting to deny the facts. He was like the horses refusing to advance down the streets of Paris because they had smelled the dreadful odor of the slaughterhouse. From that moment on, Fragonard did nothing; he considered himself dead. The most refined sensibility and the gentlest painter in France refused to even look at a canvas. The end of a perfumed world was ushered in by a tenacious odor of death.

Nineteen years earlier that same odor of death had filled the château of Versailles in the final hours of Louis XV. All doors and windows had to be kept open. The ordeal for the few loyal souls who approached the dying man was close to unbearable. The Dauphin Louis, duc de Berry, and his wife, Marie Antoinette, gazed briefly from a safe distance, then withdrew to their apartments, where they heard the news that made them the new king and queen of France; they went immediately to the royal residence in Choisy.

Hardly had the death been certified—the priests were still praying—when the stinking corpse, whose decomposition made embalming impossible, was set in a double-lead coffin after being doused with hydrochloric acid and swiftly carried off to the tomb of the kings of France in the crypt of Saint-Denis. But the remains of the king ironically known to history as Louis the Well-Beloved were not permitted to cross through the capital. The corpse, reeking despite the coffin, was hastily carried to the grave under cover of darkness in a carriage used for the hunt. The funeral procession contained only two others, one for the dukes of Aumont and Ayen, the other for the chaplain and a priest of Versailles. Pages covering their noses with handkerchiefs and carrying torches and fifty guards brought up the rear. The route chosen to go from Versailles to

Saint-Denis avoiding Paris bore the symbolic name of the Route de la Révolte.

It had been a wise decision to avoid ceremony for the funeral of Louis XV. Going through Paris would have risked provoking unfortunate demonstrations damaging to the position of France as a great power, for Louis the Well-Beloved had long ceased to be loved by his people. It was not so much the loss of India and Canada following the disastrous Seven Years' War, nor his disputes with the *parlements*, nor the expulsion of the Jesuits that was held against him: opinions were divided on these questions. What had made the king lose the respect of the majority of the French, especially of the population of Paris, the best informed in the kingdom, was the scandal of his private life. Dominated by his senses, the monarch had sacrificed the duties of his office to his pleasures. The trouble was not that he had mistresses—all kings did—but that he imposed his favorites on the court and that they interfered in policy. And the fact that they procured for their illustrious lover ever younger bedmates, often recruited from Paris brothels, went beyond all bounds. With the last of the "sultanas," Mme du Barry, to whom even the Dauphine had to defer, a disreputable world of procurers and swindlers had infiltrated the anterooms of power through the Deer Park and her notorious "little suppers."

Despite its pastoral name, the Deer Park so stimulated historians' imaginations that some of them thought it was a real château surrounded by a park. Jean-Charles de Lacretelle gave voice to this rumor: "It was said that the king had young girls of nine or ten brought there to be raised. Their number was beyond measure. They were given dowries and married off to base and credulous men." This image befitting a prince of pleasure and sovereign of sexuality was, however, far from the reality. At the time, the king had lost much of his vigor, and although he still had a fair number of mistresses, the Deer Park was by no means Bluebeard's Castle.

The Deer Park was neither a château nor a park dating from the reign of Louis XV but an enclosure set up by Louis XIII for the raising of deer. The walls were torn down late in the reign of Louis XIV, when a number of private residences were built in Versailles and new avenues laid out. A new quarter of the town had sprung up, and all the houses built there kept the name Deer Park. In 1755, a minor court official bought a small house on a dead-end street on behalf of Louis XV, declaring in the deed that it was "for the benefit of the king." A historian of Versailles, J. A. Leroy, notes the modest dimensions of the house: "In such a small house, it was impossible for more than one lady at a time to stay with her lady in waiting and one servant. It must be said that each one stayed for at least a year, because most of them left only to give birth to a child." When it is said of Mme du Barry that she went "from a place of debauchery to the royal bed," this refers to her activities before she knew Louis XV. As the Goncourt brothers point out, she worked as a prostitute for Jean du Barry. She may also have been under the control of two madams just a few days before encountering the king. At the time, everyone wanted to please the king by supplying young flesh. The Deer Park was known in licentious circles. Young women who had spent time there had increased value in the pleasure market; they were more desired and sought after than those who had not. The king's liaisons with lower-class women were numerous. His entourage sought discretion, but accidents did occur, for example at the time of the La Chalotais affair. It was feared that a secret exchange of love letters between the king and Mademoiselle de Romans might be revealed, provoking a political scandal. Activities continued in the Deer Park despite these dangers. In 1753, Marie-Louise Murphy became the king's mistress at the age of fourteen. She was the daughter of a cobbler and a street seller, whose sisters, according to the police, were on the game. Two of them had been camp followers with the army in Flanders, and three had been involved in various notorious licentious parties. The king's valet de chambre, Le Bel, who was in charge of populating the Deer Park, was heavily solicited, and the girls who pleased him were likely to be introduced to the king. Marais tells of Mme de Montréal, who had "a young girl she wanted to place in the Deer Park, and did everything in her power to succeed." Procurers sought out Le Bel, the king's provider. Even Casanova joined in, priding himself on offering Louis "a little slut who would be cleaned up for love." From 1755 on, women followed one another at the Deer Park at ever shorter intervals; the king was declining, caught in the web of the basest prostitution. A whole network had been established to serve his pleasures, including procurers, madams, and even great nobles such as Richelieu, all of whom labored to bring women and girls to Versailles for the king. The marquis d'Argenson wrote in 1756: "The king surrenders to nature and tries to stimulate his appetite with very fresh young girls brought to him from Paris. He takes pride in carrying off prostitutes of fifteen: they brought him one the other day who was half naked."

So the king's death inspired among the people, who were crushed by taxes, nothing but sarcasm, jeering, and rhymes in dubious taste, such as this very popular one:

> Smallpox a victory has won,
> And Louis now is gone.
> In ten days the small has got
> What the great pox in twenty years had not.

Idlers were heard mocking even on the steps of the abbey of Saint-Denis as the coffin was carried in: "Here comes the ladies' pleasure." On this day of mourning, under a bright spring sun, the cabarets and dance halls were full of customers.

In a sumptuous château in Touraine where he had been confined since late 1770 in great luxury, the lord of the manor shed no tears when he learned of the king's death; it might even be said that he greeted the news with quiet delight. This luxurious and brilliant great lord, a friend of Voltaire and the Encyclopédistes, whom Catherine II of Russia nicknamed "Europe's coachman," who was adored by the empress of Austria and a few other monarchs and feared by the others, was the duc de Choiseul, who had been the most powerful man in the kingdom, after the king. At the head of successive governments for a period of twelve years he had knitted the threads of international policy, sometimes without his master's knowledge, until the day when the king, under the urging of a peculiar coalition between the friends of the Jesuits and the friends of Mme du Barry, exasperated by Choiseul's thirst for power and his independent initiatives, decided to send him into indefinite exile on his estate of Chanteloup near Amboise. There he could meditate, indulge his taste for gardening, interior decoration, and reading, not to mention music, since he had an orchestra with which to charm his guests.

Having served with unquestionable brilliance—he can be credited with the acquisition of Lorraine and Corsica and the Dauphin's marriage—before being sent into luxurious retirement in a gesture of royal ingratitude, Choiseul in his memoirs judged the king with a severity that no historian of today would fully adopt.

After extensive study from which nothing ever distracted me, I saw the king, a man with no soul and no spirit, loving evil as children love to torture animals, with all the defects of the basest and least enlightened soul, but lacking the strength at his age to enable his vices to flourish as vigorously as nature drove him to express them; for example, he would have been delighted to watch Paris burn from Bellevue, but he would not have had the courage to order it done. He is incomparable in his vanity, a valet's vanity, raised to the highest possible pitch, but he does not have the strength to assert it, for he has the virtue of sensing that he is capable of nothing, and he inwardly acknowledges that his unfortunate character is lower than all characters in nature. I have heard him say that he was thoughtlessness incarnate, for, through foolish vanity, being jealous of his authority, he has no will and surrenders out of weakness to the will of the various ministers working with him; he shows them the most disgusting indifference no matter the issue and no matter the individual concerned; his vanity leads him to believe that to maintain his authority it suffices for him periodically to dismiss the ministers in whom he has shown trust, which is always enormous because he does everything they wish.

He believes that the splendor he displays in his love affairs is evidence of his authority and the servility that results a sign of submission; he regards resistance against the object of his fantasy as a lack of respect for the royal person; in this regard, he recognizes neither decency nor rank, shows neither consideration nor honesty; he believes that everything must give way before his mistress because he honors her with his intimacy.

The weakness of his soul, his timid air which is largely accounted for by his stupidity, his handsome figure which has the appearance of decency, his age, the example he should give to children as young as his, and the coming marriage of his grandson all pointed toward the rejection of the uproar caused by such a contemptible action as the [official] presentation of a woman said to be married, against all decency, to the infamous brother of a nobody, who ran a public school of swindling and prostitution in Paris.

It is understandable that rancor brought forth such merciless language from a great dignitary who had demonstrated loyalty and effectiveness. But setting aside his qualities as a statesman, Choiseul's morality was not so exalted that he could speak with such disdain of his former master. Had he not attempted to slip his own sister, Mme de Gramont, into the king's bed to increase his hold on the monarch? He, too, kept mistresses, while happily spending the fortune of his tender, intelligent, and patient wife, the daughter of a farmer-general and financier. But one should not forget that the age was marked by a libertine view, allied with the intelligentsia and with culture. The time of austere virtue had not yet come, if it ever truly would.

There was, however, one point on which the late king and Choiseul had been in complete agreement and that he might have recalled: the necessity of taking revenge on arrogant England, and of rebuilding a powerful navy for that purpose. The king and his minister also shared the conviction that a conflict between the British throne and the North American colonists was inevitable. Events over the preceding four years had confirmed their belief but had not produced their reconciliation. Five months before the death of Louis XV, in December 1773, angry Americans had dumped the cargo of tea on the British ship *Dartmouth* into Boston harbor. George III had responded to the Tea Party with very harsh repressive measures, which the Bostonians labeled the "Intolerable Acts." The port of Boston was shut down and local courts were barred from trying cases involving offenses against the Crown. By the time the king of France died in May, agitation had spread through most of the North American colonies outside Canada. The news, had it reached him in time, would have given the king a final pleasure. Within four months the first Continental Congress met in Philadelphia, and within eleven months the first bloody confrontations between British troops and American militia erupted in Lexington and Concord, signaling the beginning of a new era.

As his enemy's stinking corpse was hastily being buried, Choiseul hoped that he would play a prominent role in this new era. The new queen, Marie Antoinette, whose qualities and political intelligence he had the presence of mind to praise publicly, seemed to look favorably on him. Moreover, he was the friend of Voltaire, and the American patriots, whose action he had anticipated, were working for him. What happened to those hopes will be considered later.

We turn to an adolescent of sixteen, to whom the death of the king gave much food for thought. He knew everything about it from the account of one of the most respected and influential men of the court, who had had the signal and fearsome privilege of escorting the royal coffin from Versailles to Saint-Denis, and of having borne more than most the odor of the decomposing corpse. This distinguished figure was Duke François d'Ayen, and the young man, despite his youth, was the duke's son-in-law, married a month earlier to his daughter Adrienne, who was only fourteen and a half.

Himself the offspring of a notable family from Auvergne, the son of a colonel in the king's grenadiers who had died at the battle of Minden in 1759, the young husband was very interested in what happened in Versailles. Besides, he had had the honor of being reviewed by the late monarch when he was a cadet at the Military Academy.

Even though he was an accomplished courtier, the Duke d'Ayen was an enlightened man, who was very cultivated, fascinated by science, and in some ways close to the philosophes and liberal aristocrats with whom he fraternized in Masonic lodges.

The son of Marshal Louis de Noailles, the Duke d'Ayen had married Anne Louise Henriette d'Aguesseau in 1755. They had eight daughters, only five of whom reached adulthood, and two sons, who died young. Marie Adrienne Françoise, the third daughter, was the bride of the Marquis de Lafayette. The future hero could look on his father-in-law with sincere respect. His military record was impressive: a colonel of cavalry at sixteen, brigadier in 1770, and lieutenant general in 1784. He had fought at Fontenoy, Kehl, and Hastembeck, and ended his military career as Marshal of France. He was, in addition, a humane man who, when he served on the Supreme War Council, suggested reforms to improve soldiers' living conditions. A member of the Royal Academy of Science from 1777, he presented papers on physics and chemistry. But the duke also had the rare privilege of being a friend of the king's; as an accomplished courtier, he had been able to charm the monarch and become a close associate. They shared a passion for botany, and the duke often showed the king around his experimental garden in Saint-Germain-en-Laye. He was also beside the king at two decisive moments: as aide-de-camp at the battle of Fontenoy and as captain of the guards the night of the Damiens assassination attempt. His pleasant singing voice gained favor with Mme de Pompadour, and his witty remarks amused Louis XV even when they were at his own expense.

The duke spoke freely to his son-in-law, who looked on him as a father. Lafayette was told everything about the king's frightful death throes and his virtually clandestine burial. He also learned everything about the intrigues and cabals agitating the court, the role played in the final weeks by the king's daughters, ferocious enemies of the favorite, Mme du Barry. Despite their sanctimony, they were patrons of a clockmaker who had become famous (after repairing the Versailles clocks) through his talent as a dramatist and skill at public relations, Pierre-Augustin Caron de Beaumarchais, the author of *Figaro*. He would soon play a significant role in the international conflict in which Lafayette was to achieve lasting glory.

Lafayette could not, of course, predict the future. But he could reflect on both the immediate past and on what had occurred sixty years earlier. While Louis XV had indeed had a sad end, his great-grandfather and predecessor on the throne, Louis XIV, had not been mourned by the people either. They saw his death, according to Saint-Simon, as "an ardently desired deliverance." These two funereal episodes might well impel the young Marquis de Lafayette to reflect on the relative nature of absolute monarchy.

CHAPTER TWO

CHILD OF NATURE

I F THE END OF THE REIGN OF LOUIS XV CAN BE SYMBOLIZED without exaggeration by the horrible odor of the royal corpse, it is legitimate to locate the beginning of the reign of his grandson and successor, Louis XVI, and his sparkling wife under the emblem of perfumes. They were all the rage at court and in the capital. The young creator of scents Houbigant opened his shop in a fashionable quarter of Paris, drawing clients not only from the capital but from the provinces and even among fashionable foreign visitors. It was a must for women from England, Germany, Austria, Russia, Spain, and Italy, and their admirers. Everyone knew that the queen of France had a decided preference for violet and rose water, for delicate, fresh scents that were alluring rather than intoxicating. Less favored were heady, intense perfumes that were linked to perversity, love potions, and erotic witchcraft. The simplest flower scents were in fashion, in keeping with the renewed taste for nature inspired by Jean-Jacques Rousseau. Happiness moved out of confined and mysterious places into the woods and fields watered by springs and streams. Mills and sheepfolds became highly poetic places. The flowers that pretty women adorned themselves with, particularly in their hair, where they were set off by multicolored feathers, evoked youth, beauty, and the world of dreams. The reign began, with the king age twenty and the queen nineteen, in an atmosphere that fostered dreams. It seemed to be the sign of a new spring for both monarchy and nation. Exoticism enjoyed great success in literature, art, and fashion, because nature in the islands, and especially in America, was seen as richer, more favorable, more perfect, as if it were more natural than in the most fortunate regions of Europe.

One person whose almost violent attraction to nature owed nothing to fashion, to the fantasies that governed the imagination of the privileged and cultivated classes, or to the literature that nourished them was the young Marquis de Lafayette. Even though he had been in Paris for six years when Louis XVI acceded to the throne and had been enrolled (rather briefly) in a school for young nobles destined for great things, he remained in many ways a country boy, a child of nature.

He was born in the château of Chavaniac in a remote region of the Auvergne mountains on September 6, 1757. He was christened Marie Joseph Paul Roch Yves Gilbert Motier de Lafayette, baron of Saint-Romain, Vissac, and other localities, but was most frequently called Gilbert. The name was that of his father, a colonel in the grenadiers, who was fighting in Germany when his only child was born. He was killed by a British cannonball at the battle of Minden in 1759 in the midst of the

Seven Years' War, which had begun in 1756. The British commanding officer was named Philips, a name that Lafayette, who had no memory of his father, never forgot. Indeed he never forgot anything, kindnesses or offenses, although he was capable of forgiveness. His unfailing memory was linked to his great sense of loyalty that was universally recognized in his later life. Colonel Philips providentially reentered Lafayette's life, twenty-two years after his father's death, thousands of miles from Lafayette's birthplace.

The birth of a boy was at the time always a matter for celebration, especially in a household that was made up of four women: his mother, maternal grandmother, and the latter's two daughters, Charlotte and Madeleine. The four noble ladies were unsurprisingly delighted by the birth of the heir who, in two short years, became the head of one of the oldest families in France and allied to two of the most illustrious noble families in the country. Among his illustrious ancestors were a marshal of France who had fought with Charles VII against the English in the fifteenth century and, in the seventeenth, Mme de Lafayette, author of one of the greatest novels in the history of French literature, *La Princesse de Clèves*.

But this illustrious family was relatively poor, in a region that was poor and undeveloped, sometimes known as the "country of red cows," after the mahogany color of its cows. Chavaniac in the eighteenth century was a small village with houses resembling huts, with thatched roofs. In clear weather, the château, located on a height, commanded a panoramic view of the surrounding countryside. The soil was volcanic, the climate windy, rainy, and snowy, producing a sober and thrifty population that struggled endlessly to grow crops to feed itself and its livestock. The cautious and honest Auvergnats were known as peaceful people, but they were capable of fighting fiercely when called upon.

Lafayette's grandmother ruled over the château, which she had brought to the family in her dowry. It was not a fortress, nor was it an architectural masterpiece, rather a large pile with only twenty rooms, meriting the name château only because of its location, its towers, and particularly its history. At the time it did not have the appealing look it has now thanks to a series of restorations. Chavaniac was a very old building, parts of which had been restored as early as the fourteenth century. In 1701, following a disastrous fire, it was almost entirely rebuilt.

Lafayette's grandmother, Mme de Chavaniac, was a strict and kindly woman, who had an elevated idea of her duties as a chatelaine. She was hospitable when the circumstances required it but indifferent to society life. She governed the peasants as though she were a mayor, an administrator, and a company head, and when necessary, she acted as a doctor. She supervised the distribution of seeds, seedlings, fertilizer, and other farm supplies to ensure fairness; she defended the weak and comforted the suffering. She was not too proud to allow her grandson Gilbert to play with peasant children or to wear patched trousers that she had repaired herself. Her daughters assisted her in running the château and the village. Charlotte, the elder, a widow with a daughter one year older than Gilbert, who considered her a sister, was authoritarian like her mother and always wore a frilled cap. Both sisters were cultivated women interested in new ideas. They read Jean-Jacques Rousseau, who was not a model of Christian virtue but who wrote so well of the simple things around them. Lafayette's mother spent only the summers at Chavaniac, but her absence was filled for him by his grandmother and his aunts, who loved to chatter with him and read to him. Beginning at the age of five a Jesuit tutor taught him Latin. At night by candlelight, he liked to read Plutarch's Lives, the classic text that inspired generations of boys with a taste for action. After the Jesuits were banished in 1762, Gilbert was entrusted to Abbé Fayon, a modest and erudite man who was very attached to his pupil and taught him a great deal: history, math, geography, along with Latin, in which he was quite accomplished for his age.

But most of his years of childhood were spent outside the classroom in the surrounding woods, fields, and mountains. He took great pleasure in leading kids in expeditions into the country, climbing trees and cliffs, exploring the nearby forests that he knew like the back of his hand, and climbing to the bottom of the deepest ravines. He was in such need of physical activity that villagers compared him to a runaway horse that had broken its traces. He was an excellent swimmer who loved to challenge the swiftest river currents. He even knew the secrets of poaching game. Often, when his lessons were over, he would dis-appear for hours, reveling in solitude in the depths of the forest or at the top of a hill, contemplating the distant prospect like a romantic hero.

The air in Auvergne was very pure, and the scene before him was green and dark, echoing with the sounds of water. The fog covering the plains amid the volcanoes seemed to form solid waves of a blue ocean, a forecast of his future ocean voyages. The château to which he returned was surrounded by mountains populated by cows and woods full of wolves. Despite the harsh-ness of the surrounding countryside, the terraces overlooking the valley gave the château an air of Provence, or, thanks to the gar-dens, even of Italy. As an adolescent he put spiked collars on his dogs to protect them from the wolves, of which the region had many. He had great tenderness for domestic animals and hunted only to kill predators.

Aside from his times of meditation, daydreaming, or sporting activity, the countryside was not a place of leisure for him. Unlike a young aristocrat on a country holiday, Lafayette participated willingly in the work of the harvest. He did not lose consideration because of that, but was rather well-liked by the residents of the region, who remained attached to him throughout all his subsequent ordeals.

Just as the château was built on a height not as a challenge but to keep watch and protect, Lafayette saw himself as the protector of the peasants of Chavaniac and the surrounding countryside. For example, when as a child he joined in the wolf hunt, it was not only for pleasure but also to protect the possessions and the safety of the inhabitants, giving precocious evidence of the sense of chivalry that was one of the deepest and most constant aspects of his character. Even before he was ten, he dreamed of playing a great role in seeking and destroying the "beast" of Gévaudan, a monstrous animal that since 1765 had been devouring shepherds and shepherdesses as well as their lambs and sheep, not to mention calves and cows. He dreamed of the opportunity this would provide to demonstrate the heroism of his father and his ancestors, because the beast was known well beyond Auvergne. Its sinister exploits had been talked of in Marseille, Lyon, Paris, Versailles, and abroad, appearing frequently in the London papers.

This was an affair with international dimensions that had begun with a rumor. The bishop of Mende was the first person to make it credible, when, in January 1765, he spoke from the pulpit of the gravity of the danger posed by this man-eating animal and asked his parishioners to make public prayers for its disappearance. Hitherto unknown in France, was it not an expression of divine anger against the population of the region? The terror was so great that the first victim, a cowgirl, was buried without the sacraments. Deadly attacks proliferated and the most carefully organized hunts were fruitless. Even when wounded, the beast always managed to escape. Forty men on foot and seventeen on horseback, commanded by a Captain Duhamel, went through Gévaudan with a fine-tooth comb. The population was terrified, because the abuses committed by the dragoons during the repression following the revocation of the Edict of Nantes were still vividly recalled. But the unfortunate Huguenots were much easier targets than the beast. The dragoons feasted on the farms, where the frightened peasants could refuse them nothing, but there was no sign of the monster. Several people who had seen it and managed to escape were assembled, and on the basis of their testimony, excluding what seemed fantastic, a profile of the animal was drawn up. It resembled both a dragon and a hyena, with a broad black stripe on its back. An appeal was made to the greatest wolf hunter in the kingdom, M. Denneval, who had twelve hundred of the predators to his credit, with no result. The beast even attacked a horse and its rider. Emotion ran so high that the king sent his own gun bearer at the head of an experienced team, who finally killed the mysterious animal, earning him the cross of Saint Louis.

The beast was stuffed and presented to Louis XV at Versailles. There was not much resemblance to the profile—it was in fact a gigantic wolf, a monstrosity of nature weighing 130 pounds (the average wolf weighed 50) and measuring four feet eight inches from head to toe. The only element of the profile that was confirmed was the black stripe on its back.

A second beast appeared in the Margeride in 1767, and was killed by a celebrated hunter with the help of his three sons. Buffon viewed the remains and concluded that it was indeed a wolf. There was serious speculation later that a sadistic criminal had taken advantage of the wave of attacks attributed to the beast to commit murders with complete impunity.

In any event, Lafayette was much too young to join the

thousands of hunters mobilized to track down the monster, and he regretted it. And when another opportunity arose to conquer glory, he did not let it slip away.

But now the time had come for him to leave his cherished countryside. His mother, who spent most of her time in the capital with her father, the Marquis de La Rivière—an extremely rich and extremely miserly old man—insisted that he undertake serious schooling in Paris. Aware of the possibilities open to him because of his illustrious name, she had ambitions for her son. His aunts reluctantly saw him off, hoping that he would soon return to his home country, at least for vacation, although a carriage trip to Paris then took a week.

Lafayette was only eleven, so he was naturally accompanied by Abbé Fayon. His intellectual baggage was not very weighty, but the life he had led in the country had given him two assets that would influence his future. His sometimes violent physical exercise had shaped his body, and he had acquired a feeling for terrain and a sense of direction, so that he could adapt to extremely harsh conditions. Sleeping on a bed of moss or dead leaves, holding out for several days on short rations, confronting extreme cold, crossing freezing torrents, mastering a wild horse—none of it frightened or repelled him. He was therefore not in the least out of place several years later among American fighters: trappers, pioneers, woodsmen, to whom he showed that he was totally unlike the officers in powdered wigs and lacy sleeves who won their stripes in Europe in court intrigues.

Besides, his early experience of rural life in all its forms prepared him to become a model farmer when the vicissitudes of politics forced him to retreat to his land in order not to renounce his ideas.

CHAPTER THREE

A MILLIONAIRE ORPHAN

J ULIE DE LAFAYETTE, WHO HAD BEEN TRYING TO SOFTEN THE harsh character of her father the Marquis de La Rivière, had secured a place for Gilbert at the Collège du Plessis in Paris. She had no intention of allowing her son to become a country gentleman, however powerful the attraction nature held for him. The young woman, who was, of course, unaware that she was soon to die, saw herself and her grown and distinguished son at the court of Versailles, among the most brilliant figures of the nobility and noticed by the king and queen. She had no doubt that his name would secure him a prestigious position, but he had to be prepared to deal with society.

The first step was to deal with daily life in school. The building was dark and rather gloomy, and he found it especially distasteful because he had enjoyed such complete freedom in his childhood and because his mother and her interesting society were so nearby. But since the classrooms, each one identical to all the others, the dark corridors, and endless sessions of Latin conjugations were to make up his entire world for several years, he set to work with courage. His melancholy found consolation in poetry, and he even went through a phase of religious fervor that was short-lived and never returned. He got along well with his more sophisticated classmates, who looked down a bit on this countrified boy. He was not a star pupil, but he did well enough, particularly in Latin, literature, and history, and was disappointed not to be accepted in Greek class. He was an average student who satisfied his teachers, and he was proud to wear the school's navy blue uniform. He remained fond of handsome uniforms throughout his life.

The Marquise de Lafayette did not to go with her son to Versailles, did not attend his first ball, did not hear the flattering comments of the nobility about this fine young man. The winter of 1769–70 was fatal to the young woman with delicate lungs, who left Lafayette an orphan at thirteen. Gilbert may have found refuge in hard work. In any event he received scant comfort from his grandfather, who followed his daughter to the grave a few months later.

Lafayette would have had few memories of this harsh and austere old man but for the fact that, despite his youth, he inherited his grandfather's considerable and hitherto well-concealed fortune. It consisted of large tracts of land, forests, and farms in Brittany and the Val-de-Loire, shares in the Compagnie des Indes and other enterprises, and various bonds. All of these resources combined provided an annual revenue of 120,000 livres, the equivalent of more than $600,000.

Such a great fortune coming unexpectedly to a boy of

thirteen who, a few short years before, had been wearing patched trousers might have been expected to go to his head. It did nothing of the kind. This unexpected wealth did not console him for the loss of his mother and grandfather, nor cure his nostalgia for the countryside, but by providing him with the means for complete freedom of action it gave him an intoxicating sense of liberty.

From an object of slight condescension among his classmates, the marquis from Auvergne, looking oddly Scottish with his red hair, freckles, and blue eyes, became the center of attention. Although his fortune was carefully administered by his great-grandfather—who was still alive—and his uncle, they nonetheless allowed him to buy very fine horses. He generously loaned them to his classmates, who promptly forgot their earlier prejudices against him. That was his only revenge.

School discipline began to weigh on the young millionaire, but it was out of the question for him to run away. He was drawn above all to a career as a soldier, and as a compromise, while he continued his studies part time he enrolled in the training course for the king's musketeers—his grandfather had commanded a company of musketeers—while remaining a student at the Collège du Plessis. He remained a student officer until 1772, when he definitively left school.

In the summer, the wealthy orphan spent the vacation in Chavaniac. Despite his fortune, he conducted himself as before with his former peasant playmates. But although his home in Auvergne remained dear to his heart, he knew that his future did not lie in this corner of France. He was fired with ambition, felt called on to perform great deeds, and the paths of glory led through Paris and Versailles, not a small provincial town. With the end of vacation he was back in a musketeer's uniform. Like his fellows, he had taken a training course at the Military

Academy of Versailles and had had the honor of being inspected by the king. His direction remained to be determined.

The great fortune of the young student officer had, of course, drawn much greedy attention. His guardian and trustee were careful to protect him from entrepreneurs seeking capital. There were also families with daughters to marry off. In that age of arranged marriages, finding a suitable bridegroom involved serious and sometimes lengthy research, followed by difficult negotiations about material arrangements. Since divorce did not exist, consideration had to be given to the long term. If there were several sisters, the parents had to exercise a good deal of diplomatic tact and economic management. The higher one went up the social scale, the more delicate was the work of negotiation and settlement. Some families preferred to work through helpful intermediaries, family members or allies, noble ladies known as matchmakers, or worldly clerics. It was not unusual for a mother to begin thinking of her daughter's marriage when the girl tried on her first dress. In royal courts, future marriages were programmed. Marie Antoinette was promised to the grandson of Louis XV when she was only two. It would have been an anomaly had Gilbert de Lafayette—who bore an illustrious name, had a great fortune and good health, and was moreover an orphan and an only child, which greatly simplified things—not drawn the attention of families with daughters to marry.

The Duke d'Ayen was the first to set his heart on Lafayette. The elder son of the last Marshal de Noailles, he was a former soldier himself, with a pronounced interest in science. An excellent chemist, he became a member of the Académie des Sciences in 1777. He was also a great lover of opera and liberal ideas, although he was an accomplished courtier, and was married to Henriette d'Aguesseau. Of their five daughters, Adrienne, the third, was the one he thought of as a wife for Lafayette.

When he broached the idea to his wife, she was not overjoyed. This cultivated, very devout, and idealistic woman did not react with the cold, scientific reasoning of her husband. For example, Gilbert's fortune, a valuable asset in the duke's eyes, seemed to his wife to be a handicap insofar as its possessor had done nothing to acquire it and therefore could claim no merit because of it. That he was an orphan was a virtue for the duke, a drawback for his wife. Lafayette had no one to advise and direct him, and her daughter ran the risk of suffering because of that. Finally, the student officer was fourteen, and Adrienne was only twelve; wasn't she too young to get married? Thus, through no fault of his own, the unfortunate young marquis became the subject of a quarrel between the Duke and Duchess d'Ayen. But they quickly found the obvious solution: wait. Let the young people get to know one another and develop, if not maturity, at least a little more judgment and experience, and then they would see. Gilbert was invited to their home, a splendid building in a fashionable neighborhood of Paris near the present-day entrance to the Tuileries gardens. The mother, the daughter, and her four sisters all liked him, and the atmosphere was warm and welcoming. The duchess and her daughters, whom she called her "flock of doves," were a very harmonious group in which matters were discussed with a degree of openness that was rare in noble families of the time. The mother, a born teacher, never imposed her point of view but helped each of her daughters to clearly define her own and express it with elegance. They talked about everything: poetry, literature, travelers' tales, theology, all the while keeping their hands busy with embroidery or other women's work. The freedom of conscience and the sensibility of each of the children were respected. For example, when Adrienne did not wish to take her first communion because she did not feel mature enough to appreciate the importance of the sacrament, she was not forced to do so. A curious detail, considering the religious customs in a traditionalist family—although the duke was something of a skeptic—was that Adrienne did not take communion until after she was married.

In the household of the d'Ayen family Gilbert had found a home, and in Adrienne an admirer whose affections he had won without attempting to charm her; his seriousness, sincerity, and idealism quickly overcame the duchess's reservations. The marriage was celebrated in the Noailles family chapel on April 11, 1774, when Adrienne was fourteen and Gilbert sixteen. This marriage of convenience turned out to be the beginning of a great love match.

In 1773, looking ahead, the Duke d'Ayen, whom Gilbert, with touching and sometimes disarming sincerity, saw as a second father, had had his future son-in-law transferred to the Noailles regiment. The young man served there as a second lieutenant and then as a lieutenant, and after his marriage the duke secured from the king his appointment as a captain. He could not, however, actually command a company before he was eighteen. In the meantime, he developed his military skills in Metz, where the regiment was garrisoned under the command of the Prince de Poix, a cousin of the Duke d'Ayen. Poix himself was under the command of the Marshal de Broglie, the governor of Metz, another cousin of the duke.

In late May of 1774 in Metz, Gilbert learned that Adrienne was pregnant. He was overjoyed, but the pregnancy miscarried. He was finally able to rejoin his young wife in September. Emancipated by marriage and connected with the highest of high society, he lived in Paris and Versailles for the next eight months, a period when his personality began to assert itself.

CHAPTER FOUR

THE FORTUNATE BEGINNINGS
OF A TRAGIC REIGN

THE NEW KING AND QUEEN WERE WILDLY ACCLAIMED
when they arrived in Choisy after the death of Louis
XV. To demonstrate his confidence in the jubilant
population, the young king made the most felicitous gesture of
dismissing his guards. For the first time, he placed himself
under the protection of his subjects; it would not be the last,
but his other experiences did not turn out as well. For the
moment, the reign was in its euphoric phase: never had a royal
couple been so popular, so adored by all classes of society. This
exceptional level of affection should have been enough to cure
Louis XVI of his timidity and give him the assurance he had
lacked. But unfortunately this did not happen. The king was
truly frightened by the responsibilities that lay before him. As
though symbolically to put off the fateful moment when he

would take on absolute power in solitude, he postponed moving back to Versailles for three months.

⊸◇⊶

Louis XVI and the less straitlaced Marie Antoinette both admired the palace of Versailles, the glory of France that all crowned heads envied and some tried to imitate, but it was as though they were a little afraid of making it their permanent residence. Such luxury and glitter seemed hardly compatible with daily living. No setting was better than Versailles for prestigious displays designed to impress the audience, but it was much too ponderously formal for a young childless couple, themselves barely grown out of an overprotected childhood in which everything had been decided and organized for them and they had not had to think for themselves. Perhaps they felt nostalgic for such profound tranquility.

According to a well-established tradition, Versailles was the location of royal folly, where everything was sacrificed to display, formal ceremonies, and never-ending costly celebrations. In Versailles, a bloated society of courtiers and parasites of all kinds drifted from festivity to festivity and lost fortunes on gambling or mere whims, neglecting affairs of state and remaining indifferent to the suffering of the people.

The Versailles of Louis XVI did not in fact entirely correspond to this picture. The king, who had a truly complex personality, wished to reduce as far as possible the degree of formal representation incumbent on him. He was a kindly and devout young man far removed from the vanity and megalomania characteristic of men of power. He felt great concern for the unfortunate, and no king had ever been so zealous in relieving the poverty he encountered. Had he not inherited the crown in the simplest way, he would have engaged in no intrigue to win it. At the time his older brother the Duke of Burgundy died in 1761, when Louis was only seven, he was told that this family misfortune was above all a tragedy for France, because this brother, whose place in the order of succession he then took on, was vastly more gifted than he to assume the highest office a man could dream of on earth.

This ill-considered way of making the new Dauphin feel guilty affected the unfortunate development of the child's character to the extent that he seemed frightened by major responsibilities. At the age of thirteen, he noted: "The most terrible burden is the burden of absolute power." Either because of his natural timidity or because he thought a certain style of ceremony was out of date—he was a keen observer of social mores—he wished to make life at Versailles simpler than it had been in the past, all the more because he liked simplicity for itself. As for Marie Antoinette, however imbued she may have been with her dignity as queen, however haughty, capricious, condescending, or inflexible she might occasionally be, she had nonetheless been brought up in Vienna, where imperial society, though formal, was rustic in comparison with the rituals of Versailles. The rules of court protocol were so strict and complicated that the Countess de Noailles (the great-aunt of Lafayette's wife Adrienne) had to constantly tutor the queen in their operation. Marie Antoinette found them oppressive from the outset and christened her tutor Madame Etiquette. She had suffered from them when she was just the Dauphine, and things could only be worse now that she was the queen. She attempted to change the pompous, almost comical performances of the *lever* and the *coucher*, in which various items of clothing had to pass from hand to hand following a strict hierarchical order before reaching the queen. It made no sense to mobilize great ladies and numerous servants for such ordinary, everyday matters. It was not that Marie Antoinette was drawn to austerity. On the contrary, she loved luxury in every form: spectacles, diversions, gambling, any kind of amusement. She would have liked life to be one continuous party, on the condition that she could move freely and be royally at her ease. She could, however, appreciate grandiose celebrations when they marked a special occasion, such as her marriage to the Dauphin on May 16, 1770.

France had not seen such a brilliant celebration since the reign of Louis XIV. For the king and his right-hand man, Choiseul, the thoughtful and determined architect of the match, the organization of the event was to show the world that seven years after the disastrous Treaty of Paris following the British defeat of France the country had completed its economic recovery and once again become the greatest power on the continent. To impose this image, to successfully carry out what might well be called a media campaign, Louis XV had spared no expense, despite the dismal state of the treasury. No king had ever gone so far in setting the stage. The master of ceremonies insisted that the usual temporary structures be replaced by lasting transformations. An opera auditorium that could be transformed into a ballroom was created in Versailles. With the use of mobile mirrors, the palace rooms were made into integral elements of the forthcoming spectacle. Large numbers of gold statues were scattered about, along with buffet tables inside and in the park for the evening festivities, the culmination of this grand spectacle, in which the noble guests, unaware perhaps, played perfectly choreographed roles as extras. Dinner was served in the new opera auditorium, illuminated by chandeliers hanging from ropes decorated with flowers, with blue silk wall hangings beneath a ceiling representing Apollo and the muses. The royal musicians played constantly from beginning to end of the festivities. The guards were dressed in Turkish uniforms and sang exotic tunes in the galleries. The subtle play of mirrors reflected the scenes in which the guests were themselves the players. The evening festivities were postponed for three days because of rain, but they amply rewarded the people, who for once could freely enter through the gates of the château; the curious population from Paris or elsewhere could enter at will provided they were correctly dressed. Thousands of Chinese lanterns had been distributed around the park, and brightly lit triumphal arches illuminated the grand canal on which drifted richly decorated gondolas carrying musicians, behind curtains, who serenaded passengers sailing toward a dream world. Virtuoso pyrotechnics displayed unprecedented fantastic visions in the sky. Late into the night the crowd was literally transported into another world by the perfection of the celebration, forgetting that it would return to earth the next day.

Not wanting to be outdone and wishing to assert its status as capital of the kingdom, Paris organized another fireworks display on the banks of the Seine that some hoped would outshine the pomp of the nearby town, which would have been insignificant were it not for the château. Unfortunately, the great city's nocturnal triumph turned into a tragedy because of its very dimensions. The crowd on the rue Royale grew so dense and was so eager to reach the river's edge that 132 people were crushed or trampled in the confusion. The stricken Dauphin gave up the funds he received each month for his personal expenses to provide for the families of the poorest victims.

Marie Antoinette's entire life unfolded under the sign of festivities, but they were all illusory. It began when she was first welcomed in France by Cardinal Rohan at the bishop's palace in Strasbourg on May 7, 1770. The building's contrasting white and pink sandstone, harmonious proportions, and triangular pediment all enchanted her. Her windows looked out on a magnificent prospect of rows of trees and houses reminding her of the view from the palace of Schönbrunn. But this first familiar prospect was in reality an artifice designed to make the Dauphine feel at home: a painted canvas concealing little Alsatian houses on the other side of the river Ill. Even the river had been hidden by rafts and pontoons covered with banks of flowers to make the illusion complete. Thus began her reign, with a visual lie designed to hide the truth and offer her the artificial pleasure of an existence intended to resemble her dreams.

Marie Antoinette experienced an even more extraordinary celebration than her marriage with the coronation of her husband, a ceremony that lasted for several days in June 1775 in Reims, the "holy city" of the absolute monarchy. Despite his inclination toward simplicity, from a sense of duty and religious conviction, Louis XVI participated in this mystical and political demonstration in the course of which every gesture and every element of the setting held symbolic value. It was another great display in which medieval customs and the forces of modernity—nascent industry, navigation, trade—were alike glorified. The venerable cathedral was transformed into an extraordinary stage set. All the nobility of France was there, with Turgot, whose star had faded, rubbing shoulders with the illustrious outcast of the preceding reign, Choiseul, who hoped that his time had come around again, a hope that would be dashed by the end of the ceremonies.

The king, who entered the city in a special carriage inspired by Apollo's chariot, decorated with motifs from mythology, submitted to the exhausting ritual with patience and sweetness. At dawn on the day of the coronation, which had been preceded by religious ceremonies and official dinners, he was awakened, following the tradition, by two bishops. They had to be told twice: "The king is sleeping." The third time, he got up and, supported under the arms by the eminent messengers, was led to the cathedral, where he was greeted, to the sound of great fanfares, by Monseigneur de la Roche-Aymon, the archbishop of Reims, and the rest of the clergy. After taking various oaths—to maintain the peace of the Church, to uphold justice, to prevent plunder and dueling, to exterminate heretics—the king witnessed the blessing of his crown and scepter. Then the king was partially undressed and the archbishop anointed him five times with the holy oil from a vial, making him into a figure invested with religious and supernatural powers. Emotion was at its height. The envoy from the Sultan of Tripoli suffered a nervous breakdown and began to scream—he was quietly removed. Another, less noticed, incident had occurred earlier: the Count d'Artois (the future Charles X) had dropped his own crown in the church and had been unable to stifle a curse. But these lapses took nothing away from the scenic and symbolic grandeur of the event. Restoring a custom that had terrified his grandfather Louis XV and overcoming his disgust, the new king used his miracle-working power to touch 2,400 victims of scrofula. Despite having to touch purulent wounds and scabs, he held out to the last, and numerous rapid cures were recorded, justifying his brave action.

In another impressive detail of the ceremonies, after the king was enthroned, amid cheers and fanfares, eight hundred caged little birds were released. Witnesses interpreted this flight to freedom as a symbol of the freedoms the French would enjoy under the reign of an "enlightened, just, and beneficent prince.

One might have expected an enlightened prince to omit taking the oath to exterminate heretics, as Turgot had suggested in a very dignified letter. The king rejected the suggestion, not justifying the oath but pointing out that it was "less trouble to change nothing." The king indeed saw it as a purely formal oath. He did nothing subsequently to exterminate heretics and even took steps to restore to Protestants at least some of the rights that Louis XIV had taken away with the revocation of the Edict of Nantes a century earlier.

The coronation, which the king had wanted to be the same in every respect as past coronations, hence refusing to have it conducted in Paris, had certainly been a great spectacle, but it had not been enough to restore to divinely ordained absolute monarchy an unquestionable legitimacy based on unanimous consensus and total surrender to divine will. During one of the ceremonies in Reims, the solemn vespers, the archbishop of Aix preached that the king had to govern by following the laws and advised him not to fear contradiction. Contrary to custom, the archbishop's sermon was not published, and Condorcet commented that of all futile expenditures, the coronation had been the most futile and the most ridiculous.

Aside from the great official ceremonies involving visits of foreign royalty and the like, Versailles was also the scene of celebrations in the nature of pure diversions, from games of chance through balls and picnics to opera performances. The queen grew bored with a serious, stay-at-home husband whose only form of relaxation was hunting, but she had no trouble finding people ready to help her amuse herself. There was first her brother-in-law, Artois, as cheerful, carefree, and skeptical as his elder brother was serious, conscientious, and industrious. Married to Princess Marie-Thérèse de Savoie, as ugly as she was dull-witted, he, too, needed and found distractions. His mistress, Mme de Polastron, had very gay and sociable family and friends who, so to speak, conquered the queen. Most prominent among them was the ravishing Gabrielle de Polignac, who soon became so inseparable from the queen that their relationship became a subject of gossip. They included her complacent husband, Jules, her handsome lover, her sister-in-law, a constellation of nobles and party-goers, and finally the enormous Count de Guines, the ambassador to London, whom Turgot later recalled because of his scandalous conduct. What might be called Marie-Antoinette's "gang" were in complete agreement about how to pass the time in the best way possible. With her friends and some others with solid fortunes, the queen frequently risked large sums at faro, which was very popular at the time, setting up the card table in one of the salons of the palace.

She loved dance, theater, music, and opera and often had concerts in her private apartments, at which the most advanced music of the day was performed. This did not prevent her from frequenting, along with Artois and other close friends, the celebrated balls at the Opera in Paris. She was often criticized for going to masked balls, which gave rise to equivocal situations.

It was during one of these episodes that she first encountered the young foreigner who was to play an important role in her life. Stefan Zweig gave a masterly description of the romantic meeting of these two extremely attractive figures on that romantic evening. The young man was Axel de Fersen, who was Swedish, the son of a senator, and the heir to a great family; after a journey to Italy, he had just met Voltaire at Ferney. Marie Antoinette was masked and, delighted at being unknown, was able to act with complete freedom. The sylph and the handsome young man were both eighteen. This is how Zweig describes Fersen:

> To the advantages of blue blood, high personal standing, shrewdness and commonsense, wealth, and

the nimbus of a distinguished foreigner, there were added in Axel de Fersen's case the exceptional merit of being a remarkably good-looking man. Upright, broad-shouldered, muscular, he was a typical Scandinavian in build, virile without being stout or massive. In his portraits, we cannot help being charmed by his frank expression, his regular features, his thoughtful eyes, surmounted by well-arched and thick black brows. Add to this a broad, finely shaped forehead, and warm red lips—which knew the value of silence. Here was a man to arouse both the love and the trust of a passionate woman. Fersen does not, indeed, seem to have shone as a conversationalist, as a wit, as an amusing companion; nevertheless, his somewhat dry and homely intelligence was set off by sincerity and natural tact. As early as 1774, King Gustavus III's ambassador in Paris reported to his royal master: "Of all the Swedes who have visited this city during my term of office, Fersen has secured the best reception in the great world."

There was nothing morose or fastidious about this young gentleman; the ladies believed him to have a "cœur de feu" beneath an icy exterior. He did not forget to amuse himself in Paris, becoming a regular attendant at court balls and the receptions held in the best houses.

Zweig goes on to describe their first meeting:

In the course of these relaxations, he had a strange adventure. One evening, on July 30, 1774, at the Opera ball, where the "monde" and the "demi-monde" rubbed shoulders, a slender young woman who moved as if on wings and was richly apparelled, accosted him without introduction, and, under cover of her mask, opened a lively conversation. Fersen, flattered by thus being singled out, responded in kind. The conversation assumed a gallant tone. He found the lady to be endowed with a stimulating personality, and perhaps had begun to entertain fantasies of a night that would be signalized by "bonne fortune." He could not, however, fail to be struck by the fact that he and his partner had become encircled by ladies and gentlemen who were exchanging eager whispers, and were regarding the pair with lively attention. When, at length, the situation began to grow embarrassing, the young woman who had been flirting with him thought best to remove her mask. It was Marie Antoinette! Forsaking the tedious couch of her sleepy spouse, the Dauphiness had driven off to the Opera ball and had entered into conversation with this handsome stranger. Such an incident was unprecedented in the court annals of France, and Marie Antoinette's attendant ladies did their utmost to ensure that it should not attract too much attention. Surrounding the escapee, they promptly conducted her back to her private box. But what could be secret at Versailles? There was much whispering, much astonished conversation about the Dauphiness's breach of etiquette in thus showing favour to an unknown cavalier. It seems likely enough that next morning [Ambassador] Mercy may have written a distressful letter to Maria Theresa, to which the response may have been the sending of a special courier from Schönbrunn to convey one of those censorious epistles to the "giddy-pated" daughter, telling her it was time for her to put an end to her unspeakable "dissipations," and to cease from entering into conversation with unintroduced strangers at those abominable masked balls.

However that may be, Marie Antoinette had had her own way; the young man had pleased her, and she had made the fact plain to him. Thenceforward the youthful Swede, though by no means of outstanding rank or position, was always a welcome guest at Versailles balls and receptions. Are we to suppose that, as an immediate sequel of the acquaintanceship begun under such favourable auspices, the pair conceived a passion for one another? We do not know.

While Marie Antoinette loved dancing, either to dance herself or as an admiring spectator of ballet, her preferred amusements were theater and opera. She had her own theater, which moved back and forth between the Petit and Grand Trianon. The Comédie Française and the Italian troupe took turns performing every week, covering the entire repertory from Racine to Goldoni. The queen loved the stage so much that she did not hesitate to perform herself, and not in the roles of princesses of tragedy. She was applauded by an exclusive audience in the role of a soubrette in *La Gageure imprévue* by Sedaine and as Rosine in *Le Barbier de Seville* by Beaumarchais, hardly a conservative author. Although she detested democratic ideas, she ordered a performance of *Le Devin du village* by Jean-Jacques Rousseau—a writer that her executioners would invoke as a precursor—in her private theater.

As the years passed, her pastoral tastes grew stronger,

reaching their peak when she set up a hamlet with a wooded hill, stables, a sheepcote, a cheese and butter workshop, a flour mill, and a country inn where everyone sang in chorus as in the suburban Viennese inns it was modeled on, while the proud queen, wearing a bonnet and an apron, served lemonade.

CHAPTER FIVE

VERSAILLES
THE PALACE OF PLEASURE

T HE RANGE OF DIVERSIONS AT VERSAILLES UNDER LOUIS
XVI was far from the corrupt pleasures of the preceding
reign, the Regent's orgies, and the Deer Park of the aging
Louis XV. It took the malice, the bad faith, and the vulgarity of
authors of pamphlets and songs just before and during the Revolution to make the château of the Sun King into the symbol of
depravity, an aristocratic Gomorrah where the honor of the
monarchy had been overwhelmed.

This was the Versailles that Lafayette discovered when he was
presented by his mother-in-law, the Duchess d'Ayen, who loved
him "like a son." The Noailles family was fully integrated into
the court. The duke had an apartment in the château and a
house in town where he and his wife gave sumptuous dinners at
which Lafayette and his wife, and the family's other married
daughter and her husband, were the guests of honor. With such

an introduction, Gilbert, who often danced the quadrille with Marie Antoinette, became a prominent figure in a court that valued youth above all, so much so that the queen publicly declared that people over thirty ought to have the decency to no longer show themselves in Versailles. The king, of course, displayed no such insolence, obliged as he was to entrust the highest responsibilities to men of experience. In the first rank of them was M. de Maurepas, born in 1701, whom the queen treated with some condescension.

The queen no doubt found that Lafayette lacked some of the social graces, that he was a bit of a provincial, not to say a rustic, and that he failed to meet her high standards for dancing. She nonetheless thought that he must have hidden talents, since her entourage seemed to take pleasure in his company and spoke most highly of him. At first sight, it might seem strange that the serious Gilbert, who dreamed of accomplishing great deeds and who had found happiness at the age of sixteen with an extraordinarily devoted young wife, was attracted by a group of skeptical and blasé sensualists whose only law was pleasure. One might suppose that he was the victim of an intrigue out of *Les Liaisons dangereuses*, the scabrous novel by Choderlos de Laclos, friend and adviser to the Duke d'Orléans (the future Philippe Égalité), who reigned at the Palais-Royal in Paris, as his cousin Louis XVI reigned at Versailles. In this center of unbridled pleasure, gastronomy, and fashion, the duke was an amused spectator of the ferment of new and subversive ideas and a constant flow of amorous intrigue and society gossip. But Gilbert was a willing visitor to the Palais-Royal, located near the Noailles home in Paris, and there was no manipulation behind his association with lowlifes. He stepped onto the slippery slope that led to adultery only a few months after his marriage because he freely decided to imitate his new friends. Since the men around him, bearers of great names who could look forward to bright futures, were cheating on their wives, he would do the same. He followed them to the cabarets where he imitated their drinking; showing off his ability to hold his liquor became a matter of pride. His older brother-in-law, Louis de Noailles, was in no position to criticize his behavior. Recently married, and a cultivated man, he was already a confirmed sensualist who in fact set a bad example. One night as friends were carrying a drunk Gilbert to his carriage, he said: "Tell Noailles how much I drank."

It was such an accepted practice for men to cheat on their wives that a faithful husband was seen as a simpleton or a sanctimonious prig and even suspected of being impotent. Since they had often been married off without being consulted, wives may have been more justified in rather openly poking holes in their marriage contracts. The colonel of Gilbert's regiment, the Prince de Poix, was amiably cuckolded by his wife, a tall and rather attractive woman who found it inconceivable that she could remain faithful to such a short man; he accepted the situation with a great deal of detachment. Even Lafayette's father-in-law, the Duke d'Ayen, was far from being a model husband, although he had the good taste to be discreet.

It was easier to drink large quantities of champagne to demonstrate one's ability to hold liquor than it was to win the heart of a suitable mistress. Chambermaids and minor actresses were available to any gentleman, especially if he was young and amiable, but women commanding greater prestige were too sought after by the most powerful aristocrats to be susceptible to the blandishments of the young and inexperienced. Lafayette realized that to impress his companions he had to aim high. Encouraged by a few minor successes, he thought he could approach any one of the Versailles celebrities, and he did indeed aim high. He set his sights on Aglaë d'Hunolstein, whose husband commanded the regiment belonging to the Duke de Chartres. Aglaë was attached to the duchess, which did not prevent her from being the duke's mistress. Lafayette had aimed too high: Aglaë was known to love all forms of diversion and was hardly drawn to a naïve young man who was barely eighteen. But Lafayette had peremptorily decided that he was mad about her and he loudly and publicly proclaimed his infatuation, not understanding that he risked making himself ridiculous, a crime at court ever since Saint-Simon had declared: "Ridicule is more dishonoring than dishonor." That is indeed what happened when, imagining that his friend Ségur was as smitten as he with the same lady, he challenged him to a duel. Ségur managed to persuade the apprentice seducer to open his eyes, and Lafayette began to back off. For a while he was content to spend nights at the Opera with his band of friends, sometimes joined by the queen, the Count d'Artois, and the king's other brother, the Count de Provence (the future Louis XVIII). They sometimes extended their forays into nearby hamlets known for cabarets that used to cater to a popular clientele and had recently become fashionable among the aristocrats of Paris and Versailles.

When the queen accompanied Lafayette and his friends to L'Épée de Bois in the hamlet of Les Porcherons, the queen had to be extremely discreet and disguise her identity. One form of amusement they indulged in was to perform parodies; one night they put on a mock session of the Parlement, the venerable institution whose conflicts with royal authority were always in the news. The Count d'Artois played the role of the presiding officer, and Lafayette, with surprising verve, that of the prosecutor general. At the time, representation of official figures was close to aggression, if not sacrilege. Since police surveillance was thorough, the episode was known to everyone the next day, and the chief minister Maurepas seized the occasion to ask the king to bring the frivolous young aristocrats into line in the name of the respect owed to institutions.

Maurepas finally had an opportunity to slap the wrists of these scatterbrained aristocrats who, taking shelter behind the queen, thought they could freely mock him and the king's officers who had worn themselves out in his service. But Maurepas had been outflanked by Ségur, who had recounted the episode to the king. Louis found it rather amusing and answered his minister with the observation that youth must have its fling.

The Duke d'Ayen was not very pleased with the unexpected way his son-in-law was turning out. He appreciated it even less because, having planned to place him in the household of the Count de Provence, he had just found out that at a masked ball, Lafayette had pretended not to recognize the king's brother beneath his disguise and had used the occasion to make fun of him.

The disguise was not enough of an excuse, and Gilbert had gone too far. His father-in-law's plan was wrecked, and he decided to send Lafayette back to Metz to rediscover the military discipline that the ceremonies of Versailles and his diversions at the Palais-Royal and in the cabarets had made him forget. Adrienne would have to swallow her tears.

CHAPTER SIX

THE ROUNDUP IN METZ

I N THE DIM STREETS OF A GARRISON TOWN IN LORRAINE, piercing cries of distress followed by a thunder of boots on the pavement suddenly troubled the usual calm of evening. Alerted by these troubling noises, the residents opened their windows to see women in unbuttoned brightly colored dresses running down the street, holding their skirts above their knees to avoid tripping. These unfortunates were pursued by armed soldiers yelling insults and futile commands to halt. Some were caught and immediately and roughly attached by the wrist to others already captured. Others managed to get through unlocked gates and hide in the corner of a garden, in a stable, or a barnyard. But they would not be able to escape for long. After the pursuit in the streets, the soldiers would move on to searching houses, and the fugitives knew they could hardly count on the complicity or compassion of the population. The scene of these unpleasant events was Metz. The Marshal de Broglie, governor of the region, with no Prussians to fight against, had decided to launch a great roundup to rid the city of its numerous prostitutes, with whom his men were too eager to seek a solace that their lack of action did not at all justify.

Almost sixty, De Broglie, who had fought valiantly in the Seven Years' War, had allowed his time as head of Louis XV's secret service, Le Secret du Roi, to go to his head and developed a taste for international intrigue. The existence of this service had been revealed only at the death of the king, after operating for more than twenty years under various directors. It involved secret diplomacy, managed by thirty-two individuals, supervising ministers and increasing French influence wherever they could. It had ways of maintaining ties with Russia and Austria, and through oral reports, the interception of letters, and coded correspondence, it conducted parallel diplomacy. It worked successively on planning a French landing in England shortly after the Seven Years' War and on supplying arms to the American insurgents under the nose of the English ambassador, thanks to the clever duplicity of Beaumarchais. It played a major role in the American War of Independence and also strove to influence the foreign policy of European nations.

All decisions were made in the central section of the château, more precisely, in the king's apartment. It was in the ornately decorated room known as the Cabinet du Conseil after 1755 that Louis XV presided over meetings that, among other things, decided on a reversal of alliances after 1756, and participation in the American War of Independence in 1775. This apartment, in which mirrors glittered like lies, was the nerve center of the kingdom's intelligence. Struggles for influence and power, and the tools of persuasion, calumny, intrigue, information, and propaganda, influenced the course of world events. It is strange to realize that this secret chamber was so close to the king's private apartment that every morning, Louis XV and then Louis XVI went through a mirrored door to the right of the fireplace to go from this room full of dark plans into the chapel, while the door to the left of the great window led to the bathroom, where the king could wash his hands of the stain of politics. Meetings of the council to formulate the secret plans of the intelligence service for the glorious future of the kingdom of France were held in early morning or late evening. It is easy to understand De Broglie's regret at no longer running this prodigious machine that organized striking actions in silence and seemed decidedly to govern the world.

A lover of mystery and a touch megalomaniacal, he was bored in Metz, where he continued to dream of glory, awaiting a sign of his destiny. To pass the time he subjected his soldiers to great numbers of drills. His strictness and the brutal zeal he brought to defending the virtue of men in uniform made some of his officers smile. One of them wrote to his young wife about the 1775 raid described earlier: "We are in a state of uproar and desolation. The whole garrison is going into mourning. The marshal has seized the girls, driven them off, locked them up. He is the sworn enemy of those ladies who curse him from the bottom of their hearts." The author of the letter was none other than Captain Gilbert de Lafayette, who had been sent to Metz to improve his rather superficial military training and to acquire under the tutelage of vigilant superiors a sense of responsibility that he still seemed to lack. The letter seems to show that the discipline that the marshal was seeking to impose had not yet taken full effect. The comments, in a letter to his very devout and prudish wife, who had just told him that she was again pregnant, might seem out of place and even in very dubious taste. But the remarks were not those of a cynical libertine, because Lafayette had never been, and never would be, drawn to prostitutes. His reaction to their being hunted down merely expressed the compassion he spontaneously felt for hunted creatures, the proscribed, the marginal. This remained a constant trait of his character throughout his life.

He was truly bored in Metz, despite De Broglie's efforts to keep his men alert for the day when they might be needed. Hoping to attend the coronation ceremonies and following the advice of the Prince de Poix, he had ordered a sumptuous costume for the great days. Unfortunately, the Metz troops had to remain in station, prepared to march to Champagne in case conspirators might take advantage of the situation to launch an adventure.

The Duke d'Ayen had been very optimistic in counting on the Prince de Poix to straighten out his son-in-law. The prince was an amiable man, not uncultivated, and not too opposed to the liberal ideas that were fashionable among some aristocrats. He liked everything around him to function smoothly. Lafayette inspired friendly feelings in him and he was pleased that the young captain spent his time reading the great authors everyone was talking about—Rousseau, Voltaire, Diderot, Raynal—rather than wasting his time gambling. There was in fact little for bored officers to do in the dreary garrison town of Metz but to gamble and try to seduce women.

In this town where nothing ever happened, however, an event occurred on August 8, 1775, that was to count in Lafayette's life. That evening, the governor, as representative of Louis XVI, had as a dinner guest an important traveler who had decided to stop at Metz on the way from England to Italy. The traveler, accompanied by his wife and a large entourage, who bore the title Royal Highness, was the Duke of Gloucester, the brother of King George III.

To honor his guest, the governor invited to his table the most titled and distinguished of his officers, including the Prince de Poix, the Viscount Louis de Noailles, and the young Marquis de Lafayette. The reception was sumptuous, with Baccarat crystal gleaming brightly. Champagne, Louis XVI's preferred drink, and wines from Alsace and Moselle flowed freely. Toasts were even drunk with wine tinted with rose water. De Broglie and his subordinates were intent on showing the English prince that the men who had been defeated in the Seven Years' War were great lords who knew how to treat guests, not at all troubled by their past defeats, men with whom the English would soon have to reckon again. The message was received, but the Duke of Gloucester was not the right audience. As arrogant, harsh, and stubborn as George III was, so was Gloucester open-minded and inclined to conciliation. He gave proof of this by mentioning a matter that was extremely embarrassing for the British crown: the conflict between the royal government and the rebellious colonists of North America, known in Europe as the Insurgents, or the Bostonians, after the birthplace of the revolt. Far from condemning his rebellious subjects, the duke showed himself to be rather understanding toward them. After all, why should they be obliged to pay taxes decided on by Parliament in London without being consulted? And why should they accept that, because of these taxes, their products would be sold at higher prices than products imported from England or from other British colonies? These two issues were in fact at the source of the conflict.

As soon as the subject was raised, Captain Lafayette abandoned his silence, and stopped distributing friendly smiles and wine to his neighbors at table intended to make them appreciate the charm of French hospitality. Although his subaltern rank and his young age should have impelled him to open his mouth only to answer a question, he did not hesitate to question the duke about the details of the conflict. It seemed that this story had truly captured his interest. The duke was surprised to see that a young French captain serving in a backwater garrison was following so closely a quarrel in a distant country among people whose language he did not know and in which his own country was not at all involved. It seemed as though what was happening on the banks of the Delaware was more important to him that what happened on the banks of the Seine. Marshal de Broglie wondered if he should not frown to indicate to the excessively curious captain that he should show more discretion. But he decided not to, since his guest seemed not at all offended. The marshal allowed the conversation to continue, which he and Louis de Noailles, who joined in, also found interesting. He himself listened impassively, but what he heard gave him food for thought. He was a man who saw far, very far, or at least he thought so.

As for the Duke of Gloucester, this fervent curiosity and emotion expressed in Metz about the revolt of the North American colonists became clear to him only from information he received two years later. He understood even better when he read this account written by the young captain: "From the first moment when I heard the name America, I loved it. From the instant I found out that it was fighting for freedom, I burned with the desire to spill my blood for it; I will count the days when I will be able to serve it, in all times and places, among the happiest of my life."

CHAPTER SEVEN

A YOUNG MAN WITH A GRUDGE

I N A LIBRARY RESERVED FOR HIS USE ALONE, A LITTLE
messy—many books not put back on their shelves, files
scattered on table and chairs, and sometimes on the floor—
a tall young man with very blue eyes was slowly turning a globe
of impressive size, and then he moved on to another one.
Nations, continents, seas, and oceans revolved beneath his fingers. He seemed fascinated by this splendid pair of globes, true
works of art, that he had just acquired and installed in this room
where he loved to spend time, like a pair of domestic animals. As
they turned, he traveled in his imagination from one country to
another, changing climates or sailing down long rivers. As a child
he had already been fascinated by geography, and he admired
beautiful maps almost as much as works of art. Guided and
encouraged by his tutor in the subject, Philippe Buache, he had
learned at a very early age to draw maps to scale as elegant as they

were precise. For example, at the age of eleven, he had drawn a map of the forest of Fontainebleau in which no pertinent detail was omitted, so that a lost traveler would easily have been able to find his way by using this document. Had the circumstances of his birth been different he might well have become one of the great explorers of his time, leader of a scientific expedition opening unknown lands to French influence. He would have to realize this dream through a glorious intermediary. Aside from his Mercator maps, his copiously illustrated books, and his globes, he had a precious tool for anyone curious about the outside world: a powerful telescope set up in the highest room in the château. From this observatory, he could watch everything that was going on in the courtyards, the park, on the roads, and in the neighboring hamlets.

This young man enamored of his solitude, even though he was married, was, of course, the new king, Louis XVI. The château was the huge Versailles in which he had resigned himself to living in September 1774. His library, located in the *petit appartement*, was the room where he spent the most time, studying dossiers submitted by ministers, reports from spies, and letters stolen by the secret service, and reflecting on the decisions that he wished he did not have to make, delaying them as long as possible. It was here that he also carefully recorded every detail of his latest hunting party, a sport to which he had an almost neurotic attachment, forgetting not a single swallow killed for pleasure nor the dogs killed by accident, and setting out a precise plan of action for the next expedition. He also very succinctly recorded the events that had marked his day along with even the slightest expenditures.

When the problems confronting him seemed too complex and his responsibilities too burdensome, he went up one flight to find relaxation in a workshop he had fitted out and equipped with a forge, which gave the room its name. Wearing a leather apron around his already substantial girth, Louis XVI took great pleasure in making locks in his workshop. Professionals considered him skillful and competent, although his technical training was insufficient to allow him to copy the splendid decorated locks with complicated mechanisms that he collected.

His innocent mania of indulging in humble manual labor, which was not at all a source of vanity, later became an activity for which the melancholy monarch was criticized. Weren't there better things for him to be doing, in light of the crisis the country was going through, than wasting time reading maps, dismantling locks, or exhausting himself in endless hunting parties, sometimes spending eight hours on horseback? These criticisms—except perhaps with regard to hunting—seem misplaced, in view of the king's constancy as a faithful husband and the fact that he spent less time in his library and his forge than his predecessors had devoted to their numerous mistresses.

This rather awkward young man with a fleshy face and a gangling stride, who was embarrassed by his powerful frame (he could lift a shovel with an adolescent sitting on it), sincerely loved his subjects. He wanted to work for their happiness and preserve the popularity that marked his first encounters with crowds. Unfortunately, he did not know how to go about achieving a goal that seemed within his reach. It was as though everything had been working together since his childhood to make it impossible for him to exercise the office of king that his tutors mistakenly prided themselves on having prepared him to assume.

As though it had not been enough to crush him by comparing him to his elder brother, the Duke de Bourgogne, dead at fourteen, who had embodied all the hopes of the royal family, he was led to believe that even his younger brothers, Artois and

Provence, were more brilliant than he, and that it was a pity he preceded them in the order of succession. After his father died, his grandfather, Louis XV, showed little interest in him, and the little comfort he received from his very devout mother, the inconsolable widow Marie-Josèphe de Saxe, was swept away when she died of tuberculosis when the Dauphin was only ten. Envied by his brothers, as he was throughout his life, receiving few signs of tenderness from his sisters or his amiable but sanctimonious and distant aunts, it was inevitable that Louis would turn in on himself. When he did venture to talk, however, he clearly demonstrated some cleverness. David Hume, the Francophile historian and philosopher, who had had the opportunity to converse with the Dauphin when he visited Versailles, lavishly praised his precocious intelligence.

Louis was interested not only in geographical maps and the flora and fauna of distant countries; he read a good deal: ancient and modern history, and works on law, economics, and trade. He did not forget the Encyclopédistes and the philosophes, although he tended instinctively to mistrust their arguments, which, although seductive in some respects, seemed to him to endanger the established order, dictated, in his view, by God and Christian faith. For, although not a fanatic, the prince was a sincere believer who always followed his religious duties. His chaplain, Abbé Soldini, unfortunately treated him as a fragile creature who had to be protected from the devil's snares; he advised the Dauphin against reading novels, loathsome books that could only trouble the spirit of honest readers. As for the man in charge of his education, the vain and hypocritical Duke de La Vauguyon, his pedagogical system had the most negative effects. Not only did he exalt the memory of Louis XVI's prematurely deceased father, leading his pupil to think that it would be difficult to live up to this admirable model, but most important, La Vauguyon

58

provided contradictory advice. On the one hand, he demon-strated the necessity of calling on the advice of older figures endowed with experience; on the other, he tried to persuade Louis that an absolute monarch was a man who had to exercise his crushing power in solitude, not place too much trust in his ministers, and suspect even his friends, because everyone around him had a particular interest to protect or promote. The result was that the king, who had a kindly and amiable nature, became suspicious, while he lacked confidence and dreaded above all having to decide. Without realizing it, those in charge of his edu-cation had turned the terrible grandeur of the power of an absolute monarch into a kind of bogeyman for the man who was going to have to wear the crown. The historian Nicolas Moreau, who intended to portray for the Dauphin men as they were in reality and to show the development of ways of thinking toward the aspiration for more tolerance and freedom, was removed by the lugubrious La Vauguyon; it was fortunate he did not do the same to the geographer Buache.

When rule over the country fell to him, Louis XVI thought about establishing a new government to replace the trio made up of Chancellor Maupéou, the Duke d'Aiguillon, and Abbé Terray, who had been administering France with some difficulty during the last part of the reign of Louis XV. The dispute between the Parlement and royal authority was not really over, the Jesuits' friends continued to hound the men who had contributed to their expulsion, and the finances were in a pitiful state. The young king needed to have by his side men who owed their ascent to him alone and who would not be tempted to remind him at every moment what his grandfather had done or said.

A significant portion of the ruling class and of public opinion thought that the moment was ripe for Choiseul to return in tri-umph. He had been dismissed by Louis XV in December 1770 and was still, theoretically, required to live on his sumptuous estate, Chanteloup. He had many supporters and far from negligible assets. After all, the queen owed him her marriage, and he had been dismissed primarily because of his hostility to Du Barry, whom the royal couple detested—one of Louis's first acts as a king was to have her confined to a convent.

Impatient as he was to return to public life, where he thought he would have no trouble manipulating the young king, Choiseul was unaware of Louis's antipathy toward him. Louis XVI had not forgotten that "Europe's coachman" had considered his father sanctimonious and narrow-minded, and had held Louis himself and his brothers and sisters in contempt because their mother came from Saxony. Nor had he forgotten hearing that Choiseul had been behind the poisoning of his parents, an absurd accusation that gives some idea of the rumor factory of Versailles, where the wildest stories were circulated by the most prestigious figures.

The director of Louis's education, La Vauguyon, was an enemy of Choiseul, and he warned his pupil against the danger he represented. The influence of Marie Antoinette, the most eminent of Choiseul's supporters, was ineffective against this hostility and prejudice, although not entirely: the king agreed to remove the prohibition against Choiseul traveling outside his estate. This was enough to lead Choiseul to believe that everything would work out in the end, although Louis had already chosen the seventy-four-year-old Maurepas as his chief adviser. As a political virtuoso, Choiseul thought he would be able to make short work of Maurepas. He hastened to Versailles to declare his gratitude and devotion to his new sovereign, certain that he would be appointed to some ministry that he could use as a springboard. Louis XVI overcame his timidity and found enough self-confidence to chill Choiseul's enthusiasm with a single sentence. As the king passed through the Hall of Mirrors and the former minister bowed in front of him, the crowd of courtiers anticipating a scene of reconciliation and already murmuring in approval were surprised. Louis XVI said in a contemptuous tone: "Well, M. de Choiseul, you've gotten fat, you're losing your hair, you're going bald." That was enough to tell Choiseul that he would have no success, and he returned to his estate the next day. But he tried again the following year on the occasion of the coronation in Reims. All of French nobility had traveled to Reims to declare their loyalty to the king, along with accredited diplomats and envoys of foreign powers. It was inconceivable that such a great nobleman as Choiseul could remain in a sulk at home. The queen, assisted by Artois, laid the groundwork. The court was abuzz when it was announced that an audience had been granted to Choiseul, and it was thought that the days of the government in place were numbered. But the king suspected he was being manipulated, and when the duke bowed to kiss his hand, Louis, as though horrified, withdrew it immediately, turned his head away, and expressed his feelings in a grimace that witnesses found frightening. This was the end of Choiseul's political career, and the queen accepted her defeat. In subsequent years, the king had ministers of varying qualities. Vergennes, who moved from the post of ambassador to Sweden to head the Ministry of Foreign Affairs, was particularly remarkable. But none had the brilliance and imagination of Choiseul, which would have been of great help. He and the king might have found a basis for coming to an understanding in naval policy. Even before the signing of the Treaty of Paris, Choiseul had begun discreetly working to restore a powerful navy, and Louis XVI, with his enthusiasm for geography and adventurous expeditions, was determined from the moment of his accession to show the French flag on every ocean in strong rivalry with Britain. He turned out, despite his lack of naval experience, to deserve the name he was given of "sailor-king."

Nonetheless, because of his open-mindedness and his connections with the philosophes of the Enlightenment, Choiseul might have been able to keep the king from making many mistakes and to set the French monarchy on the path to the modern world.

CHAPTER EIGHT

HONOR TO THE SPY

O N A SNOWY EVENING IN PHILADELPHIA IN DECEMBER 1775 two men were walking on Chestnut Street. The smaller of the two, who had a limp and was short of breath, had trouble keeping up the pace. When they reached a rather large brick building they were quickly and discreetly admitted. The building, well known to the 35,000 residents of this model city, better lighted than London, Paris, Vienna, or Rome, was Carpenters' Hall, headquarters of the Carpenters' Company and the site of many political meetings, including that of the Continental Congress. The building also housed the largest library in the colony, if not in all thirteen colonies, the Library Company, which loaned books to all citizens. One of the two men was the library's director, Francis Daymon, a librarian, teacher, and translator of French origin, who enjoyed the confidence and esteem of the leaders of Pennsylvania who had rebelled against George III. It was precisely because of the position of trust he occupied that he was leading the shorter man to Carpenters' Hall. They were expected, and were swiftly ushered into a small room where five serious-looking men were seated around a table as though they were members of a council or a tribunal. They all had major responsibilities: Benjamin Franklin, John Jay, and John Dickinson, along with two less celebrated men. Francis Daymon introduced his companion, who was also French: the Chevalier Julien Achard de Bonvouloir et Loyauté, lieutenant in a regiment based in the West Indies, who was traveling privately in North America for health reasons. The military title was honorific, bestowed in order to facilitate his mission. Despite the disfigured face that risked making him easily recognizable, Bonvouloir was an authentic secret agent hired by Foreign Minister Vergennes through the French embassy in London and with the king's approval.

The younger son of an ancient Norman family, who could trace his ancestry back to one of William the Conqueror's soldiers, physically handicapped because of a childhood accident, Bonvouloir had not been a brilliant student. Since his handicap kept him from the army, and he felt no inclination for the church, his demanding father had sent him to Saint-Domingue (then a French possession), counting on connections he had with some notables on the island to help the young man with no particular qualifications make his way. One of the advantages of the colonies was to offer opportunities for marginal figures from good families. But Julien was mainly interested in the charms of the island's mixed-race women, and spending time in taverns with other young men who had been conquered by the mild climate and the luxurious vegetation and were in no hurry to find regular employment. But however much like paradise the island might be, and because he did not have the resources to buy land

and slaves for a plantation, the young man had to do something. He had learned from officers on merchant ships plying the waters between the West Indies and the North American colonies that strange things were happening on the continent, and he decided to see for himself. A rather marginal figure such as Bonvouloir, who in addition detested Britain, could only feel sympathy for the rebels. He had landed in Boston and traveled down the East coast, claiming to be in America for his health. In Philadelphia, he had met his idealistic compatriot Francis Daymon, an enthusiast for Enlightenment philosophy, who was only to happen to explain what his friends the Insurgents were doing and what they wanted. Dazzled by the brilliant and candid thinking of Daymon, Bonvouloir thought he would be able to find a fitting place that accorded with his tastes in this country in turmoil. Not by joining the American army as some suggested to him, but by becoming the eyes and ears of the king of France in a theater of operations that must be of interest to Versailles. If, as he thought would happen, the insurgents won, Great Britain would come out of the conflict weakened and diminished, whereas France would again become a great power, all the stronger because it had been able to establish privileged ties with the victors, who would then become major trading partners. It would be useful to keep the king informed about everything that happened, to help the insurgents, and to follow their actions down to the final victory.

Bonvouloir had not only correctly analyzed the situation he had found his vocation—intelligence—and he had done so with no tutoring and influenced by no one. The first stage of the underground career that he now planned to undertake was, of course, to gain approval from the authorities of his country. He sailed for England, and through the French ambassador in London, the Count de Guines, whom he contacted through a cousin, he presented his plan to the government. Vergennes, convinced as Guines had been, submitted the plan to the king, who agreed in principle. Bonvouloir therefore received, along with very precise instructions, a secret code and details about how to send his messages, the most confidential portions to be written with milk, which would be decipherable at the other end only when a heated shovel was applied to the paper. A commission as lieutenant that he requested was provided along with an annual budget of 200 louis. Duly mandated by Guines, Bonvouloir sailed on the *Charming Betsy* in September 1775, on a crossing that took 100 days.

Vergennes had given him a dual role: he was to be first an informer and then, while insisting that he was nothing but a private individual, act as a diplomat would. This meant essentially that he was to convince his high-level American interlocutors that while Louis XVI and his ministers were very sympathetic toward the rebellion and hoped that it would be victorious, they did not intend to take advantage of the situation to attempt to recover Canada, which France had lost in 1763.

Bonvouloir, then, presented himself as a disinterested friend of the cause of the insurgents, more enthusiastic than ever, and asking nothing for himself. With very well placed friends in France, he could, if the leaders of the insurrection wished, give them the most precise information about what was happening in the colonies in order to combat British propaganda, and possibly make known the colonists' wishes, although he could make no commitments on his part or the part of anyone else because he was not involved in any mission. Franklin and the others, of course, like Daymon himself, were persuaded to the contrary, but as well-brought-up men, they pretended to believe him. They would appreciate his propagating a good image of their rebellion in France and throughout Europe, but they wanted a good deal more. They were responsible and clear-eyed leaders, who knew that they could win out over a very powerful enemy only with significant foreign help. They also hoped to become a solid partner for France, and even for Spain, and spoke not only of immediate aid in the form of matériel and specialists, but also of trade treaties and treaties of defensive and offensive alliance. In short, while taking note of Bonvouloir's assertions, they acted as though he could put them in touch with the French government. The spy carefully took note of everything without for an instant abandoning his initial attitude. He would transmit the content of this conversation to his friends, and they would see if they could pass it on to the proper authorities. Two further meetings followed the first one, also in December. Bonvouloir took advantage of them to get a precise idea of the rebel organization and its plans; he sketched for his superiors a picture of the military situation, about which he shared his hosts' optimism, since American troops had had great success in Canada and had occupied Montreal. He would also support the request by the Committee of Secret Correspondence to send a representative of the Continental Congress to Paris; his role would be unofficial, so that France, which still had good diplomatic relations with Great Britain, could not be accused of dealing with rebellious subjects of a friendly king. Franklin drew up a questionnaire and presented it to Bonvouloir, who sent his report on December 28. It was addressed to a merchant in Antwerp through a municipal officer in Calais, who in turn passed it on to a French citizen living in London, who handed it over to the ambassador. This was the circuit that had been set up in advance. Guines embellished the report with his own remarks and commentaries—he had another informer in the British Colonial Office—and sent the material to the Foreign Minister in the diplomatic pouch. Vergennes received it toward the end of February 1776. He chose a high official in his department to write a memorandum for the king based on Bonvouloir's report, titled *Réflexions*. This document and another memorandum titled *Considérations*, also dealing with the rebellion in Britain's North American colonies, made it possible, when the moment seemed ripe in 1778, for the least decisive king in the history of France to make the most difficult and most courageous decision of his reign, a decision that would restore France to the front rank of the great powers, a decision whose consequences would change the face of the world in the coming centuries.

In the meantime, the first request the insurgents had made to Bonvouloir, to send an unofficial representative of the Continental Congress to Paris, was granted. A few months later, in the summer of 1776, in the guise of a Connecticut merchant wanting to do business in France, Silas Deane, the member chosen, landed in Lorient.

CHAPTER NINE

FIGARO AND AMERICA

"**W**HAT A WICKED MAN! WHAT A NAUGHTY WOMAN!"
In a hotel room in London in June 1775, the
man freely expressing his rage was a
Frenchman, a dramatist of immense talent. His name was almost
as well known in London as in Paris, where he was constantly in
the news because of his agitation, his projects, his trials, and his
vigorous and salty writings about the damage he suffered because
of the arrogant stupidity of some and the hypocrisy of others.
This figure, whose company was sought after by men of the highest
rank, even those close to the throne, was Beaumarchais, the former
clockmaker, the protégé of Louis XV's daughters, whose clocks he
repaired, to whom he gave harp and viol lessons, and for whom
he organized concerts. The author of plays that were the source of
operas was also a musician.

After an interminable trial, Pierre-Augustin Caron de Beaumarchais found himself in an unfortunate position. Having been deprived of his civil rights in April 1773, he could no longer hold public office. His financial situation was catastrophic; moreover, because he had attacked the new Parlement created by Louis XV, he felt his safety in danger. In the spring of 1774 he went to Flanders and from there to England, where, thanks to the good offices of his friend La Borde, the king's chief valet and a farmer-general, he began a new career as a secret agent. His first mission was to persuade a journalist operating in London, Charles Thévenau de Morande, to destroy a pamphlet, *Mémoires secrets d'une femme publique*, which harshly abused the king's favorite, Jeanne du Barry. Beaumarchais succeeded in buying the pamphleteer's silence, and the three thousand copies of his work were burned in a lime kiln. Louis XV had just died when Beaumarchais returned to Paris, and he decided to offer his services to Louis XVI through his friend Antoine Gabriel de Sartines, Count d'Alby, chief of police and future navy minister: "For everything the king would like to know in private and promptly, for everything he would like to have done quickly and in secret, here I am. I place at his service a head, a heart, my arms, and a silent tongue." This charming man, both a financier and a dramatist, an arms dealer and a music teacher, gallantly offered his services to protect the reputation of Marie Antoinette, also threatened by the publication of a pamphlet. Louis XVI sent him to London for that purpose. In accepting his mission, Beaumarchais wrote: "A lover wears the portrait of his mistress around his neck, a miser attaches his keys, a pious man his reliquary; as for me, I wear a golden oval box in which I have enclosed Your Majesty's orders."

But who were the targets of Beaumarchais' rage that day in London? There seemed to be two of them, but the wicked man and the naughty woman were in fact a single person, alternately man and woman, at a time before there was any talk of transsexuality. This strange individual, whose escapades were the talk of embassies, elegant salons, and taverns, was the Chevalier d'Éon, on some official occasions known as the Chevalière d'Éon. Beaumarchais was enraged against this strange creature merely out of exasperation. His anger had nothing to do with d'Éon's sexual ambiguity but simply because the chevalier's prevarications had interfered with the mission on which Beaumarchais was embarked. He knew the city well, and had already disposed of libelous writing against Mme du Barry and others attacking Marie Antoinette. London was a nest of slanderers and blackmailers—often manipulated from Paris—who took advantage of the relative freedom that prevailed in the country to publish attacks against prominent people, even against the highest authorities in France. Beaumarchais's current mission was to get his hands on correspondence from Louis XV clearly alluding to possible revenge against England and the necessity to prepare for it.

Was Charles-Geneviève-Louise-Auguste-André-Timothée d'Éon de Beaumont a man or a woman? This was the question everyone was asking in London and in Paris. Wild bets were made everywhere in England on the answer. The Home Secretary had the chevalier followed every day in the hope that a gesture or a moment's inattention would reveal his/her true nature. This diplomat and writer, a former valorous captain of dragoon and secret agent for the Marshal de Broglie, had briefly been France's chargé d'affaires in London and had taken possession of this correspondence that was so embarrassing for the court of Versailles. He wanted to get the highest possible price for it. Beaumarchais endeavored to cajole him into accepting reasonable or at least minimally decent conditions. To make things absolutely clear, d'Éon went so far as to undress so that Beaumarchais could see with his own eyes that "he" was in fact a woman, an experience the dramatist found troubling. But this intimate scrutiny did not prevent d'Éon from going back on his agreement with the tantalized dramatist. In the end, the former diplomat and spy handed over the correspondence only in exchange for authorization to return to France and the receipt of a pension that would enable him to live like "a noble lady." (In reality, d'Éon was, of course, a man, definitively settled by an autopsy after his death.)

Buoyed by the success of his mission, Beaumarchais was again sent to London by his patron Navy Minister Sartines to gather thorough intelligence on the state of the British fleet, anticipated shipbuilding, and government plans for action. He gathered that the crisis between George III and the North American colonists bore some connection to his mission. He was well informed about the crisis, in part because every time he traveled to England, he met with Lord Rochford and other opposition figures, including the brilliant journalist John Wilkes, with whom he spent long evenings in intense discussion and drinking fine French vintages. These men did not conceal their sympathy toward the insurgents, which Beaumarchais, as a natural rebel, shared. He also met Arthur Lee, an American living in London, who was officially a lawyer but in reality an agent of influence for the Continental Congress, of which his brother was a member. Lee led Beaumarchais to believe that, after crushing the American rebellion, the British intended to conquer the remaining French islands. Half convinced, Beaumarchais sent alarmist messages to Sartines and to Foreign Minister Vergennes, who was inclined favorably toward him and advocated overt armed action by France in support of the insurgents. When he was informed, Louis XVI merely strengthened the navy and waited. The situation on the ground did not seem clear enough to him, nor did he think France strong enough to embark on the adventure. But things changed after the report from Bonvouloir and the arrival of Silas Deane in Paris, and Vergennes thought of Beaumarchais for a very special secret mission. France was determined to offer matériel (rifles, cannons, uniforms, and ammunition) to the insurgents, but because it wanted to maintain normal diplomatic relations with London, such aid could not be provided officially. A screen had to be found: a private import-export company, for example, could purchase the matériel for an American customer. French ships would carry it to a port in the French West Indies, where American ships would take delivery at their own risk. Vergennes thought Beaumarchais would be the ideal man to set up and manage this fictitious French company, to be named Roderigue Hortalez and Company, sounding vaguely Spanish. It might seem surprising that Vergennes chose a dramatist and occasional spy for the job. In fact, this extraordinary man also saw himself as an entrepreneur, promoter, and big businessman. He had already been involved in commercial operations, notably the provision of all sorts of supplies to the army, along with one of the greatest financiers of the time, Paris du Verney, who treated Beaumarchais almost like a son, and on whose behalf he had engaged in financial operations in Spain. In addition, he was motivated because he was a warm supporter of the American cause, and he found the mission especially attractive. His notes from London about the situation in North America, once their alarmism had been discounted, turned out to be very useful. Just as he had used Bonvouloir's report as the basis for his first memorandum to the king on the American rebellion, Vergennes used Beaumarchais's notes for the second, which influenced the king's decision to provide clandestine aid that could only weaken Britain, even if the rebels were not in the end victorious.

The clockmaker/dramatist/businessman/secret agent was the

right man in the right place. He was discreetly given one million livres to enable the company to begin operations, and he feverishly set out to locate partners, suppliers, and ship owners to set the rather large enterprise in motion. With the enthusiastic participation of Silas Deane, he visited ports, offices, and workshops. With some assistance from luck, British privateers did not capture too many of the transport vessels, and operations were so successful that for nearly two years, 80 percent of the supplies of the rebel army came from this clandestine source. It is not certain that the British were deceived. Lord Stormont, the British ambassador in Paris, had too many spies to remain in the dark about the operation. British intelligence even had an agent in the American delegation headed by Franklin, Edward Bancroft, the mission's trusted doctor: he placed his reports inside a bottle in the trunk of a hollow tree in the public part of the Tuileries gardens, where an agent regularly picked them up.

CHAPTER TEN

THE DUKE'S SURPRISE

AFTER THE DUKE OF GLOUCESTER HAD PASSED THROUGH Metz, the dull life of the garrison town resumed: drills, inspections, long marches. The late summer trees bent beneath the weight of glowing ripening fruit, which would provide plentiful supplies of brandy, jam, and tarts. But there was one officer in the Noailles regiment who was thinking of anything but the comforts of winter quarters in Lorraine. Captain Lafayette's mind was elsewhere, far away. Younger than his brother-in-law Louis de Noailles, he had managed to communicate his enthusiasm for the American rebels to the older man, and both had resolved to leave everything to join the fight. They knew almost nothing about the New World, but they already saw themselves in the vast plains described by travelers, on horseback, swords drawn, ready to charge the British cavalry. Lafayette spent most of his time learning about the flora and fauna of the East coast and of the South. He imagined himself under a sassafras tree in Pennsylvania smoking a peace pipe with Indians whom he had persuaded to join the cause. He had openly confessed his intentions to the commander of the region, the Marshal de Broglie, who had not discouraged him. Quite the contrary. But the marshal had recommended that he be very discreet about his plan and that he should keep in touch in the event he had to leave Metz, advice that might be expected from a former head of the secret services.

In December, Lafayette went to Paris on leave in time for the birth of his daughter Henriette on the fifteenth. Adrienne was more devoted than ever, having forgiven his infidelities, if indeed she had ever held them against him. The young officer, who was more in love with his wife than ever, had no difficulty making her share his enthusiasm for the rebel cause—she may well have been its first active sympathizer in France. While she was surprisingly public in her praise of the great deeds of the countrymen of Washington and Franklin, her husband had not informed her that he intended to join them; there would always be time for that, he thought. For now, Gilbert was reading all the history, philosophy, and geography he could. His scholarly father-in-law was surprised by this sudden intellectual craving. His uncle by marriage, Ségur, was equally surprised. Perhaps because of this intellectual curiosity, Ségur, with the consent of the Duke d'Ayen, suggested to his enthusiastic nephew that he be initiated as a Freemason. Lafayette was initiated at La Candeur Lodge in Paris at the age of eighteen, and unlike many of his contemporaries who joined because it was fashionable, remained an exemplary Mason throughout his life. He was dazzled by the atmosphere of freedom and the high level of culture that characterized the best Paris lodges under the reign of Louis XVI, where he was enthralled by his encounters with scholars, artists, and philosophers.

Soon Count Alexandre de Ségur decided to join Louis de Noailles and Lafayette on their mission to fight for freedom in America. When they informed the Duke d'Ayen, he encouraged Noailles and Ségur but not Lafayette. Despite the improvement in the conduct of his youngest son-in-law, and the interest he had shown in philosophy and science, which could not fail to touch so cultivated a man, he still considered Lafayette too flighty and immature. The duke used what he thought was a persuasive argument to divert Lafayette from his plan. He explained that Ségur and Noailles were not very rich, so they risked nothing by undertaking this adventure, whereas Lafayette had a significant fortune, which imposed certain obligations on him. This showed a remarkable lack of psychological insight on the part of such an intelligent man. The hint of bourgeois morality it expressed had the opposite effect from what the duke expected. Lafayette would undertake the risk when the time came, not despite his wealth but precisely because of it. The misunderstanding was complete, and it was not the only one that marked relations between Lafayette and a father-in-law for whom he had the warmest feelings and whom he treated as a father. Fortunately for Lafayette, if he did experience a moment of doubt, another man of age and experience, the Marshal de Broglie, was there to support him. Living in semi-disgrace in Paris, the former governor of Metz also wanted to play a prominent role in America. Overestimating his abilities and, more important, his prestige, he dreamed of being appointed general-in-chief of the rebel army, since he thought his name and his international reputation were such as to discourage the enemy. Depending on circumstances, he thought, he could win a decisive victory in the field or negotiate a peace to the advantage of the rebellious colonies.

Untroubled by any doubts, he began putting together his

brilliant staff, including Ségur, Noailles, Lafayette, the Viscount de Mauroy, who was devoted to him, and a Prussian officer in French service even more closely attached to him, Johann de Kalb. De Broglie, as head of the secret service, had sent Baron de Kalb to America in 1768, and he was fluent in English. De Broglie thought that, with this group, all it would take was a green light from the king and a little help from government ministers for him to bring his career to a spectacular conclusion.

But neither the king nor Vergennes was willing to fall in with De Broglie's plans. His "ingenious" idea seemed to them pure fantasy and could only interfere with the policy they intended to follow. He was advised to give up his ambition and to tell his lieutenants to do the same. Noailles and Ségur immediately submitted. The government's instructions were to do nothing for the moment that might antagonize Britain. For his part, the marshal pretended to give way before royal authority, while still counting on the loyal Mauroy and De Kalb, and on the young hothead Lafayette, to go to America and report to him on what was happening. Perhaps he would find an opportunity to revive his plan.

The clandestine delegate of the Continental Congress, Silas Deane, had arrived in Paris in June 1776. Although his knowledge of French was slight, it did not take long for him to set to work. At the same time that he was loading ships with matériel bought in France with his partner, the indefatigable Beaumarchais, he endeavored to recruit volunteers, sometimes enticing them with appointments as officers in the American army, although he had no such authorization from the Continental Congress. De Broglie suggested to Lafayette that he contact Deane to offer his services. The name Lafayette, a figure at the court of Versailles, could not fail to dazzle the American, who was obliged by circumstances to operate discreetly in France.

After taking the wise precaution of securing unlimited leave from his regiment to avoid charges of desertion if things turned out badly, Lafayette went to see Deane and his right-hand man William Carmichael and told them that he was the leader of a group of gentlemen with the best references who were, like himself, prepared to put their swords at the service of the American cause out of their love for freedom. He demonstrated his complete sincerity by offering to cover all expenses for the transport and equipment of this group of volunteers. To avoid any risk of indiscretion or interference, he was himself prepared to use his personal wealth to charter a ship for the operation.

Deane may not have been familiar with the country or the language, but he immediately understood that this proposition bore no resemblance to the others he had received. Until then, the volunteers who had come forward had been, with rare exceptions, adventurers, vagabonds, has-beens, and demanding braggarts. Lafayette and his companions represented the flower of high society. Flattered, the least he could do was encourage his visitors (De Kalb had come with Lafayette), and he presented them with documents appointing them to high rank. Lafayette and De Kalb were thereby made generals from the outset, while the others were promoted to various lesser ranks.

When Benjamin Franklin came later in the year to oversee Deane, he hastened to ratify the decision regarding Lafayette, to whom he gave a warm letter of recommendation addressed to the president of the Continental Congress.

All that remained was to organize the departure with maximum precaution in order not to attract the attention of enemies of the plan at the court of Versailles, nor that of the British ambassador, Lord Stormont, who had a remarkable espionage network in France. Lafayette sent an emissary named Dubois-Martin (incidentally a secretary of the Marshal de Broglie) to

Bordeaux with the mission to purchase a ship. He found one that seemed suitable for the price of 112,000 livres, and bought it. The vessel would be ready in March 1777 and bore the name *Victoire*.

To cover his tracks, Lafayette innocently (or so it appeared) spent a few days in London with the Prince de Poix, visiting the French ambassador, Adrienne's uncle the Marquis de Noailles.

He may have succeeded in deceiving the English about his intentions and his opinions about the conflict raging in North America. In any event, he was very well received. The Colonial Minister invited him to a ball. Lord Shelburne, a friend of Beaumarchais, invited him to lunch. Even General Clinton wanted to meet this distinguished young Frenchman, whom he would soon encounter on the field of battle. The ambassador himself, who was full of indulgence for his niece's husband, even presented him to King George III, who found him quite likable. While he was being celebrated in London, in a French port, a ship was being outfitted that would take him and his companions in arms to the declared enemies of the hospitable kingdom. Lafayette no doubt savored the irony. When they learned that he had tricked them, the members of the British establishment had enough of a sense of humor to smile.

Out of naïveté (or extraordinary cynicism), Lafayette wrote from London to his father-in-law: "You will be surprised, dear father, at what I am about to tell you; it has cost me more than I can tell you to have not consulted you. . . . I have found a unique opportunity to distinguish myself and to learn my profession: I am a general officer in the army of the United States." He announced his imminent departure with his friends on a ship belonging to him, saying that he rejoiced at having found "such a glorious opportunity of occupying myself and of acquiring knowledge." The duke was outraged. Not content with subjecting a French ambassador to ridicule, he was ready to abandon a young wife who was again pregnant. The duke was so furious that he asked the chief minister, Maurepas, to do everything to prevent his son-in-law from leaving, if necessary by locking him up in the Bastille or some other establishment for hotheads. Lafayette, who was in Paris for three days, did not even dare to go to his in-laws' to see Adrienne. He left for Bordeaux without taking leave of her. In Bordeaux, he received an order from the government to go to Marseille and wait there for his father-in-law and his aunt Mme de Tessé, with whom he was supposed to travel to Italy. It was thought that this cultural expedition would divert him from his plans and reconcile him with the Noailles family. Rather than complying, the young rebel sent the ship on to the Spanish port of Los Pasajes, and crossed the frontier disguised as a courier to join the ship. He had to encourage De Kalb, whose enthusiasm had begun to flag when he learned that the expedition was against the king's wishes. Moreover, orders had been given to seize the ship and arrest its passengers at the first port of call. These orders had gone out as soon as the flight into Spain became known. Captain Le Bourcier, who commanded the *Victoire*, feared British warships and privateers and now had to worry about being stopped by a French ship. He hesitated to raise the anchor. But Lafayette, the ship's owner, had the last word: they would cross the ocean without making landfall. On one side lay adventure leading, if everything went well, to glory. On the other was a pious return to the nest and months, if not more, inside four thick walls. Even though he, too, had a family to look after, De Kalb recovered his enthusiasm. The other companions placed their trust in their young leader's star. There was dancing at Versailles, where some fully supported the young rebel, Lord Stormont wrote his report stigmatizing the flighty French, the

Duchess d'Ayen tried to console Adrienne without ever speaking a word of reproach against her son-in-law, the duke fretted with his mistress, hoping that the ship would be stopped, and Marshal de Broglie built castles in the air, while the *Victoire*, under full sail, left the port of Los Pasajes and set out on the unpredictable Atlantic Ocean.

CHAPTER ELEVEN

DREARY VISTA

I N May and June of 1777, on board the *Victoire* between Europe and America, a solitary young man stood in the bow. He had never seen anything as monotonous as the ocean, which he described in a letter to his wife as a dreary plain.

He stared at the beautiful and wearying prospect, and the movement of the waves made him feel alternately enthusiastic and discouraged. As time passed he grew increasingly bored. Realization of his bold plan seemed so distant that his hopes began to fade. Contemplating the vast blue expanse before him, his thoughts turned back to the Auvergne summits of his childhood.

Lafayette had in the last few days overcome the seasickness that had immobilized him in his cabin. He felt pleasure at standing in the ship's bow. He scrutinized the horizon that was full of threats; a British privateer might appear at any moment, and the clouds above might portend a storm. When he felt reassured, he devoted himself to the study of English, repeating words that he would find indispensable, with an atrocious accent.

Below decks, his companions played cards, read, talked, and, when they came on deck, refrained from disturbing their leader if they found him motionless in the bow. Lafayette's relations with Captain Le Bourcier had been rather tense at first, when the captain had again tried to get Lafayette to agree to make landfall at the Leeward Islands, and had been met with a second categorical no, accompanied by a threat that if he insisted, Lafayette, as ship's owner, would dismiss him and replace him with the first mate. Lafayette had made another, more troubling, decision. The *Victoire* had only two cannons and a few rifles to deal with an attack: not very much. Because the courage of the sailors and the volunteers would not be enough to save the ship, it would have to be destroyed to keep it from falling into the hands of the enemy. A Dutch sailor whom Lafayette trusted was charged with making sure that the plans to sink the ship quickly that had been established were ready to be put into operation at any time. Fortunately, the *Victoire* never had to confront that situation; it seemed to be protected by providence from all the predators plying the Atlantic in the service of George III.

Days and weeks passed without sight of land. Believers began to pray for the voyage to end. Rations were down to salt pork and biscuits, with the occasional fish they managed to catch. Water had to be conserved, but morale remained high. De Kalb, whom Lafayette sometimes asked for help with his English, and who was old enough to be the father of some of his companions, provided an example of perfect calm. He was wondering what he could do to satisfy his patron, Marshal de Broglie. The others—

Viscount de Mauroy, Jean-Joseph de Gimat, Louis Saint-Ange de la Colombe, Chevalier du Buysson, Charles-Antoine de Valfort, Jean-Pierre de Fayols, Guillaume de Lesser, François-Augustin Dubois-Martin, Charles Bedoulx, Louis Candon, Jacques Franval, Jean Capitaine, Léonard Price, and Louis Devrigny—wished only for De Kalb, who alone among them had been there, to tell them more about America.

Lafayette appears not to have felt very guilty over having left Paris without seeing Adrienne: he offered some apologies for his strange conduct, nothing more. In the end, he believed that his wife was delighted because he had easily succeeded in indoctrinating her. The letters he wrote to her on board ship were more concerned with having her share his passion than with asking for forgiveness that he seemed to take for granted. Would she have been proud of him if he had been touring Italy with the duke like a nervous adolescent?

The letters to his wife from the ship contain some of the language that best defined his attitude. He saw himself as an American, and he asked Adrienne to follow his lead: "I hope that, for my sake, you will become a good American, for that feeling is worthy of every noble heart. The happiness of America is intimately connected with the happiness of all mankind; she will become the safe and respected asylum of virtue integrity, toleration, equality, and tranquil happiness." He acknowledged, of course, that he sought after glory, but that was not his only purpose. Referring to America, he wrote: "Her happiness and my glory are my only incentives to the task."

His few remaining regrets, if any, would have been immediately dissipated had he known that most of the great families that frequented the court of Versailles, rather than blaming him for being a rebel, praised him and criticized the Duke d'Ayen for having had the bad taste to put obstacles in his way. He would have been delighted to learn that Adrienne, far from being shunned, was sought out as the wife of a hero. Lord Stormont wrote to George III that, despite the order against his plans sent by Maurepas, everyone who counted at court was applauding his adventure.

For the moment, the adventure was stalled by contrary winds and the impossibility of advancing in "the most dreary of all regions," the "melancholy sea." Impatient to join the battle, the future general continued studying English, and read works on military strategy, his knowledge of which was full of gaps. He hoped that his courage and high spirits would compensate in the field for his lack of training and experience.

On June 15, 1777, he was still contemplating the dismal prospect, and everyone on board was suffering from the heat. Suddenly a sailor cried out: birds were circling the tops of the masts. Flocks of different species came one after the other, a sign for the crew. As the sun was setting, one could distinguish a line on the horizon that might well be the coast. The captain and the ship's officers were not certain they were approaching their intended destination, Charleston, South Carolina. In the humid atmosphere, the relief of knowing that land was so near was mixed with vague anxiety. No ships were visible through the telescope, and there was nothing indicating the proximity of a port. No one knew which power controlled the flat coast that seemed very accessible. In Paris, Silas Deane had not concealed from Lafayette the unfortunate turn that recent military events had taken. After brilliant victories, the rebel army had had to retreat in Canada, New York, and other theaters of operations. During the seven months of the voyage of the *Victoire* when they had been without news, the situation might have deteriorated even further. Nothing told them that the British, who enjoyed a crushing naval superiority, had not landed on the Carolina coast or that the loyalists had not resumed the upper hand. In any event, they had to find out or risk throwing themselves into the lion's den. Lafayette ordered a landing craft to be launched as night fell. The lights of houses could be seen in the distance. Strange installations dividing the area into sections appeared on the surface, making them think traps had been laid. One of the sailors reassured the passengers: they had happened by chance on oyster beds. Despite the thickening evening fog, human forms could be distinguished moving from one clump of oysters to another. They froze in place when they saw the boat approaching. The sailors rowed faster, and when the oyster gatherers were in hailing distance, De Kalb asked in English: "Where are we?" In answer, the dark-skinned men dressed only in shorts ran toward dry land. De Kalb, who knew the country, and Lafayette, who had learned a lot about it, had identified them as Negro slaves assigned to the oyster beds. The arrival of strangers had frightened them, and the strangers soon learned that at first they had been taken for British spies on a mission to the Southern coast.

It was strange that the first contact with the New World was an encounter with slaves. Chateaubriand was to have the same experience a few years later. The first human being he saw was "a half-naked Negress of extraordinary beauty." And he exclaimed, as Lafayette might have: "I was welcomed to the land of freedom by a slave."

The French hastened to land and headed toward a house where they had seen light. Luck continued to favor them: the owner was a patriot, the rebel Major Huger. When he learned that these unexpected visitors were volunteers who had come to America to fight, he was overjoyed, and he welcomed them as his guests at South Inlet. Reassured by their master, the slaves rapidly set to work preparing dinner, which was copiously washed down with wine. The party welcoming these providential French volunteers lasted until dawn, and the workers in the oyster beds could hear, ringing through the night air, songs in a language they did not understand.

CHAPTER TWELVE

THE SAILOR-KING

I N THE FALL OF 1777 IN THE PALACE OF VERSAILLES, A GREAT
foreign lord who had just been received by the king with all
the honor due his rank strode through the galleries with a
good deal of authority, preceded by the presenter of ambassadors
and serious-looking high officials. The visitor was rather handsome, young, and distinguished-looking. He glanced around
him like a man used to this kind of formality, smiled fleetingly
at dignitaries and courtiers he recognized as he passed by, and
bowed gracefully to a few pretty ladies whom he also seemed to
know. The people who were the objects of his attention showed
him their satisfaction by marks of respect that, to a practiced eye,
were a little too emphatic not to have a slightly mocking intention. Those familiar with the court of Versailles had long been
past masters of the art of subtly coded messages delivered
through shows of exquisite politeness. And the ambassador of

Great Britain, the high-spirited Lord Stormont, was not taken in. In the diplomatic, political, and social playacting that made up daily activity at court, the only dupes were new arrivals from the provinces or a foreign country, regardless of their merits and their titles.

To the renewed protests of George III's envoy against the sympathy shown by France toward the rebellious British subjects across the Atlantic, the king had responded with assurances that these were rumors, attitudes held by private individuals who held no official responsibilities. As the sovereign, he held and would continue to hold to a strictly neutral position on the question, the only way to maintain the friendly relations between Versailles and London to which he was devoted.

Lord Stormont had pretended to believe him, to take what he said at face value, but had in fact not believed a word. He knew from reports from his secret agents that war matériel shipped from French ports to the French possession Saint-Domingue was in reality intended to be shipped in American vessels from the island to American ports. He knew that almost all of French high society applauded the slightest victory of the rebels. The king may have informed Stormont that Lafayette, in sailing off to join Washington's soldiers, had disobeyed formal instructions from the court not to leave national territory; the ambassador knew, regardless of what Maurepas and Vergennes might say, that everyone who counted in Versailles and Paris greatly favored the adventure. While Lafayette was officially an outcast, his gracious and timid wife Adrienne was treated everywhere as the wife of a hero. In cafés, literary salons, and Masonic lodges, everywhere that people talked—and the French talked abundantly and incautiously despite their frequent complaints that they lacked the freedom enjoyed by the English—one heard praise of the rebels and the brave men who had joined their fight. The French authorities spoke only of peace and good relations between France and Britain, but public opinion, from the royal family to the lowliest notary's clerk reading the *Encyclopédie*, supported the enemies of George III.

It is hard to believe that Louis XVI, despite appearing innocent, weak, and indecisive, really thought that Lord Stormont was unaware of his real views and passions. The king required no urging from his ministers or his family to become anti-British, for the simple reason that he was more anti-British than anyone in his entourage, even though he had been able to conceal that fact from inexperienced men such as Lafayette.

No informed observer of French affairs could be unaware of the monarch's predilection for the navy from his early youth, of his special interest in the navy department from his accession to the throne, or of the pressure he exerted on the ministers who had been charged with rebuilding and reorganizing the fleet. To be sure, the 1763 Treaty of Paris had imposed humiliating constraints and limitations on France. In 1769, for example, Great Britain had prevented the transport of 900 French soldiers to Mauritius; and in 1770, it had prevented the launching of six ships to combat piracy in the Mediterranean. Warships were rotting in the harbors of Toulon and Brest, unable to go out to sea, and they were pitiful in number because Louis XV had suddenly lost interest in Choiseul's magnificent program for the presentation of ships to the king by large cities, provincial Estates, merchant guilds, and other sponsors.

Hardly had Louis XVI been crowned when he ordered that wood be secured from Prussia to build new naval units. He ordered the admirals d'Orvilliers and du Chaffault to take the fleet on maneuvers in the Mediterranean. Under pressure from the king, Navy Minister Sartines asked Necker, who was in charge of finances, for a special appropriation for shipbuilding. By the end of the year, 52 ships of the line and 45 frigates complete with excellent artillery were ready for use.

The king's zeal regarding the navy did not stop there. He thought of sailors as well as of ships, and made some significant decisions in that regard. In 1775, he abolished the death penalty for navy deserters and proclaimed an amnesty for those who had not been sentenced and were not on the run. A decree the same year prohibited any commander of whatever rank from making insulting or humiliating remarks to his subordinates on pain of dismissal and being declared ineligible for service in His Majesty's Navy.

A second in command who had struck a cabin boy was put in irons for two days and required to serve for a time as a simple sailor, despite intervention by powerful people on his behalf. Louis XVI made certain that sanctions were applied against officers to the same degree as against the men. These measures led to the establishment of genuine discipline. The king also made sure that the families of battle or accident victims received assistance, and he surrendered to ships' crews the one-third of prize money that traditionally went to the crown.

Louis XVI had been passionately drawn to the sea ever since his adolescence. He collected and avidly read travel narratives and was an assiduous student of Nicolas Ozanne, a great naval draftsman. His interest in geography was such that he learned how to draw charts. So great was his devotion to the cause of the navy that shipbuilding in France was multiplied by four between 1774 and 1778. Even recruitment was improved, and the reign of Louis XVI produced a host of elite naval officers and remarkable characters ranging from Charles de Fleurieux, director of ports and dockyards, to the Chevalier de Borda, who invented instruments used to determine longitude. Ship building also launched such production facilities in France as metallurgical factories for the manufacture of cannons and anchors. The king's activities were both concrete and humanitarian. It is well known that Louis XVI fostered the creation of the port of Cherbourg, which Calonne called "a useful splendor." It is not so well known that it is thanks to the king that the pensions granted to old, disabled, or crippled sailors became a right. With regard to naval policy, the sailor-king was not limited to an aggressive vision of a combat navy. He also thought the navy should be engaged in commercial and scientific exchanges. It was under the reign of Louis XVI that the most brilliant chapter of the French naval epic was written.

The monarch made no attempt to disguise his interest in the Navy Council, which brought together specialists, officers, commissioners, and engineers. Among the duties he assigned to it was the investigation of responsibilities for accidents. And he could not conceal from British agents that he imposed sanctions for naval errors and that he had created a new class of "blue" officers, transferred from the land forces. Equally widely known was his interest in geographers, researchers in all scientific disciplines related to the sea, and navigators seeking to discover and explore new territories. And the king himself prepared the logistics for the expedition of La Pérouse, for whom he felt admiration and friendship, and to whom he supplied ample funds for his expedition to the Pacific. La Pérouse may have been the first European to contemplate the colossal statues of Easter Island; he rectified the map location of the Hawaiin Islands; and he discovered Necker Island. He learned of his promotion to the rank of squadron chief when he landed in the Russian Far East, and he gave Jean-Baptiste de Lesseps the assignment of taking his maps and ship's log to France. He sailed past Samoa and headed for Tonga.

It seems that the apparently timid and indolent—except for

his passionate devotion to hunting—king had never been able to stomach the declaration of the First Lord of the Admiralty, Lord Sandwich, on February 3, 1775, in which he asserted that several countries in Europe wanted to take advantage of the state of rebellion of the American colonies to support the colonists' plan to trade freely and equally with everyone, a plan that "King George III could not accept." And precisely what Louis XVI wanted to establish for France and other countries was the freedom of the seas.

Lord Stormont was not mistaken about the king's determination, as his dispatch of February 27, 1777, indicates: "M. de Vergennes said to me with the greatest apparent openness and candor: 'I repeat, Monsieur, what I have already told you. The king, my master, will not launch a war of ambition or policy; he will not be the aggressor, but if he is attacked, he will be more stubborn and determined than his grandfather, because of the firmness of his character.'" The assessment is surprising, yet it appears to have been true.

It is likely that Lafayette was unaware of this backdrop to the American affair. He was also unaware, while he had been fighting since the summer of 1777, that thanks to Benjamin Franklin, the cause of his American friends had made great strides in Paris and Versailles. Nor did he know that the great Voltaire had asked the Duchess de Choiseul to introduce him to Adrienne so he could pay tribute through Lafayette's wife to the man he called the "Hero of the New World," in the hope that he would become the "Hero of Two Worlds," through his fight for freedom. While he was unaware of the intricacies of French diplomacy, he had no doubts about the deep intentions of some government ministers, if not of the monarch himself. He had so little doubt that despite his outcast status, he took it upon himself to write to Vergennes in person that he was getting ready to weaken Britain and force it to withdraw some of its forces from America and transfer them to the East Indies; Lafayette would lead a small force to fight them there. Of course, this mad project, suggested to Lafayette by an intriguer, the Franco-Irish colonel Thomas Conway, to get rid of Lafayette so that he could assume his place as the principal French officer, after Washington was replaced by General Gates, came to nothing. The episode does reveal Lafayette's naïveté whenever it was suggested he undertake an adventure that might make him known around the world. It was a dangerous inclination, but it is important to recognize his exceptional ability to take hold of himself and rectify his course of action whenever he recognized that he had gone astray. When he became aware of the conspiracy of Gates and Conway against Washington, he helped his commanding officer, spiritual father, and friend, with a good deal of lucidity, firmness, and humility—recognizing his own mistakes— to foil these ambitious leaders and the members of Congress who were backing them. He forgot his project for an expedition to the Indies, and after the fall of Philadelphia in September 1777, he provided, in a letter to Adrienne, a whole argument that she could use to answer those for whom this defeat raised doubts about the ability of the rebels to win in the end:

> I must now give you your lesson, as wife of an American general officer. They will say to you, "They have been beaten." You must answer, "That is true; but when two armies of equal number meet in the field, old soldiers have naturally the advantage over new ones; they have, besides, had the pleasure of killing a great many of the enemy, many more than they have lost." They will afterwards add: "All that is very well; but Philadelphia is taken, the capital of America, the rampart of liberty!" You must politely answer, "You are

all great fools! Philadelphia is a poor forlorn town, exposed on every side, whose harbor was already closed; though the residence of congress lent it, I know not why, some degree of celebrity. This is the famous city which, be it added, we will, sooner or later, make them yield back to us." If they continue to persecute you with questions, you may send them about their business in terms which the Viscount de Noailles will teach you, for I cannot lose time by talking to you of politics.

CHAPTER THIRTEEN

CHARLESTON

FOR THE FRENCH, AS FOR EVERYONE ELSE, CHARLESTON was the large American port in the South where Lafayette had planned to land, and the guests of Major Huger sailed the short distance from South Inlet to Charleston on board the *Victoire*. Those who had thought it would resemble Bordeaux or Nantes were disappointed. The great Southern port was in 1777 still a town with terribly paved roads, made up primarily of small wooden houses. The shops were gloomy, and everything was sacrificed to immediate utility. There were no squares, or monuments, or public gardens. The taverns, crowded with sailors from everywhere, provided little comfort. But the docks and the town itself were very lively. The setting was, moreover, of relatively little importance to the passengers of the *Victoire*, because the local authorities, informed by the diligent Major Huger, were there to welcome them with full honors.

The welcoming committee included Governor John Rutledge and Generals Robert Howe, John Calder, and William Moultrie. Lafayette was received with as much respect and warmth as if he had been the commander of the French army. The official speeches extolled the policies of the great King Louis XVI and praised the French volunteers, who were treated to banquets, patriotic songs, and religious ceremonies. The volunteers who had defied the authorities of their own country were treated as conquerors even before they had undergone their baptism of fire. The Americans admired them for having managed to reach Charleston even though two British frigates had blockaded the harbor for several days. In fact, a violent wind had driven off the watchdogs, enabling the *Victoire* to make its spectacular appearance under the blazing noonday sun. This lucky chance was a good augury, but once the festivities were over, the volunteers under Lafayette's command, who intended to offer their services to the Continental Congress in Philadelphia, chose not to tempt fate a second time and decided to travel by land. Lafayette, already feeling like the general he was to become, bought horses and carriages, divided his men into small groups, and before leaving Charleston donated 17,000 livres to the combatants of South Carolina. On the journey over badly maintained and sometimes barely existing roads through the two Carolinas, Virginia, and Delaware he was universally celebrated and applauded. From Charleston and every principal stop along the way he wrote to Adrienne. It is not surprising that, despite potholed roads, stifling heat, mosquitos, broken axles, falls from horses, and food that was sometimes bizarre for French tastes, he described the country he was discovering in idyllic terms. "The American women are very pretty, and have great simplicity of character; and the extreme neatness of their appearance is truly delightful. . . . What gives me most pleasure is to see how completely the citizens are all brethren of one family. In America there are none poor, and none even that can be called peasants."

The slaves he encountered caused him concern; the problem would continue to trouble him throughout his life, but he made no allusion to it in his first letters to his wife, no doubt in order not to tarnish the bright image he was presenting.

CHAPTER FOURTEEN

STRIPES?
WHAT STRIPES?

I N Philadelphia on Sunday, July 27, 1777, despite their fatigue, a group of French officers in full dress uniform, wigs powdered, boots gleaming, to do honor to the capital, strode through the streets. They had finally come to a city resembling its European counterparts. There were no imposing monuments, but the architecture was pleasing. The streets were well laid out, lined with trees, with wide sidewalks, squares, fountains, and many watering points, and the façades were bright. Most buildings were constructed of red or beige brick, with small-paned windows painted white. Taverns and restaurants had furniture of good quality, usually polished, and the food was varied and served in copious portions. Soldiers and civilians were coming and going, and families in their Sunday best were attending church services of every denomination, the meaning of which was still obscure to the new arrivals from

France. But the atmosphere was far from joyous. The news from the nearby front was bad. Matériel was insufficient and quickly worn out, and desertions were numerous. How could a handful of men overcome the powerful British army supported by a navy that was ravaging coastal cities and blockading the harbors, and might land reinforcements whenever it liked. Lafayette and his little troop may well have crossed paths with some Frenchmen who had come from the West Indies or metropolitan France, called themselves officers, claimed all sorts of exploits and skills, and offered their services in return for high pay and elevated rank with no justification except that, since they came from a French territory, their value could be taken for granted. With a few exceptions, these men had become hateful to the American leaders, who no longer wanted to deal with isolated individuals not guaranteed by their governments and who soon turned out to be liars, swindlers, and schemers ready for any escapade to amass money. Lafayette did not mention those Frenchmen, although he suffered from their unfortunate presence. In any event, he soon understood that the Americans would rather get rid of them by sending them back to where they came from, and he did everything he could to distinguish himself from them.

After visiting the city—it is not known whether they attended a religious service—they presented themselves at the residence of John Hancock, president of the Continental Congress. It was to this important figure that Silas Deane in Paris had written a letter of introduction.

Considering the way he and his friends had been welcomed in America since their encounter with Major Huger, Lafayette thought Hancock would greet him with open arms. The assistant to the president of the Continental Congress to whom he spoke displayed no particular warmth. He was advised to get in touch with the financier Robert Morris, the man who was known as the "banker of the Revolution." Lafayette again felt hopeful, because Morris was precisely the man on whom his agent in France had relied for the transfer of Lafayette's funds to America. But he was disappointed, because the financier was too busy to meet with the French volunteers. He made an appointment to meet them the next morning at the entrance to Independence Hall. The rich and influential Morris treated him rather brusquely, pointing to a man passing by, James Lovell, chairman of the recently established Committee of Foreign Correspondence. He seemed to be the man who could do something for the passengers of the *Victoire*. Moreover,, he was fluent in French. Morris went on his way, and Lafayette turned hopefully to Lovell, who dismissed him almost as quickly, on the pretext that while America had needed foreign military help, it no longer did. As for the commissions Silas Deane had handed out bestowing various ranks in the American army, this was a flagrant abuse on the part of the Continental Congress's representative in Paris, because he had never received instructions on the matter and had acted on his own, which meant that the documents had no value. Lovell, however, cordially thanked the Frenchmen for their good intentions toward his country. If they wanted to do some sightseeing, they could of course stay and travel freely as friendly visitors.

The French were dismayed. Had they been manipulated from the very beginning? If so, by whom and for what reason? Perhaps British agents had told the Americans they were clandestine envoys of Marshal de Broglie in reality assigned to foster his ambitious plans, that no one in America wanted to have anything to do with. If Mauroy, along with De Kalb, had really been given a secret mission by the marshal, it was up to him—since he was soon sent back to France—to inform his patron that his great plans had no hopes of being realized. As for De Kalb, he remained with Lafayette and met a glorious death in battle.

The enthusiasm of the French volunteers seemed to have suffered a serious blow. The leader of the expedition sat in his room thinking while his companions took a melancholy stroll along the banks of the Delaware on the hot summer day. For Lafayette, the adventure on which he had embarked, drawing honest gentlemen in his wake, could not end in such a pitiful way. It would be impossible for him to confront the humiliation and ridicule of returning to France as he had come, after having boasted of being appointed general at the age of nineteen. He would never dare show himself at court after such an episode. And how could he present the affair to his severe father-in-law, who wanted to have him locked up in the Bastille? Lafayette could already hear his scornful laugh. And he could not face Adrienne after all his letters full of exalted declarations of faith, worthy of a hero preparing to perform great deeds. There must have been some misunderstanding, some conspiracy by Machiavellian British agents. But all was not lost. He had to try again, present the basic problem to men with the highest authority. Above all, he had to distinguish himself from his self-satisfied and arrogant compatriots who had come to America out of self-interest, looking for personal advancement. He and his companions had crossed the ocean only to serve, at the risk of their life, the great cause of freedom embodied by America. His motives were disinterested, and he had undertaken the voyage at his own expense, taking the risk of disobeying his king, because he was at heart a rebel, just as the Americans were rebels against George III. He aspired only to the honor of fighting as a free man and dying, if necessary, as a free man, sword in hand.

The Americans had already begun to understand him; while Lafayette was preparing his next step, Lovell and his colleagues had looked closely at the letters from Franklin and Silas Deane and at other messages concerning the unusual volunteer. They were disturbed. Lovell wondered whether he had been too hasty. Benjamin Franklin had presented things very clearly. They ought not to discourage a man whose presence would facilitate a connection with Versailles at a time when the Continental Congress was hoping for help from France, indispensable both militarily and diplomatically.

The next day, acknowledging his mistake, Lovell personally went to see Lafayette, along with fellow delegate William Duer, to apologize for his chilly reception, to welcome him to the country on behalf of the Congress, and to invite him to speak to a congressional committee. Reassured, Lafayette made his case, eloquently insisting on his love of freedom.

Lovell could recognize his difference from the other French volunteers, more accurately mercenaries, that he had encountered. Lafayette insisted that he was completely disinterested, and that if he was not given the promised rank, he would serve as a simple soldier. Convinced of his sincerity, Lovell and Duer became his advocates. Congress passed a resolution recognizing the great merits of the Marquis de Lafayette and, in response to his zeal, awarded him the rank of major-general. But his troubles were not at an end. Although he had been personally praised by Congress, he still had to argue forcefully so that at least some of his companions could join the fight with him. Only De Kalb, De Gimat, and La Colombe, Lafayette's aide de camp, were allowed to join the ranks of the army. All the others had to return to France, one can imagine with what disappointment.

Lafayette had not yet recovered from this setback when he had to confront another. Although he had been appointed major-general, he would not command a division against the enemy. He would wear a general's uniform, receive the honors due his rank, and be admitted to staff meetings, but his position would be as an honored guest, an observer of high rank dispatched by a friendly country. This flattering but passive role was, of course, not what he had hoped for. What good would he do if he were not fighting? His hosts did not say so openly, but they would find him extremely useful. Sharing the feelings of the combat officers, Lafayette, as a politically engaged and enthusiastic observer, would certainly provide the kind of information the Philadelphia leaders wished to convey to Versailles. That is, he would help to have their struggle taken seriously enough so that sympathy would be transformed into a formal defensive and offensive alliance. This was hardly the kind of glory that he thirsted after, and again he protested. Had they not understood that all he wanted was to fight? The only thing to do was to turn to the military authorities. The Continental Congress turned the matter over to the only man who could make a definitive decision: the commander in chief of the army, George Washington. It happened that Washington was in Philadelphia for a few days.

CHAPTER FIFTEEN

THE TAVERN OF DESTINY

IN THE PROVISIONAL CAPITAL OF THE NATION THAT HAD declared its independence on July 4, 1776, the City Tavern was one of the places most frequented by military and political leaders.

They met for dinners, as formal as the circumstances permitted; food was plentiful and of high quality. The atmosphere was a blend of officers' mess and comfortable restaurant where representatives and government officials could invite important guests.

On August 1, 1777, Lafayette was invited to a dinner that was considered important because Washington would be present. When the young volunteer arrived at the City Tavern, most of the guests were already in the room reserved for the meal. The protocol was not as strictly regulated as, for example, with dinners given by the Marshal de Broglie in Metz. Etiquette here was

106

reduced to a minimum, and conduct was governed by simplicity and cordiality. There was no heel clicking. Lafayette had no difficulty recognizing the commander in chief in the group of uniformed men, and moved toward him as though attracted by a magnetic force. His natural majesty and the benevolent and reserved courtesy he displayed toward all the guests, regardless of rank or office, were unmistakable signs. Although he was not yet twenty, he had already met kings, princes, commanding generals, and high dignitaries of all kinds, in Britain and in France, and none of the figures he had approached had had the dignity and presence of this leader of a band of rebels. He seemed a worthy embodiment of the movement that would transform the New World and give the Old World food for thought. Lafayette bowed respectfully before the man who would decide his fate, and the fate of four million Americans. Washington smiled and seemed, with a single glance, to evaluate this anxious and awkward adolescent, the celebrated marquis who had come from France at his own expense, the talk of the town. He had difficulty imagining that this young man had frequented the court of Versailles, and had discussed events in America with George III's brother in a garrison town in eastern France before being presented to the king himself by his wife's uncle, the French ambassador in London. This was the man to whom his attention had been brought by Silas Deane, Benjamin Franklin, and John Lovell, because of the unusual quality of his adventure (that the British press had not failed to note) and the services he could render through his connections. The general might have been amused by the contrast between Lafayette's appearance and his reputation. But, a sharp observer of men, Washington was struck by the impression of openness and determination he presented. Despite Lafayette's still hesitant and awkward English—Washington knew no French—and the twenty-five-year age difference, the two men struck up an instant rapport. They felt they were destined to understand and respect one another and to confront the future together. One of the greatest friendships of the late eighteenth century began on that August 1, 1777.

George Washington's strength lay in his placid majesty. Everyone was happy to acknowledge the virtues of the warrior hero, the commander in chief of the continental army, who would later participate in drafting the Constitution, and would be the unanimous choice as the first president of the United States. George Washington was born in Wakefield, Virginia, on February 22, 1732. His parents were of English origin and belonged to the economic and cultural elite of slave-holding planters in Virginia. He learned topography as an adolescent and helped map the Shenandoah Valley. When Augustine died, George's half brother Lawrence became something of a mentor, and George later inherited Mount Vernon from him. He became a Freemason at the age of twenty, in 1752. Four years later, George Washington joined the Virginia militia with the rank of major and helped build a series of forts on the western frontier. The Ohio Valley was at the time a theater of battle between the British and the French and the governor gave him the mission of driving out the French. Meeting opposition, he attacked and killed a group of ten scouts. He built a small fort at the site of the future city of Pittsburgh to prepare for reprisals, but because it was built on a flood plain and had insufficient defenses, it was of no value. Washington surrendered on July 3, negotiated his return to Virginia, and left the French in control of the valley. This was the first American engagement in the Seven Years' War. Even Washington had a dark side to his existence. He committed his most serious mistake on May 27, 1754, when he ordered the execution of a French officer, Joseph Coulon de Jumonville, who had come to talk under protection of a white flag and with the status of emissary, charged with delivering a demand to withdraw from land belonging to the king of France. Washington later claimed that he had taken Jumonville for a spy, incompatible with his status as an emissary. Jumonville's death provoked a scandal in France, and even an Anglophile like Voltaire declared: "I am no longer of the English party since the English have become ocean pirates and assassinate our officers in New France." Claude de Contrecœur then sent a detachment of 500 men to capture Washington, under the command of Jumonville's brother. Washington was captured at Fort Necessity, but released even though Contrecœur was supposed to try and execute him for murder. The gesture of generosity was all the more striking because the future alliance between French and Americans was, of course, as yet unknown. It is interesting to note that Washington acknowledged his mistake in writing. A town bears the name of Jumonville in memory of the sad event.

By 1774, Washington was one of the richest men in the colonies. He was elected as a delegate from Virginia to the First Continental Congress, and to the Second in the following year. On June 15, 1775, on a motion by John Adams, Congress voted unanimously to appoint him commander in chief of the continental army. He joined the ragtag forces stationed near Boston, confronting a 12,000-strong force of well-trained redcoats, one of the factors that led him to order his recruiting agents to accept free blacks. In 1776, Washington took Boston and forced the British troops under Howe to evacuate to Halifax. He then marched to New York to prepare for the British counteroffensive. He lost the Battle of Long Island but managed to hold his troops together and retreat through New Jersey. The future of the Revolution seemed in jeopardy until the remarkable Christmas crossing of the Delaware to attack the Hessian mercenaries in

Trenton. He surprised the British forces under Cornwallis at Princeton in early 1777 and retook New Jersey. He was a man and a military leader who knew how to make time his ally, to withstand hardship, and to return to the battle. He possessed determination, calm, courage, obstinacy, a sense of organization, the ability to resist, and the will to take the initiative after defeat. His victories had strengthened the morale of the colonists in favor of independence.

This was the man the young French aristocrat had chosen as a guide, and the two are appropriately memorialized by the Bartholdi statue in Paris (a replica can be found on Morningside Heights near Columbia University in New York). The commander in chief had fully grasped the situation in which the newcomer found himself. He invited Lafayette to join him at his headquarters, gave him the insignia corresponding to his promised rank, and took him along to inspect the forts erected to protect the approaches to the Delaware. Observing his behavior and reactions, Washington introduced him to his chief lieutenants, showed him the arrangements of the rather rudimentary rebel military organization, and sent him for a period of training in a military camp. There, as at Washington's headquarters, Lafayette made a very favorable impression, even on generals such as Horatio Gates, Henry Knox (head of artillery) Nathaniel Greene, and William Alexander (who claimed the title of Earl of Stirling). He was full of good will, never complained, and never displayed the slightest pretension or made the slightest demand. He conducted himself throughout like an eager trainee, intensely experiencing everything his companions in battle were going through, and sharing their moments of exaltation and disappointment at bad news from the front. One day when they were inspecting a unit notable for the shabbiness of its uniforms, the scarcity of its weapons, and the ineptitude of its soldiers, Washington remarked that he must find the spectacle rather disappointing as a man who had belonged to one of the most highly disciplined and well-equipped armies in the world. Lafayette merely answered: "I am here not to teach but to learn." The remark spread throughout the army and greatly boosted the esteem in which its author was held.

There was, however, one superior officer who, despite his shows of politeness, did not wish Lafayette well: Colonel Thomas Conway, a Frenchman born in Ireland whose entire career had been in Europe. A valiant soldier, but extremely ambitious and conspiratorial, he thought himself destined because of his bilingualism to be the most prominent Frenchman in the American army. The arrival and great popularity of Lafayette offended him, and he tried indirectly to get rid of him by joining a political and military plot aimed at Washington's dismissal. Lafayette played a part in unraveling the plot. There were two other French officers who might be offended by the popularity of the commander-in-chief's aide de camp. First was Du Coudray, an engineer who had come through the clandestine network established by Beaumarchais and Deane. He was an engineer of great talent but had trouble adapting to the ways of the country and to the conditions of a war that was in many ways a guerrilla combat. He died in an accidental drowning. Another possibly jealous man was, like Lafayette, an aristocrat of distinguished lineage who had arrived a few months earlier than he. This courageous and generous marquis was Armand Tufin de La Rouërie, from Brittany, who became famous through his exploits leading cavalry units under the name of Colonel Armand. But although he was a little annoyed by all the praise of his young compatriot, Armand did not conspire against him.

Washington appreciated Colonel Armand for his bravery and boldness at the head of his cavalry units. He was a man of the battlefield, adept at attacking, a kind of commando leader. But he was imprudent, and however great his loyalty, he did not have the idealistic character and the passionate love of freedom that made Lafayette a being apart in this world.

CHAPTER SIXTEEN

ORDEAL BY FIRE

B Y SEPTEMBER 1777, LAFAYETTE HAD BEEN LIVING AMONG the close associates of the commander in chief for a little longer than a month. Although his time at the Military Academy of Versailles and the garrison in Metz had not taught him much about military strategy, he knew just about as much as the average rebel officer, most of whom would never attain the rank he had been awarded at the outset. But as the scion of a distinguished military family, whose father had died a heroic death on the battlefield of Minden in 1759, Gilbert du Motier de Lafayette carried the art of war in his veins. He knew what the American army was worth and the dangers that he faced: insufficient weapons, equipment, and supplies; inadequate discipline, regional idiosyncrasies, and political interference. It had been able to win dazzling victories over an army as well organized as the British Army because it contained men of exceptional courage and endurance, imaginative leaders with the ability to improvise and take risks. Confronting professional British soldiers, or mercenaries recruited in Germany, Washington's soldiers, like their French successors in Year II of the Revolution, were soldiers in the service of an ideal. This is why Lafayette felt at ease in their midst despite everything that divided them: language (though he was making rapid progress in English), food, customs. He even felt he was becoming an American. Washington had few secrets from him, even fewer when, learning that his commander was a Freemason, Lafayette told him that he himself had recently been initiated in Paris and therefore had had contact with some of the most distinguished and cultivated men in France. This bond must have helped to bring the men together and strengthen their friendship. In any event, Washington did not conceal from his aide de camp that the military situation in September 1777 was troubling and that it was feared the British forces would soon be in a position to take Philadelphia, a highly symbolic city for Americans. Washington did not imagine for an instant that Lafayette would send alarmist reports to France calling into question the rebels' desire and ability to win victory. Washington knew that the young man shared his thirst for victory, and that the harshest ordeals, far from driving him to give up the fight, would strengthen his will to continue. And so, Washington decided the time had come for Lafayette's baptism of fire.

In early July, a British force under General Burgoyne had advanced from Canada and driven the American troops commanded by Horatio Gates from Ticonderoga. It was now threatening an advance into Pennsylvania as the British fleet was landing forces in the Chesapeake Bay in preparation for a major attack from the south. General Howe's plan was to capture the rebel army in a pincer movement, and the fall of Ticonderoga had made success likely. Washington concentrated his forces around Philadelphia and immediately began attempts to weaken the enemy columns.

On September 11, a decision was made to launch an immediate attack against the British regiments under Howe's subordinate Cornwallis on a line along the Brandywine River. Commanding a few hundred men, Lafayette was ordered to join General Sullivan's division, which was the most exposed—he had been unable to break through the lines because of enemy artillery superiority. When his left flank was forced to retreat, he even had to join the central division in order to establish a defensive core that was as solid as possible. All British fire was concentrated on this core, which began to crumble. Brandywine was anything but an American victory, but the bulk of their forces was able to escape encirclement and be preserved for future combat. Lafayette played a very positive role in the battle. With rare energy and enthusiasm, and boldly exposing himself, he held together the men who were beginning to flee in every direction. He turned a band of deserters into a relatively disciplined force that retreated in good order and avoided capture. But he exposed himself a bit too much and was hit by a bullet in the leg. He fell from his horse, had himself put back in the saddle, and continued to rally his soldiers, until the excessive bleeding became so worrying that he had to be evacuated.

After having his own doctor treat the wounded man, whom he was beginning to see more and more as a son, Washington sent him to the rear and reported his brilliant conduct to Congress. Evacuated by boat to Bristol, the major-general, whose twentieth birthday had been a few days earlier, was visited by Henry Laurens, president of the Continental Congress, who personally transported him to the hospital of the Moravian

Brothers in Bethlehem. There he received excellent care and was on his feet ready to resume combat in two months.

Following another heroic defeat at Germantown, Washington had been unable to prevent the evacuation of Philadelphia, which was occupied by British forces on September 26. While Congress moved to Lancaster, American troops saved by the commander in chief were assembled in the camp at Valley Forge, not far from the occupied capital, where Lafayette joined the men he now saw as his American brothers for a terribly trying winter.

CHAPTER SEVENTEEN

THE GLORIOUS
BAREFOOT SOLDIERS

I T WAS SNOWING IN VALLEY FORGE IN DECEMBER 1777. Rather than casting a romantic glow on the setting, the snow made it even gloomier. Valley Forge was a huge improvised military camp in the middle of the woods less than twenty miles from enemy lines, where Washington had assembled the nine thousand men he had been able to save, who had been joined by civilian refugees. There were no permanent buildings or traditional military barracks, but hundreds of small huts that had sprouted like mushrooms, built by the soldiers themselves with wood from the trees of the forest. These farmers and trappers who had often settled temporarily in precarious regions knew how to build, quickly and with the materials at hand, improvised cabins that would protect them from cold, rain, snow, wind, robbers, Indians, and wild animals, often for months and, with some improvements, sometimes for years. Lafayette was astonished by the speed with which they built this precarious town, the somber setting for the army's winter quarters.

Valley Forge was a sad place for everyone there, although some were more comfortably settled than others. Almost everything was in short supply: uniforms in good condition, boots, shoes, blankets, furniture, kitchen utensils, and enough weapons to counter an unexpected major attack. Some officers were in rags, others had made boots out of thick woolen cloth. All day, when their fingers were not numb with the cold, soldiers cut, sewed, assembled, improvised, patched. They ate whatever they could. Fortunately the local farmers supplied enough gin and whiskey to hold out, especially when the snow was blowing and it was hard to stay close enough to the fire. In spite of the commanders' efforts to maintain the morale and discipline of men living in forced idleness, desertions were numerous. They had better things to do in workshops, farms, plantations, or shops. The winter was very long and the soldiers had not been paid for months. And yet many of them held on. In their combination of extreme misery and heroism, the combatants of Valley Forge prefigured the soldiers of Year II of the French Revolution. They had not forgotten that they were rebels, and for many of them, especially the officers, a defeat would mean the scaffold or long years in prison—and the reputation of British prisons was dreadful. Their tenacity was all the more remarkable because they knew that merchants in Philadelphia and elsewhere were growing rich because of the war, indifferent to the suffering of soldiers and refugees and to the ruin threatening the country.

Major-General Lafayette was intent on sharing as much as possible in the harsh ordeals of his subordinates. His youthful escapades in the Auvergne mountains had prepared him for very rigorous conditions. His ascendancy over the men under his command arose not only from his courage and coolness under fire but also from his sobriety, his contempt for comfort, and his understanding of the revolutionary situation and the course of conduct that flowed from that for everyone involved.

This young general also exerted authority through his sense of equity, his ability to command without humiliating or brutalizing his subordinates. Yet the Virginians he had been ordered to lead to Valley Forge were hard to handle, the worst soldiers in the American army according to the colonels and generals who had commanded them: vulgar, brutal, drunken, thieving, brawling, stubborn, arrogant, lacking in any form of discipline, and unable to understand anything but harsh words and well-placed blows. This was the division he had finally been given to command by Congress on December 1, 1777, in reward for his conduct at Haddonfield, where, leading a small squadron on a reconnaissance mission, he had overwhelmed three hundred Hessian mercenaries serving under the British flag. His probationary apprenticeship had lasted only four months. He himself had asked for the Virginia regiment, to honor Washington, who was rather embarrassed by the gesture, for he wondered whether his terrible compatriots would obey such a young and inexperienced commander. But Lafayette insisted, and Washington finally agreed. Lafayette was seriously disappointed, however, when he discovered that the promised division contained just a little more than one thousand men, assembled by scraping the bottom of the barrel. He nonetheless displayed at Valley Forge, where inaction was undermining the morale of many, an optimism and fervor that Washington deeply appreciated.

Lafayette was at Valley Forge in early May 1778 when he received the great news by courier: France, which had recognized the independence of the United States after the victory of Saratoga, had finally signed a defensive and offensive alliance and a treaty of trade and friendship on February 6. On March 20, the American plenipotentiaries Benjamin Franklin, Arthur Lee, Ralph Izard, and Silas Deane, were received with great ceremony at Versailles. The die had been cast. Louis XVI had chosen the time well, neither too soon nor too late.

The news was celebrated at Valley Forge. They drank large quantities of everything they could find, out of chipped glasses, dirty cups, or straight from the bottle. Had the young general commanding the dreadful Virginians at Valley Forge helped, through his presence in America, and through the reports he had sent to Vergennes, to his influential father-in-law, and to his wife whom he encouraged to repeat his remarks, to foster the progress of the indispensable alliance? The leaders of the new nation were inclined to think so, and Lafayette himself had no doubt about it. Indeed, on March 20, 1778, before a great dinner given in their honor at Versailles, Franklin and his colleagues visited Adrienne at home to thank her for the help given by her husband.

Lafayette did not spend all of the winter and spring of 1777–78 at Valley Forge. He was offered another opportunity to win the glory he dreamed of in January. He was ordered to go to Albany to take command of forces in the north to prepare an invasion of Canada and drive out the British forces. He would have a corps of three thousand men (soldiers and militia), a large budget, abundant reserve supplies, horses, and sleds. His first task would be to burn the British fleet, which was blocked by ice on Lake Champlain. Then he would march on Montreal and Quebec City. The headquarters staff who had dreamed up this campaign still believed that the French Canadians were eager to join the rebels, despite the failure of Benjamin Franklin's mission to Canada in early 1776. But nothing could be more enticing to the new general of the northern rebel forces than this plan: he imagined himself as the liberator of Canada. He, Gilbert de

Lafayette, would erase with his sword the shame of the Treaty of Paris. What would the king, Maurepas, and the Duke d'Ayen say when he appeared at Versailles as a conquering general in his splendid blue American uniform?

When he reached Albany, he was again disappointed. Instead of the three thousand men promised, there were barely one thousand. As for the reserve supplies and matériel, they were very inadequate, to say the least. It would be preposterous to launch an invasion of Canada with such paltry resources. Lafayette had the good sense, courage, and character to immediately give up the campaign from which he had hoped to gain so much. He expressed undisguised bitterness to Washington, who, at bottom, had never favored the expedition. Washington found the words to go directly to the heart of the matter: "I am persuaded that everyone will applaud your prudence in renouncing a project, in pursuing which you would vainly have attempted physical impossibilities. . . . However sensibly your ardour for glory may make you feel this disappointment, you may be assured that your character stands as fair as ever it did."

Appeased if not comforted, Lafayette managed to maintain discipline in his unit, covered his soldiers' back pay out of his own pocket, reorganized the Albany military region, and restored abandon forts, before undertaking one of the most positive actions he was to accomplish in America: reconciliation with Indian tribes that had until then been manipulated by the enemy.

CHAPTER EIGHTEEN

GENERAL KAYEWLA

O N MARCH 9, 1778, THE ASSEMBLED INDIANS WERE celebrating noisily in the broad plain near the theoretical border between the United States and Canada. Despite the uproar, old men squatting on animal skins were smoking the peace pipe. Women wearing multicolored cloth were roasting sides of meat, children were running among the tents, and the men were deep in discussion. Their face paint was so carefully designed that they seemed to be wearing masks. This exuberant and diverse crowd belonged to the League of Five Nations of the Iroquois and related tribes. On this March day they were celebrating the entry of a new tribe into what was about to become the League of Six Nations.

Lafayette, who had discussed the Indian question with Governor Clinton of New York, was distressed that the British had been able to turn the Iroquois and their allies against the

Americans with large distributions of rum and tools, along with a few weapons. Feeling supported by the British, the Iroquois had pillaged, burned out, murdered, and driven away through terror a portion of the colonial population of the northern states. Lafayette wanted to transform these turbulent tribes, whom he considered victims of British trickery, into allies of the rebel army, just as the French in Canada had earlier made the Hurons invaluable allies of the subjects of Louis XIV and Louis XV.

By appearing alone and unannounced among the Indians assembled on this solemn occasion, with no preliminary negotiations, General Lafayette was taking a great personal risk. He might have been exposing himself to scalping and torture. On the other hand, approaching them when the heads of several tribes had come together was a politically astute move, because the principal difficulty of negotiating with the Indians had been the fact that they were scattered.

Although he presented himself as an American general mandated by Congress, Lafayette decided to speak French. The language brought back pleasant memories to several of his listeners. One of them, covered with feathers and his face colorfully painted, making him indistinguishable from his companions, was in fact a former soldier of Louis XV, named Lafleur, who had decided to become an Indian after having been captured by and escaping from the British during the Seven Years' War. He stood up and, following custom, coated the speaker with grease, which didn't bother Lafayette, as a sign that he should be treated benevolently by the audience. Lafayette praised the tribes for their move toward unity, a prerequisite for their freedom and development; he exhorted them to cooperate with the Americans, friends of the French who wished to live in peace with them, whereas the British wanted to subdue them through intrigue and false promises. After his speech was translated, Lafayette responded appropriately to questions that were raised. He distributed a number of trinkets, a few gold louis, and the barrels of alcohol indispensable for an agreement, and a treaty of alliance was signed before a celebratory dinner. Now a brother in arms of the Iroquois, whom Lafayette, as a disciple of Rousseau, saw as noble savages, he was given the name Kayewla (Intrepid Knight) after one of the tribe's most celebrated warriors. The League of Six Nations was for a time a significant ally of the Americans. Kayewla could be proud of the service he had rendered, and he returned to Valley Forge with his head held high, despite the abortive Canada campaign.

Washington envisaged one day changing the nomadic Indians into peaceful farmers who could be integrated along with other non-English speakers into the new nation. He therefore had nothing but praise for his loyal subordinate's initiative. In early May, it will be recalled, news came of the alliance with France. A few days later, while his companions at Valley Forge were still celebrating, Lafayette was informed of the death of his oldest daughter, Henriette. He was deeply stricken, but this new wound, coming on top of the disappointments he had just confronted and overcome, helped to make him more mature and thoughtful, a leader.

CHAPTER NINETEEN

A DISAPPOINTMENT
ARRIVES BY SEA

I n July 1778, off the coast not far from the mouth of
the Delaware a corpulent captain with a contented face and
a comfortable double chin stood at the wheel of a French
warship, the *Fantasque*. He had removed the obligatory powdered
wig, revealing a bald head. A Provençal with dark eyes and a
piercing gaze, he was a Mediterranean to his fingertips. He was
forgiven for his slovenly appearance, his corpulence, and his foul
temper because, despite his character, he was a very fine sailor.
The man at the wheel was the Bailli de Suffren.

In addition to the *Fantasque*, sailing under his orders were
three frigates: the *Aimable*, the *Chimère*, and the *Engageante*. They
were part of a fleet of twelve vessels, including the *Tonnant* (80
cannons), the *Languedoc* (90), the *Marseillaise* (74), the *Provence*
(64), and five frigates. The fleet had been assembled in Toulon in
the spring of 1778 to come to the aid of the American rebels, the

new allies of France. It had left port on April 18 and did not enter the mouth of the Delaware until July 8. The combative Suffren had been grumbling constantly. He did not like this campaign, and he did not hide his feelings from his friends. He had limited confidence in the leader of the expedition, Admiral d'Estaing, appointed by the king as lieutenant-general of French naval forces in North America. D'Estaing from Auvergne and Suffren from Provence were of the same age and knew and appreciated one another. D'Estaing had won glory as an infantry officer in the East Indies. He was a leader of men and a firebrand who had very boldly captured forts from the British on Sumatra and Mauritius. One day he was given command of a frigate, and with this light vessel he captured several British ships in the Persian Gulf. On the basis of these exploits, he asked to be transferred to the navy, but in Suffren's eyes, he was not a real sailor. He did not know how to command at sea, and he would be even less competent as the head of a fleet than the Duke de Chartres, the future Philippe Égalité, who had learned navigation technique from Bougainville, and to prove that he was a better sailor than his cousin Louis XVI, only an armchair sailor, who had tried unsuccessfully to command a squadron.

Some saw evidence that he was not a real sailor in the fact that after first hesitating to run the blockade in New York, he decided not to land at Newport, Rhode Island. Suffren had even less respect for d'Estaing's adjutant, Count de Breugnon, of whom he said that he was a good soul but that "he had declined from imbecility into childhood." It is true that Suffren had a sharp tongue, and his judgments were not always models of equity. Yet he was not wrong to be worried. D'Estaing's campaign was a disappointment to the Americans, who had greeted the anticipated reinforcements with cries of enthusiasm.

It was also a disappointment for Lafayette, who had thought

when he saw Silas Deane, back from Paris, along with Conrad Gérard, plenipotentiary of France to the United States and one of the architects of the February 1778 alliance, disembark from one of the ships in the fleet, that he was finally going to play a decisive role at the head of a Franco-American army.

Nonetheless, the fleet had, without combat, secured an advantage for the allies of France. In June 1778, the British, who had been informed of its impending arrival, fearing a landing, had evacuated Philadelphia, and the Continental Congress had returned to the city. It is true that the rebels had already caused the British some difficulties, in which Lafayette had played a part. On May 18 at Barren Hill, assigned to isolate the garrison and the city of Philadelphia from the rest of the British Army, he succeeded in extricating his twenty-four hundred men from the grip of enemy forces seven thousand strong, who had managed to skirt the Americans.

The Americans won a qualified victory at Monmouth on June 25, thanks to Washington's cool head, and General Clinton was forced to retreat to New York. As for General Howe, who had vowed at Barren Hill that he would take Lafayette, whom he called "the boy," prisoner and bring him to England in a ship already fitted out for the purpose, he was covered in ridicule, and he organized his own departure for London.

D'Estaing, who seems to have been given no particular instructions regarding Lafayette, whose situation in France was still questionable, was urged by the Americans to attack New York. He declined, on the pretext that his large vessels had too deep a draft to attempt the operation with any chance of success. Suffren, for his part, had been ordered by his commander to remove a British naval division from Newport Harbor. He advanced full sail as though he were going to board the enemy ships with no prior combat. Surprised and panic-stricken, the

British ships retreated and ran aground on the coast, where their crews burned them. The battle lasted for only a few hours on August 8. On August 10, at ten in the morning, thirty-six British ships appeared and dropped anchor. Not losing a moment, D'Estaing ordered flags raised, and his fleet, with the wind at its back, sailed beneath the nose of the immobilized and dumb-founded British. Unfortunately, a powerful storm spoiled this exemplary withdrawal and avenged the enemy by damaging several large French vessels, making it necessary for the admiral to sail to Boston for major repairs. The British fleet sailed for New York, a base its commanders considered impregnable. Even though repairs to the damaged French vessels were necessary, and Boston was the only port with shipyards large enough to carry them out, his allies did not understand D'Estaing's attitude. General Sullivan questioned his abilities. A British commission that was there to attempt to negotiate a compromise peace took advantage of the situation to cast doubt through its propaganda on the value of the French alliance. Had the Americans forgotten the "perfidy" of Lafayette's compatriots? The campaign did have some effect: French officers were thrown into Boston Harbor. Lafayette, who had refused to sign a motion disavowing Admiral d'Estaing, sent a card to Lord Carlisle, head of the British commission, challenging him to a duel because of the insulting remarks he had made about France. George III's envoy replied ironically that the matter would be settled by the confrontation between the two navies. Annoyed that his challenge had been rejected and ridiculed but supported by Washington, who wanted to preserve the alliance at any cost, Lafayette was unstinting in his efforts to clear up misunderstandings and calm resentments, earning in difficult circumstances even more esteem and admiration from his hosts.

Disconcerted by the coldness and suspicion he encountered in contrast to the enthusiasm and warmth that had greeted his arrival, and aware of the weakness of his resources, Admiral d'Estaing ordered his fleet to sail to the Caribbean. There he carried out operations against islands owned by the British, but with surprising lethargy. When Suffren, who was living half naked on his ship under the tropical sun, saw the admiral wearing a broad-brimmed felt hat belonging to his brother, the Bishop of Sisteron, he said: "We backed down in New York, we collapsed in Newport, and now we're snoozing in the Leeward Islands." But Suffren had managed to bring back a living souvenir from D'Estaing's campaign: a young American woman disguised as a sailor, who lived discreetly on board and provided him with the warrior's reward. He continued a life of ease at sea until he was sent to the East Indies, where he won great glory.

Cooperation between France and the United States could not be limited to the visit of D'Estaing's fleet. Washington and most members of Congress wanted to revive the alliance, and they thought of sending Lafayette, who was exhausted from his exertions in a variety of missions and needed rest, to Versailles. No one was in a better position to speak for the Americans, whose ordeals he had continued to share, and to secure really substantial assistance in men and matériel.

Lafayette, who had been on edge ever since he had had to defend his compatriots against the suspicions of his comrades in arms, sensed that he needed to relax and to see his family and friends. On October 21, 1778, the Continental Congress authorized him to return to France to participate in another way in the war against Great Britain. Washington assured him that he would recover his position as major-general on his return. Henry Laurens, president of the Congress, wrote a letter to Louis XVI praising the volunteer's merits. Instructions were given to

Franklin in Paris to have a luxurious sword forged, decorated with emblems commemorating the great deeds accomplished by the young general, which would be solemnly presented to him as a sign of the gratitude of the United States.

Invigorated by the marks of confidence he had received, the future Hero of Two Worlds set off on horseback for Boston, where he was to embark on a ship named the *Alliance*. On the way, he fell ill and was bedridden for a month with a serious intestinal inflammation. They feared for his life, and Washington's personal physician, Dr. Cochran, was once again at his bedside.

A large hemorrhage that frightened his companions saved him. He recovered his strength and reached Boston, from which the *Alliance* sailed on January 11, 1779. A few days later another event put his mission in danger. The crew contained British deserters and Americans of doubtful patriotism, and some of them mutinied. They believed promises made by the British that navy deserters would be pardoned if they seized an enemy ship and that they would be given a sum of money equivalent to the value of the prize. An Irish sailor, loyal to the rebel cause, denounced the plot in time. The mutineers were disarmed and put in irons, and Lafayette managed to exchange them for American prisoners of the British.

On February 6, the frigate *Alliance* reached Brest. Its entry into port coincided with the first anniversary of the Franco-American alliance.

CHAPTER TWENTY

A VERY PAMPERED PRISONER

A RUMOR WAS CIRCULATING IN THE ARISTOCRATIC QUARTER of Paris known as the Faubourg Saint-Honoré during the winter of 1779. A man was being held prisoner in the Noailles house, one of the most handsome and luxuriously furnished on the street that shared its name with the quarter. The rumor was not entirely without foundation.

Someone was indeed being held by a decision that had come from the king himself. But it was anticipated that he would stay there for only ten days. He had not been locked up in a dark, cramped cellar but, rather, enjoyed all the comfort of the rich residence he could not leave, but where he could be visited by friends and family, a large number of visits in ten days. It was simply appropriate that Paris and all of France be made aware that a man of quality had been confined to this spot because, two years earlier, he had violated an order of the king and that, in

France, the king is the king. One is tempted to add: for the moment.

This benign, symbolic punishment, which was more a social ritual than a sanction strictly speaking, was all Louis XVI thought it necessary to inflict on a man returning from America with a well-established reputation as a hero. In return, all of fashionable Paris paraded through rue Saint-Honoré to express their admiration for the star of the hour, or to make his acquaintance. There was talk of nothing but this prisoner. Free to move about the house, he behaved simultaneously like a grand ambassador and a general. He transmitted instructions from Congress to Franklin and conferred with Maurepas and Vergennes, giving them abundant advice about the pursuit of military operations and trying to revive the idea of a campaign in Canada under his leadership. Learning that a landing on the British Isles was under consideration, he asked to participate so he could be the first Frenchman to set foot on British soil, as though that honor was his by right. When he confronted hesitancy, he proposed as a fallback that he be given command of a planned operation against Ireland. In the meantime, he was celebrated in salons, Masonic lodges, at the Opera. At the Théâtre-Français, the author of *L'Amour français* added a passage in his honor on April 17, 1779, the day Lafayette attended a performance. The Duke de Chartres, jealous of this extraordinary fame, arranged to have the play withdrawn.

Now that the hero's glory was universally proclaimed, the beautiful and calculating Aglaë de Hunolstein, on whom he had dared cast his eyes when he was discovering Parisian life, and who had not bestowed a single smile in return for his compliments, said to herself that she should offer him the fullest reward in a woman's power to give to a conqueror. Lafayette received it as he would receive a fully ripened fruit that he had patiently awaited.

Adrienne was, of course, informed of this wounding infidelity, but she was not a woman to show bitterness or dismay. Her forgiveness was another proof of love, and instead of shedding tears she proceeded to give him a son. He was born in December 1779 and given the name George Washington.

Marie Antoinette, who had been disdainful of Lafayette before his departure, treated him with consideration on his return. She even helped him get a regiment, the King's Dragoons, so that he might have in France a rank more in tune with his American career than that of captain, which he still held.

Louis XVI and several members of his entourage, however, found that really too much fuss was being made about this young man. He was ordered to go to Saintes, where his regiment was stationed, and to seriously reorganize his troops. At the same time that he conducted maneuvers and training sessions, the newly appointed colonel bombarded his high-level connections with urgent letters. He sensed that the liberation of Ireland had as little chance of being realized as the liberation of Canada. Authorized to go to Paris to receive the sword that was supposed to be presented to him by Benjamin Franklin in the name of the American nation, he saw Vergennes and tried to persuade him that it was necessary to send another expeditionary force, much larger than the one under D'Estaing, to the American allies, who were counting on the French. Then complete victory over Britain would be possible, provided the forces were well led. And who could command them better than he himself, who knew the terrain and enjoyed the absolute confidence of the American allies? Besides, they would not understand if someone else was chosen in his place.

Vergennes promised nothing, and for good reason. But it did not take Lafayette long to understand that, in the eyes of the king and his ministers, despite his enthusiasm and his genuine merits, he had neither the experience nor sufficient authority to command a large-scale naval and land force that would require a huge budget. The old and wise Marshal de Rochambeau (he called himself "Père Rochambeau) would be placed in charge of the forces. Lafayette—whom some people wanted to get rid of as soon as possible—would be sent to America for reconnaissance. He would arrange the logistics of the reception of French forces, and organize cooperation between the rebels and their allies.

He spent a few hours with Benjamin Franklin, who always provided him with good advice, in his garden in Passy. Franklin was a charming and captivating man, for whom the summit of intelligence seemed to be kindness. Perhaps even more precocious than his visitor, Franklin could read at the age of five and write at seven. He left school at ten and went to work in his father's candle-making business. He soon changed to printing and worked under contract with his brother. His manual dexterity made him what was known as an "operative" in Masonic language. His passion was the acquisition of classic books; he adored Xenophon but also read such moderns as Defoe. He learned Italian and Spanish and familiarized himself with astronomy and the art of navigation. He was an inventor and a musician. He opened a bookstore and stationery shop where one could find naval sextants. He created *Poor Richard's Almanac*, and invented the lightning rod, and a rotisserie. He was democratic, but with a touch of snobbery, and he took his son born out of wedlock with him to England, where Pitt refused to receive him. He toured Europe and was received in France in 1767. Invited to supper by the king, he became the friend of Mirabeau the elder and Turgot. Kings and intelligent rulers understood that he was worth knowing. The king of Denmark visited Franklin in his small house in London. A scientist, philosopher, and writer, he was elected a delegate from Pennsylvania to the Continental Congress on May 6, 1775. He was appointed postmaster, worked to improve rebel arms, and traveled to Quebec to attempt to foment revolt. In Congress, he helped Jefferson draft the Declaration of Independence. His popularity in Paris was enormous—his face was reproduced on dishes and glassware.

After visiting Franklin, Lafayette left for the Île d'Aix, where he boarded the frigate *Hermione* on March 9, 1780. There he might have met an artillery officer stationed at the island's fort who often took melancholy walks along the ramparts, dreaming of America, where he would have liked to join Lafayette and show the rebels his mastery of cannons. But when Lafayette took ship, this career captain, who did not become a general until the reign of Bonaparte, was on a mission on the continent. The two men did not meet until several years later, when the absent man had earned only one stripe but had gained fame in another domain altogether. When he returned to the island, Lafayette was gone, and he continued his lonely vigil, feeling vaguely ashamed that he was living in peace.

From time to time he could see a sentinel below, close to the shore. It was hard to imagine from what direction the enemy might come, but his duty was to wait. In the calm, fair weather, the artillery captain's libertine imagination took wing, and he transferred his military imagination into the domain of amorous intrigue. His name was Choderlos de Laclos, the author of *Les Liaisons dangereuses*. Like the Marquis de Sade imprisoned in the Bastille, Laclos in his fortress gave free rein to the wildest erotic imaginings.

CHAPTER TWENTY-ONE

THE INDIAN SUMMER OF VICTORY

O N MAY 2, 1780, TWO YOUNG UNIFORMED OFFICERS who had ridden flat out from Versailles in less than three days dismounted in the port of Brest. They gazed searchingly around the harbor and looked crestfallen when they realized that a French squadron under full sail was about to go through the narrows. "Too late!" exclaimed the younger of the two. The people around them immediately understood that the captain and second lieutenant had not arrived in time to join the disappearing fleet, and they sympathized. But was it really too late? The two young officers were unwilling to accept this fatalistic conclusion. They jumped into a small boat, held out fistfuls of gold pieces, and promised all of them to the oarsmen if they managed to reach one of the large vessels that could be seen clearly sailing into the distance. Miraculously, they reached their goal. Or so they thought. They were taken on board one vessel and then transferred to the flagship, the *Duc de Bourgogne*, and presented to M. de Ternay, the commander of the fleet transporting a large portion of M. de Rochambeau's six-thousand-strong expeditionary force to America. The two officers explained that they had been given an oral order by the minister of war to join the Soissonais regiment to participate in the fighting under the command of Colonel de Saint-Mesme of that regiment, who had offered them their commissions. M. de Ternay refused to keep them on board. He had no written instructions regarding them. Although Rochambeau very tactfully intervened on their behalf, the admiral would have none of it. He was commander of this ship and of the entire fleet, and he intended to show it. A boat was lowered, and a few hours later the two men, holding back their tears, were back on the Breton coast. They were brothers. The elder, the captain, was Louis-Alexandre Berthier, future Marshal of France, future Prince de Neuchâtel, and Prince de Wagram, a trusted adjutant of Napoleon. He was twenty-seven and had been appointed an engineer-geographer at the age of sixteen. Charles, the second lieutenant, was later killed in a duel in Curaçao in 1783.

Alexandre and Charles could have waited for the sailing of the second naval division, but they were so eager to fight they decided to board a ship headed to the West Indies. From there they thought they would find a way to get to North America, which is indeed what they did. They had a stormy crossing and Charles fell seriously ill, but they finally set foot on United States soil on September 28 and were able to join Rochambeau's forces.

The determination of the Berthier brothers, who after being rejected by the admiral had even said they were willing to serve as simple sailors, was simply an extreme example of the enthusiasm displayed by the bravest and most distinguished young French officers for fighting on the side of the rebels. The fervor and the large numbers of these volunteers, some of whom belonged to families that frequented the court, indicated how popular the American cause was in France and showed that the 1778 alliance expressed something more than the national egoism of Louis XVI and his devoted servant Vergennes.

Lieutenant General Rochambeau, commander in chief of the French forces, had a brilliant staff. The Chevalier and future Marquis de Chastellux, a major-general, was both a soldier and a man of letters, a devotee of the sciences, and a follower of the Encyclopédistes who became a member of the American Philosophical Society. Baron and Count de Viomenil were brigadiers. D'Aboville commanded the artillery, Dédendrouins the engineers, and Tarlé the supply corps. Among the colonels commanding regiments were the Marquis de Laval, assisted by Rochambeau's son, and the Prince de Deux-Ponts, M. de Custine, assisted by Viscount Louis de Noailles, Lafayette's brother-in-law. Among the distinguished figures serving as aides de camp to Rochambeau was Axel de Fersen, whose relationship with Marie Antoinette had stirred so much jealousy and gossip in Versailles. Not everyone at court was sorry to see him leave, and some thought that his incorporation into the expeditionary force, facilitated by Vergennes, was not accidental. The Swedish ambassador wrote to King Gustave III: "The young Count de Fersen has behaved admirably in this situation, in his modesty and moderation, first of all by his decision to go to America. By going off, he has staved off the danger posed by his position. It took strength beyond his age to overcome such a temptation. During the final days, the queen was unable to take her eyes off him, and when she spoke to him, they were full of tears."

Fersen was quite fluent in English and served as an interpreter for Rochambeau on several important occasions. When called upon to do so, he fought with courage and served with honor in all circumstances, but unlike the French aristocrats who had already been won over to liberal ideas, he did not admire the Americans and the society they had created. It seemed to him too mercenary. He wrote to his father about the Americans: "Money is their god," and thought the war redounded rather to the credit of the British.

There was, of course, a good deal of fraternization between the French volunteers and the women of America. The French were fond of Rhode Island, where vineyards reminded many of them of home. They admired the honesty, hospitality, and civic spirit of American citizens and respected the way they lived. Aristocrats who had given free reign to their libertine instincts in Versailles behaved with remarkable sobriety in the society of Newport.

The arrival of the expeditionary force had been fully prepared by Lafayette, and none of these valiant officers ever equaled his place in the hearts of the rebels. At bottom, he was delighted to be serving under Washington and not to be dependent on the French hierarchy. But this freedom of movement led him to make a major blunder when he contacted Rochambeau in New-port, where the commander had set up camp with the bulk of his forces in September 1780.

Claiming to speak in the name of the Americans, he seemed to be dictating Rochambeau's conduct to him, ordering him to quickly attack New York, although he had not yet met Wash-ington. Rochambeau, an experienced old soldier, put the rash young man in his place with gentle irony tinged with paternal benevolence. It was just the right tone to take with Lafayette, one that Washington would have mirrored. The impatient young officer immediately acknowledged his mistake and wrote a touching letter of apology, accepting with sincerity and dig-nity the older man's authority in the common interest of the two countries. And this was the right tone to adopt toward

Rochambeau, who assured his "dear son Lafayette" in return that he "loved him, would love him, and esteem until his last breath."

From then on their cooperation was complete, even though Lafayette remained a United States general until the final victory, representing that country beside Washington and other leaders sitting opposite the French at conferences between the allies. A first meeting was held in Hartford on September 20, 1780. The French were represented by Rochambeau, Ternay, and Chastellux, and the Americans by Washington, Knox, and Lafayette. The decision was made to ask Versailles to send more troops and ships before launching an offensive, because the balance of forces was still favorable to the British. Rochambeau's son and La Pérouse were sent to France with that mission.

The British, for their part, seemed to prefer conspiracy to combat. While some London agents continued to sound out the possibilities for a compromise peace, others managed to convince one of the most brilliant American generals, Benedict Arnold, to betray the cause. He was about to deliver the fort at West Point, a vital communications link between northern and southern rebel forces, to his new masters, when he was unmasked following the fortuitous arrest of his principal British contact, Major André. Arnold was able to escape and take command of a British army in the south, but André was sentenced to death and executed. Washington rejected all requests for clemency from his closest associates, including Hamilton and Lafayette.

While waiting for reinforcements to arrive, Lafayette sought an opportunity for French forces to engage in some brilliant action rather than staying in quarters in Rhode Island, although they were on the best of terms with the local population. The residents were full of praise for the honesty and civility of Louis

XVI's officers and men, who paid promptly for everything they bought and rivaled one another for their politeness to their hosts. Dinners, balls, and public concerts brought officers and prominent families together. The French even invited twenty Iroquois to supper on the flagship, the *Duc de Bourgogne*, and their chants and dances after the meal astonished the crew. This was quite different from the tense atmosphere that had prevailed two years earlier after D'Estaing's fleet had sailed for Boston. Rochambeau's tact and affability, and even his sobriety at table, not to mention his elevated notion of cooperation between allies, left a lasting impression in the United States.

An operation was launched late in 1780 on the Chesapeake, but fortune did not favor the French fleet. On December 15, the head of the fleet, Admiral Ternay, who had been ill for several months, died. He was temporarily replaced by his second in command, Des Touches, who was charged with supporting the planned operation with his guns. Lafayette, at the head of the American forces was given the mission of attacking the enemy forces stationed on the banks of the Chesapeake River, with the backing of Des Touches's ships. The French fleet faced contrary winds once again and had to withdraw in the face of the much larger British fleet under Admiral Arbuthnot. The planned junction of Lafayette and Des Touches at Hampton did not take place. Des Touches returned to Newport, while Lafayette faced the hard task of continuing the battle in Virginia, where the traitor Arnold was fighting against his former brothers in arms at the head of a large enemy force. The Virginians under Lafayette seemed ideally suited to defeat the traitor and, with a little bit of luck, capture him. But the contest was at first very unequal. Facing a heavily equipped force, the Virginia division was short of everything. With no uniforms and often with no shirts, the men looked more like refugees from a natural disaster than troops preparing for battle. Lafayette once again personally borrowed funds to buy matériel, and he called on the patriotic ladies of Baltimore to set up workshops. They set to work without pay making shirts and other clothing for his soldiers. These enthusiastic auxiliaries even made shoes. Their zeal was rewarded with a grand ball, and the decently clothed Virginians marched toward Richmond. They managed to reach the city before the British general Philips, for whom it was also an objective. This was sweet revenge for his opponent, because Philips was thought to have been the officer commanding the troops who had fired the shot that killed Colonel de Lafayette at the battle of Minden in 1759. Lafayette's revenge was complete a few weeks later when he learned of the death from illness of the enemy general. This event did not slacken the fighting. With his two thousand men, Lafayette had to struggle to inflict serious losses on a powerful adversary well versed in the art of maneuvering, who declined engagement when he found it appropriate. On his side, Lafayette knew that he could not expose himself to the frontal attacks that the British persistently attempted to launch against him. There then began a great game of cat and mouse. The enemy had to be kept ignorant of the number of Virginians under arms, and everything was done to deceive him on the question and to try to give the impression that they were many. Arnold asked for a parley. Lafayette defiantly refused, but he had the wisdom to evacuate Richmond to avoid the risk of being trapped in the city. As he went through patriot towns and villages, he attempted to enlist volunteers. Speeches, dinners— he used every recruiting device, and many young men swelled the ranks of his division. It soon included a cavalry unit composed of horses stolen from the enemy at night or purchased from farmers. The reputation of this force continued to grow. It operated primarily through skirmishes, appearing where it was least expected, launching surprise attacks, Indian style, against the enemy when they were small in number, which caused great damage. Cornwallis, the adjutant of the commander in chief of British forces, was sent to Virginia to take command over Arnold, destroy the elusive enemy, and to capture the "boy" in person, to avenge the honor of General Howe, who had mistakenly boasted that he would succeed in doing so. In this subtle combat, the brilliant lord had his fingers singed.

The young general who held his own against the British was, however, wondering when he would be summoned to the north to be given a command in the final offensive against New York. Because he was an American general, like all his American colleagues, Lafayette believed that the decisive battle would take place in New York. He knew that Rochambeau's son and La Pérouse had secured from Maurepas and Navy Minister De Castries, backed by the king, a promise that reinforcements would soon come. An allied offensive against the great port that the British considered impregnable, Lafayette thought, must certainly be in preparation, and he was obviously eager to take part in the battle.

He was unaware that, at a meeting in Westerfield on May 20, 1781, Rochambeau had, with some difficulty, succeeded in persuading Washington and his lieutenants that a very different strategy was required. The British should, of course, be led to believe that a major attack against New York was in preparation so they would be forced to keep troops there, but in the meanwhile the allied divisions would join the great battle in the south, in Virginia, the soft spot in the enemy defenses. This offensive would have even more likelihood of success because French and American soldiers would have the support of the fleet under Admiral de Grasse, who had sailed from Brest on March 21 and was organizing his forces in the West Indies. The squadron under Barras de Saint-Laurent, who had sailed with him, had gone to reinforce the fleet that had been stationed at Newport for almost a year.

The plan was adopted and De Grasse informed. For it to succeed, Lafayette, along with the generals Greene and Wayne, who had joined forces with him, had to hold the British at bay.

The head of the Virginia division grasped the sense of the operation being put in place. He said nothing, but he played the game, to the hilt and with extraordinary determination. Fortunately, General Clinton, the British commander in New York, had not figured it out. He ordered Cornwallis, who had been vigorously attacked by Lafayette in early June at Bird's Creek, to break camp at Elk and take up position first in Williamsburg and then in Yorktown. From the banks of the York River, Lafayette observed his enemy fortifying Yorktown and Gloucester, where he had received reinforcements under General O'Hara, who had come from Portsmouth.

In reply to Rochambeau's message, De Grasse said that he would lead the fleet, aboard his vessel the *Ville de Paris*, into Chesapeake Bay around August 28. The French expeditionary force left Rhode Island and joined Washington's army on the Hudson. A five-hundred-mile march, conducted in perfect order, complete with parades accompanied by drums through the cities, brought them to Virginia.

In an attempt to protect Yorktown, 27 British ships commanded by the admirals Hood, Drake, and Graves attacked De Grasse's fleet on September 6, 1781. De Grasse forced the British to retreat after an artillery duel that lasted for an entire afternoon. The French admiral was master of the bay. Sensing that the tide of history was turning, Benedict Arnold hastily boarded a frigate heading for Europe. A Franco-American force of fifteen thousand, with fleurs de lys and stars and stripes fluttering side by side in the clear air and soft light of Indian Summer, advanced on Yorktown with the mission to capture the fortified town. The French infantry had never seen such resplendent fall colors as those displayed by the maples and oaks along the way. French and American soldiers' songs blended as they marched. Alongside the flags of the two allied nations, the residents of the villages they passed through saw the eagle with wings spread wide on the Polish flag carried by the volunteers under Kosciuszko, who, like his friend Lafayette, had come to fight for the cause of freedom at his own expense. The American ranks included black soldiers who had decided to follow Washington rather than listen to British promises of later emancipation if they fought in the army of George III. Also fighting with the Americans were Indians drawn by the prestige of Kayewla to join the battle in Virginia. Not all the Germans were on the British side: the Prussian general von Steuben led a large number of his compatriots. Lafayette's early companion De Kalb was absent—he had died in bloody fighting in South Carolina in 1780.

The forces under Cornwallis and O'Hara were equal in strength, and they had significant artillery support. Bombardments began at the very start of the siege on October 9 as the allies sought to force the British to use up their powder. Rochambeau, who took every opportunity to recognize that Washington was in overall command, offered him the honor of firing the first cannon shot. Lauzun, at the head of a cavalry force, assisted by Choisy, attacked Gloucester, located across the river from Yorktown, overwhelmed the British under Turleton, and took possession of the town with minimal casualties: three dead, and eleven wounded. Naval and land artillery continued their bombardment of Yorktown, causing significant damage and igniting fires. But to obtain a quick surrender, the allies had to take the redoubts protecting the fortified camp. Lafayette led his Virginians in the capture of the one that seemed the hardest to take. He was helped by Polish, Indian, and German forces. A French force under Viomenil captured the second redoubt but suffered significantly higher casualties than Lafayette.

Lafayette had offended Viomenil by expressing his intention to attack with bayonets, swords, and even knives in order to overcome British resistance. But the impact of artillery fire deprived him of the opportunity to engage in bloody hand-to-hand combat. On October 17, under sustained fire setting his camp and British ships in the bay and on the river ablaze, Cornwallis asked for a cease-fire. Washington refused. The next day, Cornwallis let it be known that he was prepared to capitulate. Louis de Noailles and John Laurens for the allies and Colonel Dundas and Major Ross for the British drafted the surrender agreement, which was signed on October 18 by Cornwallis and Symonds under the impassive gaze of Washington and Rochambeau.

Cornwallis handed over to O'Hara the painful duty of surrendering the sword of the conquered to the victor. Wishing to indicate one last time, on this solemn occasion, his contempt for the rebels, the British general held out his sword to Rochambeau who, gracefully and as though he had anticipated the gesture, turned and pointed to Washington as the true victor in the battle and the war, to whom by right was due the honor of receiving the weapon of the defeated enemy. O'Hara had no choice but to comply.

Rochambeau's gesture was a perfect expression of his personality. He was born in Vendôme in 1725. Originally intended for a career in the church, he was educated by Jesuits at the University of Blois. It was not until after his older brother died that he joined the cavalry regiment in which he served in Bohemia and Bavaria and on the Rhine. He was noticed for his bravery while serving as aide de camp to Louis-Philippe d'Orléans, and he began to be talked about in the army because of his skill in maneuvers. Promoted to the rank of colonel in 1747, he distinguished himself at the siege of Maastricht in 1748. He did not hang back from confronting enemy fire and received several wounds at the battle of Clostercamp, where his actions were decisive for victory. He was named brigadier and inspector of cavalry in 1761, and cabinet ministers began to consult him on technical matters. When he was sent in 1780, with the rank of lieutenant-general, in command of six thousand French troops to assist the colonists under George Washington against the British troops, his American adventure began. And it had reached its summit with the graceful act of recognition he had shown to Washington. Congress expressed its gratitude to him and to his troops. On his return to France, Louis XVI honored him with the Cordon Bleu and named him governor of Picardie and the Artois. But his career was not at an end, and in 1789 he adopted the new principles. A decree of December 28, 1791, awarded him a marshal's baton, a few days after he had been appointed commander of the Army of the North. He directed its first operations, but when his plans were frustrated by the minister of war, he resigned on May 15, 1792, and returned to Touraine. He was arrested under the Terror but escaped the guillotine at the last minute. Napoleon had great esteem for this servant of the Republic and named him a superior officer in the Légion d'Honneur. The great soldier whose victory at Yorktown had brought the American War of Independence to an end spent his last days peacefully in the château of Rochambeau.

After the defeat at Yorktown, the British general had to parade with his defeated troops as a drum and bugle corps played the cruelly appropriate tune "The World Turned Upside Down." It might perhaps have been more accurate to say that a new world had just come into existence, because a tyranny had been shattered.

Although two years separated the victory at Yorktown from the signing of the Treaty of Paris that consecrated the advent of the United States, the battle practically ended the fighting. It had two other immediate consequences: in England, the fall of the North government; in Versailles, the promotion of Lafayette to the rank of brigadier in the French army. Louis XVI was pleased with him, but the promotion did not keep Lafayette from wearing his American uniform when he was back in Europe, ornamented with the Croix de Saint Louis and the medal of the Order of the Cincinnati. Lafayette did not stay long on the territory where he had won his laurels. He once again asked Congress—which had recognized him as an honorary citizen of the United States—for authorization to return to France to serve his king. A frigate, the *Alliance*, was put at his disposal, and after a moving farewell from Washington, he sailed from Boston on December 23, 1781, as onlookers cheered.

Suffering, disappointments, ordeals, anxiety were all erased by the final triumph. The boy whom first Howe and then Cornwallis had thought they could take prisoner had had the pleasure of seeing the first leave America in bitterness and the second sign the surrender.

Lafayette's popularity in the new nation was immense, and he would have two further occasions, in 1782 and again in 1824, to measure it firsthand. The bonds he had established with the Founding Fathers of the United States were ties of friendship and complete confidence; his relationship with Washington was exceptionally strong. Never again, even though two-thirds of his life lay ahead of him, did he experience such intense feelings for a companion. Washington was never replaced as a spiritual father. In a different way, he was also the friend of Thomas Jefferson, whom he saw again in Paris, as well as the brilliant and impossible Tom Paine, whom he saw often in the years 1789 to 1792. His other American friends included Alexander Hamilton, Nathanael Greene, and Henry Laurens.

At the age of twenty-four, Lafayette wanted to harvest in the Old World the fruit of the glory he had won in the New. It seemed to him that matters were settled in the United States, and the inhabitants had nothing left to do but to work for their own happiness. But in France and elsewhere great struggles to conquer freedom remained to be waged. He felt compelled not to be absent from them because he thought those struggles would change the face of the world. His vision was noble and generous, even though his concern for his reputation played a great role in it. But with the benefit of hindsight, when one analyzes the course of his life, one might wonder whether, from the perspective of his real abilities and his own full development, he had not, by leaving America, committed his greatest mistake.

CHAPTER TWENTY-TWO

THE SWEET SMELL OF SUCCESS

I N JUNE 1782 THERE WAS A GREAT CELEBRATION IN
Versailles. Tsarevich Paul, son of Catherine II, visiting
France under the pseudonym the Count du Nord, was
attending a masked ball, one of the favorite entertainments of a
large part of the court. The choice of costume was left to individual discretion, which gave free reign to all kinds of fantasies.
In an atmosphere normally as straitlaced as that of Versailles,
cross-dressing and disguises operated as a kind of safety valve for
the rigidity of etiquette. One did not address a marshal disguised
as a janissary, for example, as one would if he were in formal
uniform.

Among the highborn people amusing themselves on this
June evening was a young woman who aroused universal
admiration for the originality and perfection of the costume
she had chosen. She was disguised as the beautiful Gabrielle

d'Estrées, the mistress of Henri IV, whose grace and amorous talents far exceeded her virtue. All the best-looking men in the kingdom unabashedly cast their eyes on the reincarnation of Gabrielle. They contemplated her with admiration, barely concealing their desire, and more than one attentive witness caught a momentary glimpse of concupiscence in the gaze of the future Tsar Paul I. The reactions of the dancing courtiers, however, remained reserved and even respectful, because the triumphant Gabrielle was none other than the prudish and haughty Marie Antoinette, Queen of France. Some longstanding courtiers who recalled the humiliations that Marie Antoinette, when still Dauphine, had inflicted on Mme du Barry could not keep from smiling ironically at the sight of the haughty Austrian princess in the costume of the mistress of her husband's forebear. But this was the way of Versailles.

The recent birth of the Dauphin had provoked in the queen an unusual state of euphoria and might in part explain her attitude during the ball. For years she had been an unwilling victim of an intimate and painful tragedy, what now would be known as a sexual disorder. Louis XVI at first experienced difficulty in consummating the marriage, so much so that he appeared to refuse to attempt it, and when he did finally take the plunge, the consummation was incomplete. Many people in court and capital knew and talked about it. When he was still alive, Louis XV had already had the young husband examined by doctors, who had not dared suggest an operation. It was finally Archduke Joseph, the queen's older brother, who came to France under the name of Count Falkenstein, who played the role of sex therapist. His sister provided him with the intimate details of her marital relations. The king was also forthcoming about details, and allowed himself to be persuaded by his brother-in-law to undergo surgery, the effect of which was primarily psychological, as the archduke said in a letter to his brother Leopold. The extremely coarse tone of this letter is surprising coming from a prince who had twice been widowed and had the reputation of being melancholy and particularly virtuous. "He is content, and says quite frankly that he was doing it purely from a sense of duty and that he did not like it. Oh, if I could only have been present once, I would have taken care of him; he should be whipped so that he should discharge sperm like a donkey. My sister, moreover, has very little temperament and together they are two complete fumblers." Whatever her brother may have said, nothing points to the conclusion that the queen was lacking in temperament, and her successful childbirth was for her a happy event that cleared her of all the accusations of frigidity and sterility that had been launched against her, even though she had already given birth to a daughter in 1779.

Other courtiers were wondering why the queen, who had the reputation of being harsh and unforgiving, had suddenly invited a tall young red-headed man, said to be an American general, to dance the quadrille with her, even though a few years·earlier she had openly found him to be clumsy. The fact was that General Gilbert de Lafayette had recently become a frequent visitor to, if not a friend of, the royal couple. His wife, Adrienne, was also a recipient of royal favor. In fact, she was at the Hôtel de Ville at the celebration of the recent birth of the Dauphin, in the presence of Louis XVI and Marie Antoinette when she heard on January 21, 1782, that her husband had arrived in Paris after landing at Lorient. The king and queen immediately escorted her in their coach to the Noailles residence to avoid any delay in the happy reunion.

Gilbert could savor his triumph in France, and Adrienne shared in it. She was applauded at the Opera when they attended together, and in many other places. But she was not the only one who shared the glory. Aglaë de Hunolstein, who had been the warrior's reward when he came back from America in 1779, and whom social circles had begun to shun—perhaps because she had been indiscreet—attached herself to the victorious general for whom she had taken the risk of deceiving the very powerful Duke de Chartres. She hung on, but he soon grew tired of her. He judged that he needed a more brilliant liaison, something that was not recycled. Perhaps he should raise his sights, not be content with easy women, but focus on those who appeared to be inaccessible. After an episode with the Princess d'Hénin, a passing fancy about which very little is known. Gilbert was taken with a sudden passion for the beautiful and much courted, though never conquered, Diane Adélaïde de Simiane, reportedly the faithful wife of the Count de Simiane. His compliments were favorably received, and this success in love soon made its contribution to the glory and reputation of Lafayette. After Yorktown, Diane de Simiane: two strongholds captured one after the other, a fitting triumph in a nation and at a time when Mars and Venus were more closely allied than ever.

Adrienne once more stifled her tears, at least in public, merely offering her husband as a gift for his return another daughter, their last child, who was named Virginie in further homage to Lafayette's American friend. Born out of pride and to satisfy his vanity, the liaison with Mme de Simiane nonetheless resisted the passage of time, even surviving the death of Adrienne in 1807 in the form of a loyal and affectionate friendship.

The adventure did not, in any event, prevent the Lafayettes from presenting an image of a remarkably harmonious household. In their new home they received not only their French friends but all the distinguished Americans in Paris, whether temporarily settled or merely on a visit. Adrienne had learned English, and her son and two daughters spoke it regularly, often even among themselves and with their parents. Franklin, until he left Paris in 1784, John and Abigail Adams, Jefferson when he represented his country in France, and later Thomas Paine and Gouverneur Morris, along with many others, frequented the Lafayette salon, which became one of the centers of the liberal and cosmopolitan spirit in the capital, lasting through the first years of the Revolution. It was moreover a rather open salon, since William Pitt the Younger and his wife dined with Lafayette, whom he would soon engage in political combat.

While peace talks dragged on, further attacks against Britain were being seriously considered in Versailles. Lafayette saw himself very close to being again beside Admiral D'Estaing in a planned operation against Jamaica, with the assistance of Spanish forces. Although he had been sent as an envoy to Madrid, and despite a friendly meeting with Charles III, Lafayette's proposal to take up a position on a Spanish island in the West Indies was rejected because he was suspected of being a republican. This well-established reputation often created ambiguity in the monarchs he encountered, who at first seemed to appreciate him. The ambiguity was all the more acute in Madrid because the French brigadier appeared in an American uniform, an unusual detail that was taken as a declaration of faith or a provocation.

He nevertheless succeeded in persuading the Spanish king to accept the opening of a permanent United States diplomatic mission in Madrid, to which William Carmichael was appointed. Wherever Lafayette went, he acted as a representative of the interests of the young republic. The memory of his adventure with the rebels constantly weighed on everything he undertook, so much so that he gave the impression that his heart and soul had remained on the other side of the Atlantic. In France itself, he secured duty-free status for the United States in five ports:

Dunkerque, Lorient, Bordeaux, Bayonne, and Marseille. While he did not succeed in modifying the French monopoly on tobacco in favor of the Americans, his intervention on behalf of the whale oil exporters of Nantucket was crowned with success. He was rewarded with a 500-pound cheese made by the local farmers, who had made a gift to him of the production of all their cows for twenty-four hours.

Lafayette had invited Washington to come to France, but because of the latter's reluctance to travel outside America, Lafayette set sail once more in July 1784 for the country for which he felt nostalgic three years after his return. (Washington may have been unaware of another reason he had to come to France besides his friendship for Lafayette and other French companions in arms. He was a direct descendant of Nicolas Martiau (1592–1657), a Huguenot, the first French settler in Virginia, who had landed on May 11, 1620, five months before the Pilgrims arrived on the *Mayflower*. A highly symbolic detail is the fact that Martiau purchased land in Yorktown 150 years before the battle in which his descendant was to win glory.) Adrienne was invited to come along, but she felt it was her duty to stay with her children.

The reception the honorary citizen of the United States received perhaps exceeded his expectations. In every town he passed through there were enthusiastic crowds, banquets, celebrations. He could not decide where he felt most at home: in Philadelphia, where Congress received him several times; in Baltimore, where a great ball was held to commemorate the one he had given there in April 1781, when the ladies of the town had banded together to make clothing for his soldiers; or in Albany, where he was once again Kayewla for a few days, the idol of the Indians of the Six Nations. He seized the opportunity of his meeting with the Indians to rekindle their enthusiasm for the new nation, which was in danger of weakening. They gave him a precious gift, a boy of thirteen named Kalenhala, whom he took back with him to France. Kalenhala lived in Lafayette's house and called him father.

Lafayette revisited all the places where he had fought and spent ten days with the Washington family at Mount Vernon. He bade farewell even more regretfully than in December 1781, to return to France, where he thought great things awaited him, as though he felt that this meeting with the man to whom he owed so much was really the last.

CHAPTER TWENTY-THREE

FROM ANIMAL FLUID
TO ELASTIC SHOES

I NTERIOR DECORATION IN THE PARIS OF THE 1780S AMONG people of quality uniformly followed the dictates of fashion: round tables of darkened pear wood by Nicolas Petit, furniture with tortoiseshell and soft metal inlay by René Dubois, armchairs with lyre or medallion backs by Georges Jacob, hangings of cloth from Lyon.

A group of men and women was gathered around a tub, which contained iron filings and a series of bottles arranged in a circle, filled with magnetized water. Each member of the group was connected to one of the bottles by an iron rod. It was through this channel that he or she received the "fluid." They were to apply it to the part of the body where discomfort was localized. The assembled people were all ill, and the application of the metal rod conducting the fluid to the organ affected by disease was a new therapy that was said to have brought about a large number of cures, some of them almost miraculous, in the most diverse forms of pathology: neurasthenia, inflammation of the throat or the lungs, severe myopia approaching blindness, diseases of the skin, and malfunctions of every kind.

Another peculiarity of the treatment was that the patients gathered around the tub were connected to one another by a cord that was wrapped around them. They touched thumbs and index fingers together, and the fluid flowed through them as though they made up an electric circuit, which the initiated called a Mesmeric circle, from the name of the inventor of the method, the Austrian doctor Franz Anton Mesmer, who had come to Paris in search of fame in 1778 and had found it.

According to this strange figure, who spoke French very badly (which did not prevent him from persuading women of the highest society and very cultivated men of the depth of his views), the entire universe was bathed in an extremely fine fluid that penetrated every physical entity. He claimed that this fluid was the source of heat, light, electricity, and magnetism. Whenever an obstacle of any kind blocked its circulation in a human body, illness appeared. The purpose of the treatment described above was to eliminate obstacles, to restore the free circulation of the fluid through the entire body, and to put the patient in harmony with nature.

The application of the fluid might provoke trances, sleepwalking, or fits of hysteria, which sometimes required the treating physician to lock the patient affected by these disorders into a carefully padded "crisis room." The patient was then calmed down with massages. Treatment might also involve attaching patients to previously magnetized trees.

Because of more or less believable reports of cures, Mesmerism experienced swift and widespread success in the fashionable society of Paris, which was always on the lookout for new discoveries and new theories. The craze for natural science and for gibberish with scientific pretensions went hand in hand with the ferment of political ideas. People hoping for a change in the social order had no qualms about embracing the language and practices of visionaries, miracle workers, or simply thinkers who moved from physics to metaphysics as though one were nothing but an extension of the other. In Masonic lodges and literary and philosophical salons previously dominated by rationalism, illuminism was greeted with interest. Mesmer and his disciples did not merely cure patients, they claimed to explain the great mysteries of the universe and even to establish bridges to the beyond. From magnetism, one moved to spiritualism and theosophy, for which Cagliostro had opened the way. Real scientific advances, such as the invention of hot-air balloons, gave rise to the idea that the possibilities of the human mind were unlimited and that even the invisible world was open to the investigations of scientists.

The sensation created by the balloon flights of the Montgolfier brothers, Pilâtre de Rozier, the Marquis d'Arlandes, and Blanchard (who crossed the English Channel in 1787), made the sciences the center of public attention, often without method and in a very confused manner. It seemed legitimate to dream, if what had seemed impossible yesterday was possible today. Scientific publications and lectures proliferated, involving both snobbery and commerce. Women wore "balloon" hats and children nibbled "balloon" candy. Balloonists were treated as heroes and stars and celebrated everywhere. When a balloon made a forced landing in a field, peasants ran up and asked the passengers if they were men or gods. Balloonists themselves were a bit intoxicated by their success. Before dying in an attempt to fly across the English Channel, Pilâtre de Rozier claimed he could fly from Paris to Boston in two days if the winds were favorable.

Louis XVI, who was a strong supporter of scientific endeavors and accepted the boldest suggestions when it came to improving the matériel available to France (he had, for example, agreed to have the largest warships lined with copper), bestowed spectacular rewards on the courageous balloonists. He no doubt had high hopes for this new means of transport. But he was able to distinguish between science and daydreams or charlatanism. Despite Marie Antoinette's sympathy for her compatriot Mesmer, and the favor he enjoyed from a number of prominent courtiers, the king refused to take Mesmerism seriously. Lafayette, who was seized with a sudden passion for the theories of the Viennese doctor, paid a price for the king's irony.

The former American general had become a supporter of the idea of animal magnetism and had not expressed the suspicion one might have expected from him with regard to the extravagant notions connected to Mesmerism. This attitude is difficult to understand if one does not consider the role Freemasonry played in his education and would play in his mature life. There is no doubt that Lafayette, who was initiated in Paris when he was very young, was a dedicated Mason, unlike many aristocrats of the time, for whom membership in a secret society was a social obligation, an easily acquired certificate of liberalism and intellectualism that imposed no requirements other than a small financial contribution and the pleasant ritual of occasional attendance at a meeting followed by a banquet. But Lafayette seemed conscious of what he owed to the Masonic order, to which he remained loyal throughout his life. Since his formal education had not been very thorough, it was the enlightened men he encountered in Masonic lodges who led him to discover the major writers and thinkers of the Enlightenment, whose works made a strong impression on him. His meetings with Franklin, Washington, and other American Masons helped to convince

him that scientific research went hand in hand with the democratic ideal and that obscurantism was one of the weapons tyran-
nies used to seek to maintain their power. By nature he seemed
to incline toward rationalism; while he dreamed of liberating
oppressed peoples and creating equality among men, mystical
adventures were foreign to him. He was a man of the country
with his feet firmly planted on the ground. But it was also part of
his character to get quickly caught up in anything he encountered that seemed new and likely to spread. This was true of Mesmerism. He saw it less as merely a promising therapy than a way
in which man might gain more power over nature and make
despots who wanted to maintain servitude look ridiculous.

He wanted to communicate his enthusiasm for Mesmer—incidentally not shared by Franklin—to his friends in the United
States, and before embarking on his visit in 1784 he wrote to
Washington that he intended to tell him about the discoveries of
the "brilliant" Viennese doctor. When the king was informed, he
mockingly put Lafayette on his guard. "What will Washington
think of you," he asked, when he knows that you've become the
chief assistant apothecary to Dr. Mesmer?"

Lafayette paid no attention. He firmly intended to establish on
the other side of the Atlantic branches of the Société de l'Har-
monie Universelle, to which the most fervent Mesmerists
belonged. He failed completely, first because of the amused
skepticism of his spiritual father and subsequently because after
Jefferson replaced Franklin as ambassador in 1784, he wrote to
his correspondents in the United States to denounce the misdeeds of Mesmerism; he transmitted to leading figures the report
of the commission made up of members of the Academy of Sciences and the Academy of Medicine whom the king had ordered
to conduct an objective investigation of Mesmer's fluid and its
applications. Among the members of the commission were the

chemist Lavoisier, the astronomer Bailly (future president of the Constituent Assembly and mayor of Paris after the fall of the Bastille), Benjamin Franklin himself, and a doctor whose invention would soon terrify the entire country, Dr. Guillotin.

After a detailed investigation, the royal commission issued a negative verdict: Mesmer's fluid did not exist; the convulsions and other effects of the treatment could be attributed to the over-stimulated imagination of the believers in the theory.

This conclusion had no more effect on Lafayette than it did on Mesmer's other supporters. Even families were internally divided. While Franklin considered Mesmer a charlatan, his grandson William Temple Franklin was an adherent of the sect, whose supporters lashed out, denouncing the academies as bastions of reaction whose members were predisposed, out of tradition and self-interest, to oppose innovators. Duval d'Epremesnil, the turbulent member of the Parlement of Paris who was a leader in the defense of parliamentary prerogatives against royal power, was among Mesmer's supporters. In the same camp was a brilliant journalist who had been employed by Vergennes, Jacques Pierre Brissot de Warville, future leader of the Girondins. Brissot was in close contact with a bitter and spiteful doctor from Geneva who claimed to refute Newton and whose work had been rejected by the Academy—his name was Marat, and he later was one of the most vehement advocates for executing the Girondins, including Brissot and other followers of Mesmer, such as Mme Roland. There were many other prominent supporters of Mesmer among Lafayette's friends, such as Chastellux, who had served under Rochambeau in America.

Lafayette's infatuation with Mesmer can be characterized as an aberration of his youth. It demonstrated both his naïveté and his extraordinary generosity. Another example of the latter was the financial help he provided to an inventor who was attempting to make "elastic" shoes that would enable their wearers to walk on water. There was even an announcement that the man would attempt to walk across the Seine on January 1, 1784. The spectacular demonstration was in fact a practical joke, but Lafayette's reputation did not suffer, which suggests the level of confusion that prevailed at the time.

CHAPTER TWENTY-FOUR

KINGS FOR EVERY TASTE

THE CHÂTEAU OF SANS-SOUCI IS LOCATED NOT FAR FROM Potsdam. The name derives from a remark King Frederick I of Prussia made to a French visitor: pointing to the site of his future tomb, he said: "When I'm there, I'll be without a care." Sans-Souci then became the name of the royal residence. By July 1785, King Frederick II, the soldier-king, had in forty years of rule doubled the number of his subjects. But the soldier-king also saw himself as a philosopher-king whose charm matched his imperiousness. Like its master, the residence was twofold, the old and the new Sans-Souci. The gardens approaching the château were elegant and luxurious but oddly lifeless and vaguely menacing. Finally, the visitor realized the source of his discomfort: there was no sound of birdsong. All the birds had been deliberately massacred, and any who strayed nearby were shot by the guards because the king was annoyed by their song. He had ordered his entourage to make certain that they were never heard again. The absent birds cast a pall of menace over the soulless château, and the silent park created a feeling of desolation.

On that July day, Frederick II—perhaps a less brilliant strategist than Frederick I, but equally passionate about military matters—was about to leave for maneuvers in Breslau. Foreign observers would be present and he intended to arouse their admiration for the skillful deployment of thirty thousand troops. Among the invited guests he intended to impress were at least two military men whose names were known around the world. They were both noble lords who shone as brightly in royal courts as on fields of battle. Although they were divided by the fact that one had recently helped crush the other on the battlefield, they retained a degree of mutual respect. The two generals who had so recently fought bitterly against one another were Lafayette and Lord Charles Cornwallis.

The king of Prussia, who had invited them as connoisseurs and experts, was an old man wracked with the pain of arthritis. He had the reputation of being slovenly and with vulgar manners, while at the same time being suspected of homosexuality, because he spent more time inspecting his barracks, day and night, than he did in the splendid château of Sans-Souci, supposedly a smaller version of Versailles. The old king was only one year from death. Lafayette thought that he had "the most magnificent eyes I ever saw, which gave his face an expression at once captivating and brutal."

Playfully, no doubt, but with a touch of sadism, at the banquet after each day's maneuvers, Frederick sat Lafayette between the Duke of York and Cornwallis, who did not appreciate the gesture. Frederick directed all his attention to Lafayette, asking him to talk about the campaigns of the American war and the character of

Washington in the presence of his defeated adversary, frozen in polite silence. Lafayette, who was viscerally anti-British and claimed to appreciate the English only when they were defeated, perhaps went overboard. He praised the American democratic system with such enthusiasm that Frederick restored some balance among his guests: "Monsieur," he said to Lafayette, "I knew a young man who, after having visited countries where liberty and equality reigned, got it into his head to establish all that in his own country. Do you know what happened to him?"

"No, Sire."

"He was hanged," the king replied with a smile that did not trouble Lafayette but must have comforted the British.

It seems that Frederick was obsessed by the American war, perhaps a trace of the influence of Voltaire. In 1783, he had already had the opportunity to discuss the American campaigns with Colonel Alexandre Berthier, the future marshal under Napoleon, who had served with Lafayette at Yorktown. He had witnessed Prussian maneuvers along with another veteran of Rochambeau's forces, General de Custine. Berthier had been very well treated by Frederick, who had given him the grand tour of Sans-Souci. He was struck by the disorder that reigned in the royal apartments: torn curtains, armchairs and other valuable pieces of furniture soiled by dog excrement, tables covered with tobacco, and worn-out clothing scattered about.

After witnessing Prussian army maneuvers, Lafayette, accompanied by his friend Colonel Gouvion, continued his tour through central and eastern Europe in 1786. He was graciously received in Vienna by Joseph II, Marie Antoinette's very indiscreet brother, and by Chancellor Kaunitz. He also met the Duke of Brunswick, who in 1792 signed a manifesto he had not written that was intended to strike fear into the hearts of republicans in

France but had the contrary effect of encouraging them to enlist for the fight.

When Catherine II invited him to come to St. Petersburg in 1787, Lafayette regretted that the situation in France made it impossible for him to make the long journey. One wonders how the tsarina would have reacted to Lafayette's republican-tinged language. But while still in Berlin, in 1785, he had written to Washington to express his admiration for the Prussian army.

It seemed that he could do or think nothing without consulting his spiritual father. For example, he wrote to Washington to describe the deplorable situation of the Protestants who had remained in France after the revocation of the Edict of Nantes before intervening with the king and his ministers on their behalf, with some degree of effectiveness. He also wanted to improve the situation of the "black part of mankind," and suggested that Washington join with him in establishing a farm where slaves would gradually get used to living as free men who were responsible for themselves. But the emancipation of slaves in America was a complex problem, which, according to Washington, could not be resolved overnight through an individual initiative. They had to study the question and wait. But "to wait" was a verb that Lafayette had no taste for conjugating. He bought a farm in Guyana, where blacks learned how to grow coffee, cacao, cinnamon, and cloves in preparation for becoming small farmers on their own.

On a trip to French Guyana, I was able to locate the place where Lafayette had from a distance established his plantation. He had situated his utopian kingdom for emancipated slaves, which he named La Belle Gabrielle, in the Amazonian jungle. He intended to show the French nobility by example how good it was to emancipate slaves through a system that involved simultaneously rewards as incentives, the absence of punishments, and the introduction of wages. Lafayette was in favor of the gradual emancipation of his farmers, but his poetic vision was far removed from the reality of the green hell in which the men for whose happiness he wished were forced to labor. The ideal plantation he had offered to slaves to manage was indeed located in the midst of howling monkeys, bullfrogs, and wild pigs. Today, not a trace can be seen of the plantation, swallowed by the Amazon jungle.

When Condorcet heard of Lafayette's humanitarian initiative, he took an interest and even thought for a moment of going to manage it, but Lafayette's enterprise, which he ran from afar, quickly collapsed, and when the government of the Convention confiscated the property of the generous benefactor, its representatives had the unfortunate black workers sold back into slavery, which the Assembly had not yet abolished.

The financial losses in Guyana came after many others, and Lafayette had to put his affairs in order, in Brittany where he owned large estates, and then in Auvergne, his birthplace. He was very popular there, as much because of his exploits in America as because of the material help he provided to the peasants on his fiefs, distributing surplus grain when the harvest was good, and trying to make the lean years more bearable. Adrienne, who was also sensitive to the needs of the poor, helped him by setting up a weaving workshop and training school to provide work for young men and women in the region.

The year 1786 brought to this man—so sought after by many illustrious people, probably especially curious to learn about the new nation across the ocean—new sources of satisfaction.

In June, he traveled with the king, the minister of the navy Marshal de Castries, and the minister of war Marshal de Ségur to Cherbourg. This was the monarch's first significant journey, and the first and last time the sailor-king set foot on a ship. A decision had been made to construct an artificial harbor at Cherbourg to make the port a center of trade between France and the two American continents, and a naval base facilitating surveillance of Britain. The project designed by an engineer named Cessart was grandiose. The nine pilings intended to support the dike were cones 20 yards high and 50 yards in diameter at their base. Each one contained three thousand cubic yards of stone fragments. (The enterprise was not in fact completed until early in the next century.) The French monarchy gave the impression at the time that it was at the peak of its power. Louis XVI was delighted, and he seemed to forget the serious financial crisis that was shaking the country. On the three-day journey back to Versailles, Lafayette traveled in the king's own coach. Although there were other prominent guests with the king, in the course of those long hours Lafayette gained more direct knowledge of the man on whom his fate, in France at least, depended.

In September 1786, Virginia presented for exhibition in the Hôtel de Ville in Paris a bust of Lafayette by Houdon, whom his fellow Mason Franklin had the year before brought to America to execute a bust of Washington.

The month of March 1787, however, greeted the Hero of Two Worlds with a bad omen. The Count de Simiane committed suicide, and public opinion attributed his act to the despair caused by his wife Diane's liaison with Lafayette. Gossip in Versailles, Paris, and elsewhere had it that Lafayette had gone too far in seducing a woman who had until then been faithful to her husband, who was madly in love with her. Insulting pamphlets were circulated, and Lafayette's pure glory was sullied for the first time. And this was only the beginning. No public man could go through the century as a parfait gentle knight, and Lafayette wanted to be a public man, not merely a soldier in service of the

Ideal. He felt that France was in a crisis, that something was cracking, and that important changes were about to occur. He intended to play a prominent role in the process, which would open him to risks, particularly for his reputation. His relations with Louis XVI were apparently excellent, as the recent journey to Cherbourg indicated, but the king seemed to him to have too much power, and he dreamed of ways to reduce it. In a letter to Washington, to whom he expressed his deepest thoughts, he spoke of the "Oriental power" of the king, who held "all the means to constrain, punish, and corrupt." This sounds like Thomas Paine speaking of George III. The year 1787 saw the advent of a new Lafayette: the political man.

CHAPTER TWENTY-FIVE

EXCESS POWER,
EXCESS APPETITE

T HE KING WAS DINING, WITH A HEARTY APPETITE AS
always. He ate a good deal and attributed great importance to food. This was true even in the most dramatic
circumstances: after his arrest in Varennes following the failed
flight of June 1791 and in the Temple prison during his trial he
never skipped a meal. His taste, however, did not incline toward
excessive refinement. He habitually ate, calmly and systematically, preferably solid and nourishing dishes. Louis XVI was one
of the most enthusiastic and constant supporters of a vegetable
that had recently appeared in France and was making slow
progress in public taste: the potato. The potato had been
imported to Germany from South America, and growers and
consumers in Germany had quickly adopted it. While serving in
the French army during the Seven Years' War, Antoine Augustin
Parmentier was taken prisoner by the Germans and discovered

the potato. Disappointed by the reluctance of French peasants, Parmentier relied on snobbery to popularize the potato in his country. He succeeded in having it placed on the menu for a formal luncheon at Versailles. The king did justice, to put it mildly, to the vegetable, and the queen, always inclined toward pastoral fantasies, for a time wore potato flowers as earrings. The promotion was a success, and the king did not let a day pass without asking for potatoes. He liked them however they were prepared. Many courtiers imitated him, soon followed by restaurants and many families in good society.

Parmentier was given land in Neuilly to cultivate different varieties of potato. In 1789, to overcome the skepticism of many farmers, he tried a ruse that turned out to be effective. He had his fields guarded during the day by armed men who made themselves very conspicuous. Curious onlookers thought the crop must be very precious if it had to be protected with weapons. When night fell, the guards withdrew and the onlookers rushed into the fields, dug up potatoes, took them home, cooked, ate, and developed a taste for them. But it was not until the reign of Louis-Philippe that Parmentier's victory was complete and potatoes were consumed from Dunkerque to Perpignan.

Meanwhile, Louis XVI was growing ever fatter, and not only because of his eating habits and his spectacular contribution to Parmentier's success. It also appears that the king was one of those people in whom anxiety provokes weight gain. It didn't matter that he'd won a brilliant victory over Great Britain and that he was in a position to tell himself that he was the most powerful and respected sovereign in Europe; he still felt burdened with worries. The triumphal journey through Normandy to Cherbourg had been a kind of interlude set against a rather gloomy backdrop. The king sensed that there was some sort of fissure in his kingdom. When he looked at his subjects he was no longer convinced of the truth of what Benjamin Franklin had said, that he was "the greatest maker of happy men in the world." Discontent was spreading, the queen was scarcely congratulated in Paris on the birth of her second son, Louis-Charles, and satirical songs and pamphlets against the queen and against government policies proliferated, all indications that a crisis that had been brewing for years was growing acute. It had many elements, but it was first of all financial. The very costly American war had increased the state deficit, and the absence of a clear and courageous economic and fiscal policy made the situation increasingly difficult. It was, of course, the common people—peasants, artisans, workers, employees, shopkeepers—who suffered the harshest effects of inflation, the unjust system of taxation, and the stagnation of trade.

The king was torn between competing interest groups. After using Turgot, a man for whom he felt keen admiration and great respect, Louis XVI was frightened by some of the consequences of his minister's policies and dismissed him without allowing him the opportunity to adjust them. He called on Necker, a prominent Geneva banker of unquestionable honesty and sincerely concerned for the public welfare. But Necker, by bringing to the light of day the waste and abuse due to an archaic and extraordinarily complex administrative system, the unjustifiable privileges of the upper strata, and the inequity of the tax system, stirred up opposition among everyone, in court and country, who profited from the current situation. Giving in to pressure from the privileged classes, the king dismissed Necker at the very moment when he was about to bring order to the state's receipts and expenses and eliminate its dependence on borrowing. His mediocre successors, Joly de Fleury and Lefèvre d'Ormesson, were unable to straighten things out. The finance ministry

needed a skillful, competent man who was able to inspire confidence among owners of capital, producers, and foreigners. The
king thought he had found the rare bird in the person of Charles
Alexandre de Calonne, intendant of Lille, a high-ranking civil
servant with a well deserved reputation for savoir-faire and imagination. He was married to a strikingly beautiful woman, and his
own amorous exploits were numerous. Women in high society
vied for his company. Charming, flighty, unprincipled, but never
short of ideas and never discouraged, Calonne was able to communicate his fundamental optimism to others and counted on
the strength of his charm to overcome every obstacle. Louis XVI
was favorably impressed by the brilliant personality who
believed that everything could be arranged without offending or
seriously inconveniencing anyone and who strove to paint the
future in rosy tones. Provided he was not compelled to make
important decisions, the king was happy. Calonne's overall
vision and long-term objectives were far from absurd. Aware of
the lead Great Britain enjoyed in industrialization, he wanted
France, too, to modernize, to be covered with factories and workshops, to export its products, and to cease being an essentially
rural country. He urged the kingdom's great families to invest in
industrial enterprises: mines, textiles, and the like. But he wanted
to satisfy all social categories. To win over to his side the powerful clans that determined the climate at court, he paid the
debts of the king's brother the Count d'Artois, suppressed the
finance committee that was supposed to monitor expenditures,
and took other similar steps. A more praiseworthy decision was
to distribute assistance to the poor during a very severe winter.
His action was primarily psychological. He intended to produce
the impression, at home and abroad, that France was wealthy,
which, he hoped, would entice lenders and investors. In fact, he
unleashed a huge wave of speculation in the stock market and

in property, in Paris and some large provincial cities. In the capital the Duke d'Orléans acquired most of the property around the Palais-Royal, and rented out shops, cafés, restaurants, and theaters. The Count de Provence took the lion's share of the Vaugirard quarter. There was also speculation in precious metals and, as gold was draining out of France, the state found itself obliged to diminish the quantity of gold in the louis coin. This de facto devaluation undermined the confidence the authorities wanted to instill. Lenders were nor longer eager to purchase official debt, and, confronted with a dramatic increase in the deficit, the extremely flexible Calonne reversed course. He suddenly proposed to institute a property tax proportional to individual wealth, to eliminate waste and the tax privileges enjoyed by nobility and clergy; in short, in broad outline, but a little late, he adopted Necker's program. The king immediately realized as much but continued to support Calonne, and the minister, seeing himself under attack from all sides, proposed a remedy to the king. It was time to call together an Assembly of Notables, representing the different orders, constitutional bodies, local communities, peers of the realm, in short, anyone who exercised significant influence, in order to submit to them the emergency measures needed to rescue the kingdom's finances. Recourse to the notables was part of the French monarchical tradition, although the last meeting of the Assembly of Notables went back to 1626. Calonne hoped that the members of the next assembly would approve his plan, since the majority of them would be chosen by him.

Delayed by the death of Vergennes on February 13, 1788, a very painful blow to the king, since the foreign minister was the only man, he said, whom he could count on, the Assembly of Notables met on February 22. But things did not turn out as

the optimistic Calonne had hoped. The members who were prepared to make sacrifices in the name of the general interest were
in the minority. The clergy wanted to lose none of its privileges
and it held fast to what it considered its inalienable rights.
Members of the *cours souveraines*, for their part, engaged in
opposition. At the meeting of the second commission, presided
over by the Count d'Artois, one member of the assembly was
particularly outspoken, the Marquis de Lafayette, who was
engaging in his first political battle. Since the *gabelle* (salt tax)
had been abolished, he asked that amnesty be granted to
everyone serving a prison term for smuggling salt. He spoke vigorously against the disastrous contracts the state had entered
into with respect to the national forests, and when he was asked
to specify his accusations, he had no hesitation in taking on the
responsibility for naming names and affixing his signature to
his statement. But he was most vehement on the subject of
taxes: "The millions abandoned to plunder and greed are the
fruit of sweat, tears, and blood of the people." Calonne was
furious at Lafayette and considered having him locked up. The
king, frightened by the unforeseen turn discussions had taken,
regretted having summoned the assembly. He demanded that
Calonne resign and withdraw to his country estate in northern
France. Once rid of this opponent, Lafayette stepped up the
attack. He called for a tax reduction for the poorest, compen-
sated for by a significant luxury tax. He again argued for the
abolition of laws against Protestants, a step that led to the
promulgation of the Edict of Tolerance, recorded by the Parlement in 1788. To resolve the questions on which the
Assembly of Notables seemed to have difficulty reaching agreement, he spoke of the need to call a "National Assembly." The
Count d'Artois asked him if he was thinking of the Estates General. Lafayette answered in the affirmative and expressed the

hope that the Count d'Artois would convey the request to his brother.

The question of the Estates General had now been officially raised and, against his will, the king had to agree to this exceptional procedure that he thought very dangerous. The idea had, in fact, been proposed by others than Lafayette, to whom the paternity of the events that were to follow cannot be attributed, but his tense and public dialogue with the Count d'Artois contributed a good deal to giving the idea substance. Since the notables considered themselves less and less qualified to make decisions, the king finally put an end to their work.

There then began a long duel with the Parlement of Paris to force it to record the various edicts the king absolutely wanted to promulgate because he believed they were necessary to rescue the finances of the kingdom.

It was in the course of this duel, which was exhausting and humiliating for the king, that the first form of opposition, that of the members of Parlement, was openly expressed, with an insolence that the conventional polite formulas could not manage to conceal. An aggravating circumstance for the monarch was that he did not always control his conduct as he should. During a very tense *Lit de Justice* on August 6, 1787, which he had summoned to bring undisciplined judges to heel, he fell asleep during the session, and the men he wanted to subdue, hearing this thirty-three-year-old snoring in the middle of the day, said to themselves that he had probably again eaten too much (perhaps potatoes) and that he suffered from flatulence.

The more Louis XVI strove to impose his will on Parlement (which was in fact defending privileges and opposing reforms), the more—and this is the paradox of the moment—the population of Paris demonstrated its support for its members, who would in fact be swept away by the Revolution they helped to provoke. When two of the most turbulent of their number, Duval d'Epremesnil and Goislard de Montsabert, were arrested by order of the king for making seditious remarks, following the advice of the new finance minister directing the government, Loménie de Brienne, they were seen as heroes. Though it had been exiled to Troyes, the Parlement had to be called back to Paris. Upon its solemn reentry on November 19, 1787, the king again tried to force it to record his edict on government borrowing. When his cousin Philippe d'Orléans dared to cry out that the obligation was illegal, Louis XVI uttered the famous reply: "It is legal because I wish it!"

He might very well, under pressure from the queen, exile Philippe d'Orléans to Villers-Cotterêts; his outburst of authority resembled the swan song of the absolute monarchy. The king could no longer be the sole source of legality; his power could no longer be unlimited. He thought he had made a major concession to Parlement by promising to summon the Estates General in 1792, but he had to backtrack and agree that they would be called in 1789. The members of the Parlement of Dauphiné let it be known that the province would consider itself exonerated from loyalty to the sovereign if the challenged edicts were maintained. The crowd protected them from forced exile, and they met in Vizille, decreed the restoration of the Estates of Dauphiné, called for the summoning of the Estates General, and demanded the abolition of privileges. This was the first spark of the revolutionary movement that would explode in 1789. In Grenoble, a young lawyer had just taken his first steps as a political agitator, and he would soon turn up in Paris, where he would play an important role in the storm, until it swept him away in 1793. His name was Antoine Barnave. No one was able to foresee the violence of the storm France was about to go through, but every lucid mind knew the country was on the eve of significant changes, although Talleyrand later declared that "he who did not live before 1789 has never known the sweetness of life." Lafayette, however, was straining at the bit with impatience. He had been in the Assembly of Notables and he fully intended to be a member of the Estates General, especially because he had helped to bring about their summoning.

CHAPTER TWENTY-SIX

WAS THE EDIFICE
THAT WORM-EATEN?

O N MAY 4, 1789, THE SUN WAS SHINING ON
Versailles. Never in living memory had there been so
many people in the streets. Hotels, inns, and restaurants were all full. For weeks all the available rooms in private
houses had been rented in advance at exorbitant prices. People
had rented space in hallways, garrets, and even closets. Distinguished people, for lack of a bed, had to be satisfied with
sleeping on a straw pallet. Everywhere, in families, offices, and
shops, one could observe an unaccustomed excitement arising
from a variety of feelings: enormous curiosity, vague anxiety, and
intense hope, none of which seemed to dominate the others.
What did seem certain was that a great spectacle was about to
occur; but no one was able to describe how the anticipated ceremonies would unfold for the simple reason that France had had
no festivity of this kind since 1614, in the reign of Louis XIII. The

last witnesses of that event were long dead. What was about to occur was the meeting of the Estates General, summoned for May 5, 1789, after much hesitation by the royal authorities.

On May 4, the eve of the solemn inauguration of the assembly's work, the twelve hundred representatives of the three orders, clergy, nobility, and third estate, marched in a procession to Saint-Louis cathedral where, in the presence of the king, the queen, the princes, and the princesses, a mass was celebrated. The members of the clergy led the procession, followed by the nobility. Each member of the clergy wore the ecclesiastical costume corresponding to his rank in the monarchy: black for parish priests, violet for bishops, crimson for cardinals, with hats and long coats. The representatives of the nobility wore silk and velvet morning coats, with gold-flecked cloth facings and gold buttons, black silk *culottes*, and white stockings. They also wore long coats and hats with turned-up brims, "à la Henri IV," with white feathers.

To mark a clear distinction between clergy and nobility on one side and third estate on the other, the latter's representatives were required by royal order to wear black wool *culottes*, coats like those worn by lawyers, muslin ties, and black tricorn hats with no decorations. During the king's speech the following day the representatives of the third estate had to remain standing, while those of the two other orders were permitted to sit.

These restrictions did not affect the solemnity of the ceremonies. The entire length of the route followed by the procession was lined with troops at attention, and the music did not stop until it entered the cathedral, while flags fluttered in the spring air.

The king's passage did not provoke as many cheers as he had hoped. There were even a few shouts of "Vive le duc d'Orléans!" as the queen's carriage went by, an act of defiance, even an insult, for anyone who knew that Marie Antoinette detested her husband's cousin.

That evening, the king, who was worried and ill at ease, had his brother, the Count de Provence, the most cultivated man in the family, read his speech, and he found no fault with it. Since his dispute with the Parlement, the king had been constantly on the retreat. He had agreed against his will to summon the notables, then accepted the principle of a meeting of the Estates General, which he then summoned three years before the date he had set. He further agreed to double the number of representatives from the third estate in light of the huge number of families belonging to that order. Despite all these concessions, the atmosphere in the course of the preceding year had continued to deteriorate. During the winter of 1788–89, there had been riots and looting in several provinces: Brittany, Burgundy, and Provence. The violence was carried out by people without work who were starving, because shortages—sometimes due to inefficient transport of grain—had caused a rise in prices. Bread became so hard to get for the poor that some municipalities set flour prices themselves. Stores in a working-class area of Paris were looted in April. There were shouts of "Death to the rich," and "Death to the aristos," after disturbances that began at a wallpaper workshop. Repression by guards on horseback caused numerous deaths. In an attempt to restore calm, the government lifted the prohibition against the meetings of clubs that had been in force for a year. New associations, more or less spontaneously, immediately proliferated, and agitation along with them. Impromptu orators appeared in the cafés and gardens of the Palais-Royal. Small newspapers sprang up, revealing hitherto unknown talents to a surprised public. Political tendencies began to take shape. Several prominent men, who called themselves *Patriotes*, met a few times a week at the residence of the *conseiller* to Par-lement Duport: the liberal mathematician Condorcet, the econ-omist Dupont de Nemours, the magistrate Roederer (who had a brilliant career under the Empire), the turbulent *conseiller* to the Parlement of Paris Duval d'Epremesnil, the Viscount de Noailles, and Lafayette himself. All of them came under the influence of an aristocrat with a scandalous past, who had been elected as a deputy for the third estate from Aix, Marquis Gabriel de Mirabeau. This group later became the *Constitu-tionnel* club. On its left was the club of the *Enragés,* led by Abbé Sieyès, also a deputy for the third estate, even though he was a member of the clergy. This club met in a Palais-Royal restaurant, a neighborhood that became the capital of the Revolution inside Paris.

The king, then, had many reasons to be worried on the eve of the opening of the Estates General. He nonetheless hailed the assembly as a "new source of happiness for the nation," while at the same time emphasizing the gravity of the financial situation, before giving the floor to Necker. The finance minister disap-pointed the entire audience by delivering an essentially tech-nical, long, and boring speech, which, despite allusions to a plan for equality of taxation, did not answer the questions raised in the *cahiers de doléances* (books of grievances) that had come from all parts of the country.

Dissensions erupted within the assembly. The third estate rejected separate deliberation of each order for the verification of credentials. The dean of the third estate, the astronomer Bailly, asked the nobility and clergy to participate in common delibera-tions, which the nobility and the majority of the clergy refused to do. The king's brothers and Justice Minister Barentin tried to have the Estates General dissolved. The king, afflicted by the recent death of the Dauphin, Louis-Joseph, preferred to wait, but events hurried forward. On June 17, the third estate, considering that it represented 96 percent of the nation, proclaimed itself the National Assembly and set itself the task of developing a constitution.

On June 23, Louis XVI delivered a solemn speech to the three orders assembled together presenting a compromise program. Equal taxation would be applied if the nobility and clergy agreed. Individual freedom and freedom of the press were recognized, but access of all to all employments and official functions was excluded, and the deliberations of the so-called National Assembly were declared illegal and void. Disappointment was almost universal. The third estate refused to leave the hall, despite the plea of the Marquis de Dreux-Brézé, to whom Mirabeau replied that he and his colleagues would give in only to the force of bayonets. Not taking his words at face value, Louis XVI himself asked the clergy and the nobility to join the third estate. Nothing would now stop the decline of the absolute monarchy.

In an outburst of energy, the king had the capital surrounded by an army of twenty-five thousand men commanded by Marshal de Broglie. The bad news coming from the provinces, where hordes of brigands and uncontrolled elements—unemployed workers, deserters, ruined peasants—engaged in looting and attacks against châteaus and administrative offices, strengthened the monarch's ephemeral determination. Agitation was growing in Paris itself, but the French Guards refused to fire on demonstrators. The king thought it would be clever, to appease the court, to dismiss Necker and the ministers Montmorin and Saint-Priest, who favored the search for an agreement with the Assembly. Breteuil, a haughty, intransigent, and inept aristocrat, but a man of great loyalty, was promoted to the position of confidential adviser to Louis XVI. The court breathed easier. But the people saw Necker's dismissal on July 13 as a provocation. Orators at the Palais-Royal set the tone: the people had to take to arms to defend their rights. A bust of Louis-Philippe was paraded around the neighborhood. Armories were looted, and there were confrontations with the soldiers of the Royal Allemand under Besenval, an advocate of harsh repression.

On the morning of July 14, rioters invaded the Invalides and looted the weapons supplies. A few hours later came the greatest symbolic event in the history of France: the fall of the Bastille.

On July 15, the king came before the Assembly, denied that a coup was in preparation, and declared that he had given the order to the troops, that were present only to safeguard the security of all, to move away from the capital. The deputies, he said in conclusion, should go themselves to announce it to the Parisians.

A delegation of 88 members led by Bailly set out for the Hôtel de Ville, where it was greeted with shouts of "Long live the nation." Bailly was immediately elected mayor of Paris. The bourgeois militia established to maintain order was given the name National Guard. It needed a commander who was competent and respected and a man in whom the advocates of freedom could have confidence. The man who was most suitable for the post was soon found in the ranks of the deputies. Occupied at the Assembly, he had not witnessed the fall of the Bastille. He belonged to the nobility and was a career soldier, a general with a glorious past. His name was Gilbert de Lafayette.

CHAPTER TWENTY-SEVEN

THE "FAIR-HAIRED BOY"

W HAT HAD WASHINGTON'S SPIRITUAL SON BEEN
doing after the Assembly of Notables? He had participated in the provincial Assembly of Auvergne,
where he had distinguished himself by his determination to
reform the system of taxation in favor of the less well-off; but his
chief goal was to participate in the meetings of the Estates General. It seemed to him that the time had come to give his fight for
freedom in America a spectacular continuation in France. It is
not certain that he chose correctly by soliciting the votes of the
nobility of Auvergne, while the third estate which he fully supported—he had come out in favor of a doubling of its number of
deputies—had asked him to be one of its representatives. He
probably hoped to bring together the liberal nobles and to foster
disciples among his peers. In any event, although he was elected
by a hair (198 votes out of 393), he was elected. "I am pleased to

think that I will shortly be in an assembly of representatives of the French nation," he wrote to Washington, who had just taken office as president, on May 26. Throughout the Revolution, Lafayette never stopped writing to his great friend across the ocean, describing his activities as though he needed the older man's advice, if not his directions. Very conscious of his role as head of state, Washington showed in his replies all the required reserve, and the more the months went by, the more Lafayette realized that the situation in his own country was enormously more complex and difficult than the one he had encountered in America, which involved essentially fighting against invaders from afar.

In the Assembly, he came up against people of his order by systematically supporting the demands of the third estate, notably deliberation in common by all the deputies. It was as though his colleagues' irritation stimulated him, as though he took pleasure in provoking them.

Gouverneur Morris, a former member of congress who was in Paris on private business (he was appointed American minister to France in 1792), wrote to Washington of Lafayette: "He is today as loved and as hated as he ever may have wished. The nation idolizes him because he has set himself up as one of the principal champions of rights." But this champion of rights soon appeared too radical to the very conservative Morris, who was a supporter of monarchy in France. Indeed, Morris went so far as to advise Lafayette to include the recognition of a degree of authority for the nobility in the planned constitution.

But Gouverneur Morris was not the only American in Paris who wanted to influence the former combatant of Yorktown, and while he tried to point Lafayette toward more moderation, one of his prominent compatriots, Thomas Jefferson, the serving American minister in France, fostered his democratic zeal.

Though they were both members of the wealthy bourgeoisie and had fought together during the American Revolution, Morris and Jefferson had very different personalities and ideas.

A rich and cultivated businessman, Morris had been conquered by the charm of French high society at the end of the Ancien Régime. He liked the stylish houses, the luxurious furniture, the works of art, the grand dinners, the exquisite manners, and especially the pretty women. A skeptic and a sensualist, for several years he shared with Talleyrand the favors of the sparkling Mme de Flahaut, the irresistible Adèle. Welcomed in circles close to the court, he felt a sincere attachment to Louis XVI, and showed it with more courage than skill in the dark hours of the monarchy. This snobbish and worldly man wanted the constitution to leave the essentials of executive power in the hands of the king, and Lafayette's dream of an assembly exercising real government power seemed to him dangerously naïve. He attempted for as long as he could to persuade Lafayette that each form of regime ought to be adapted to the particular nature of the country that chose it, or else it could not take root, and the system would not function for long.

Lafayette, who did not wish to sever ties with the monarchy but who nonetheless aimed primarily at establishing freedom and equality in the broadest terms, paid little attention to Morris's advice and warnings. He even criticized Morris for damaging the cause of democracy by publicly expressing reservations about the struggle he and his friends were engaged in.

Thomas Jefferson was as rich and as taken with the charms of the French aristocracy as Morris, but the resemblance between them ended there. A large planter, lawyer, and political figure, Jefferson of Virginia, principal author of the Declaration of Independence and future president, was essentially an intellectual. He was a man of exceptionally wide-ranging culture, a great jurist who spoke French and Italian, read Greek and Latin, and was as interested in architecture as in natural science. He had designed one of the most beautiful buildings in eighteenth-century America, Monticello, in the style of Palladio, and he could when called upon play a musical instrument, draft a constitution, or draw up a curriculum and regulations for a university.

The aristocratic salons he frequented in Paris were not the same as those where one might meet Gouverneur Morris. They were not places where the search for pleasure prevailed over all, but places for the discussion of ideas, art, and literature. His dearest friends, Mme de Tessé (Lafayette's aunt), Mme d'Anville, and Mme de Corny, were great liberal figures ahead of their time, above social frivolity, although not at all prudish. Jefferson might be seen as a patrician of the left. His private life was very discreet, although he was socially very active. The widower of a passionately loved wife, he had brought his daughter Martha to Paris as well as a beautiful black governess, Sally Hemings, his mistress.

Jefferson had been Lafayette's friend when he was fighting in America and was aware of his failings. "His foible," he wrote to Madison, "is a canine appetite for popularity and fame; but he will get above this." Jefferson nonetheless shared Lafayette's aversion to absolute monarchy and hoped for the success of the revolution that he felt approaching. He went so far as to view its excesses as "inevitable," once he had returned to America in the fall of 1789, which led to his being seen as an American "Jacobin."

Jefferson had no hesitation in appearing at Duport's residence when meetings of the *Patriotes* were held. In addition to Lafayette, he met there men who would soon become famous, notably Condorcet and the young Barnave. His analysis of the situation was lucid. He foresaw strong resistance from circles tied to the court and he criticized Lafayette for not having been elected a representative of the third estate, as Mirabeau, an aristocrat, and Sieyès, a clergyman, had chosen to do. Sitting with the nobility when his ideas were in favor of the people, he ran the risk of losing in both camps. This was indeed what happened. In the meantime, Lafayette submitted to Jefferson a proposed *Déclaration européenne des droits de l'homme et des citoyens*, resembling the American model, which he presented to the Assembly on July 11. There is no doubt that Jefferson participated in drafting this document, discussion of which was postponed by the president of the Assembly because of the rush of events—the change of government and the dismissal of Necker. Slightly revised by a committee led by Sieyès, the *Déclaration des droits de l'homme et du citoyen* was finally adopted on August 26.

Recalled to Philadelphia to take up the post of Secretary of State, Jefferson continued to follow, as closely as contemporary communications permitted, the unfolding of a revolution that he saw as the continuation and extension of the American Revolution, which he hoped would be imitated by other countries in Europe.

Lafayette, who had had a handsome uniform made, spent the summer organizing the National Guard—his army—and maintaining order in the capital to the extent possible. He was absent from the Constituent Assembly on the night of August 4, when his brother-in-law Louis de Noailles and the Duke d'Aiguillon proclaimed the abolition of privileges that he himself had been calling for. In Paris, his courage and calm in confronting a raging and bloodthirsty populace enabled him to save the lives of the Abbé Cordier, Colonel de Besenval, and Soulès (assistant to the unfortunate governor of the Bastille), but he was unable to prevent the hanging, across from the Hôtel de Ville and before his eyes, of the state counselor Foulon, absurdly blamed for price increases, or the killing of Foulon's son-in-law Bertier de

Sauvigny, intendant of Paris. Sickened by these murders, he very publicly resigned his post, and only agreed to reverse his decision under pressure from his officers.

On August 25, the festival of Saint Louis, he presented his respects to the king, who greeted him graciously. The queen herself deigned to smile on the man she nicknamed in private the "fair-haired boy." Within five weeks her life and that of her husband would depend on this fair-haired boy.

CHAPTER TWENTY-EIGHT

GENERAL MORPHEUS

I N HIS SUMPTUOUS HOME IN THE PALAIS-ROYAL IN PARIS in early October 1789, a man at his morning toilet wore the satisfied smile of someone who was seeing events unfold in accordance with his most secret desires. He sprinkled himself with perfume, as he usually did several times a day, powdered himself, and stared at his reflection in the mirror at length. He liked what he saw, and a growing number of people seemed to share his appreciation. He had always been fond of his appearance and had taken great care of it. He was proud of his smooth, unwrinkled body—he was only thirty—that had been unstintingly admired in intimate moments by countless women. To make his body even more desirable, he had had himself depilated with wax, from his toes to his chin, on the eve of his marriage to the tender and innocent Princess de Penthièvre, the daughter of the Admiral of France and a descendant of Louis XIV and Mme de Montespan. Love, or rather pleasure, held the principal place in his life. He collected mistresses, from aristocratic ladies to actresses, and including visiting foreigners and paid professionals, whom he invited to his "little house," where strange evening parties were held.

However enamored of his own image he may have been, the libertine was not so naïve as to believe that his charm sufficed for his conquests. The path from introduction to intimacy was eased by his natural generosity; he was said to be the richest man in France, a great lord, the king's cousin. His name was Philippe d'Orléans, Duke de Chartres. He is known to history by the name he was given in the troubled final days of the Ancien Régime, Philippe Égalité.

Philippe hated the king and queen, who kept him at a distance because of their distaste for his conduct. The court never solicited his advice, and this fed his fierce jealousy. Everything that might diminish the king's authority or prestige or tarnish the people's view of Louis XVI and Marie Antoinette filled him with pleasure. He lost no opportunity to present himself as a critic, if not an outright opponent, of royal authority, in the hope that a disturbance might provoke a change of dynasty in his favor, or at least a regency.

Fairly well cultivated and very much an anglophile, but weak in character, inconsistent, and a slave to his senses, Philippe had nothing of the orator or party leader. His only hope of influencing events lay in acting behind the scenes, intrigue, manipulation, and provocation, always conceived and developed so that he would not appear implicated. To this end, he worked through intermediaries at his command. The Palais-Royal neighborhood that he controlled was an area of the capital given over to leisure, where could be found excellent

restaurants, cabarets, ice-cream sellers, dance halls, little theaters, reading rooms, gambling halls, fortune tellers,
astrologers, puppeteers, singers, a wax museum, along with
many young and not so young women in search of adventure,
and gentlemen of all ages seeking female companionship for
an hour, a night, or longer. There were many welcoming apartments in the area to easily accommodate these desires.

But this center of libertinage was also a place where the
winds of political unrest were blowing. People went to the
Palais-Royal for amusement but also to engage in the discussion of ideas. It was a blend of night life, intellectual bohemi-
anism, and student quarter. There one could meet influential
and honorable people gathered around a well-stocked table
making contacts and developing plans; impromptu orators discovering their own eloquence; previously unknown journalists
who were now being talked about because their publications—
which were springing up like mushrooms—had begun to cir-
culate; and ladies of the evening picking up unaccompanied
men on café terraces.

It was at the Palais-Royal that Camille Desmoulins, later
Danton's right-hand man, and publisher of the weekly *Révolu-
tions de France et de Brabant*, launched the tricolor cockade,
uniting the red and blue of Paris with the white that symbolized the French monarchy, which might still be seen as an ally
of the people.

A comrade of Robespierre, his childhood friend from the
Collège Louis le Grand, Desmoulins joined the Paris bar in
1785. He had few clients and, besides, he stuttered. He
demonstrated eloquence only at the Palais-Royal where he
spent the greater part of his days. His dream was to become a
great poet, and he was a talented writer. He found a muse in
the person of Mme Duplessis, the wife of an employee of the

finance ministry, but her virtue and lack of interest in this sallow and skinny suitor with disorderly black hair meant that she confined him to the role of friend of the family. He consoled himself by falling in love with her daughter Lucile, a rich heiress. He played a prominent role in the popular uprising in July, and became one of the most remarkable orators in the Cordeliers club.

Philippe Égalité savored his growing popularity and pursued his work of clandestine demolition of institutions. He financed pamphleteers who, in various more or less ephemeral publications, propagated alarmist rumors, and spoke of mysterious plots with ramifications in the court aimed at destabilizing the Constituent Assembly and the Commune of Paris, blockading food supplies to the capital, and dissolving the many clubs that had just been established.

The hidden director of this campaign of rumors, the trusted adviser of the Duke d'Orléans and apparently an expert manipulator, was artillery commander Choderlos de Laclos, the author of *Les Liaisons dangereuses*. Laclos and others had understood that as long as the court remained in Versailles, with the Constituent Assembly at its side, if not at its disposal, the centers of decision would be inaccessible to the Paris revolutionaries.

In the summer of 1789, politicians who saw beyond day-to-day politics judged that in order to prevent a backlash inspired by the advocates of absolute monarchy, who had until now retreated but were dreaming of revenge (the emigration had begun), the king had to be installed in Paris. The Assembly would follow and it would be relatively easy to control a center of power that in Versailles enjoyed a freedom that made it dangerous. There was, however, no legal means to constrain the monarch. He had come to Paris of his own free will on July 17 and had left, hailed by acclamations. The use of force was difficult to envision, since the king had regiments under his orders. The people of Paris had only the National Guard, and Lafayette would not send his men against the royal troops. Even if he had wanted to, some of them would not have obeyed him. To bring the king back to Paris, a trick had to be found, and it seems that Choderlos de Laclos was the one who came up with it.

The professional soldiers guarding Versailles would not hesitate to fire on any group of armed men trying to make a forced entry into the château, and they would only be doing their duty. But would they dare to fire on women who had come en masse to implore the king to give bread to their starving children? Thus was born the idea of Louis XVI mythically transformed into a baker, the queen a baker's wife, and the Dauphin a baker's boy. Once contact had been established between the royal family and the women of Paris through a theoretically nonviolent demonstration, it would be easy for provocateurs to shift the movement into high gear by launching the slogan: "The king to Paris."

To set up the operation, first there had to be a sufficient number of motivated women, directed (unknown to them) by experienced agitators, and then a pretext had to be found. That condition was soon fulfilled. Flour supplies to the capital had been dangerously decreasing for two days, there was a threat of famine, and the people were grumbling. Blame could easily be cast on the king, who still refused to promulgate the decrees abolishing all privileges, and on the maneuvers of his advisers. It turned out, however, that the court provided the best pretext to trigger the movement.

On October 1, the king, who had only relative confidence in the bodyguards on duty at the palace, had summoned a regiment from Flanders whose devotion to the crown was beyond question. To cement the attachment of these soldiers to the king, his advisers had suggested that a banquet be organized in their honor in the opera hall of the palace. The food and wine were sumptuous, and the atmosphere was celebratory, in sharp contrast to the gloom that had prevailed in Versailles for several months. In an unprecedented gesture, the king and the queen, with the Dauphin in her arms, came to see their guests in the middle of the banquet. Their arrival aroused enthusiasm, toasts were drunk to Louis XVI, to Marie Antoinette, and to the Dauphin, and the soldiers said they were ready to shed their blood for them. There was a rumor that officers had trampled on tricolor cockades and put on white ones. A few hours later, the news was made the most of in Paris with great dramatic effects. It was claimed that the king was threatening to retake control of the capital with this excited Flanders regiment. People could already see the Seine reddened with the blood of the people and corpses flowing on the current, and emotions were stirred to launch a counterattack.

Early on the morning of October 5, drums summoned the women to assemble to go to the king and ask for bread. Groups were formed; to defend against possible attack, they needed light weapons. Figures came out of nowhere and directed the demonstrators to caches of pistols, swords, and pikes. A few men joined the procession that was taking shape. The organizers had arranged to include a few prostitutes among the ranks in order to provoke the bodyguards. Even better, they had arranged to have cross-dressing men, whose disguises would not be penetrated, join the procession to provide an example of firmness to their fellow demonstrators, who might shrink back if thing got too risky. It turned out that their makeup was ruined by an untimely rainstorm, so that the innocent young bodyguards of the palace were startled to discover determined masculine expressions behind all the artifices of feminine grace. Nonetheless, these agitators were effective.

Only an imagination as perverse as that of Pierre-Ambroise Choderlos de Laclos could come up with such a subtle stratagem. He had always been fond of masking the truth. A paradoxical figure who was long considered as scandalous a writer as the Marquis de Sade, he was a literary man and a soldier without illusions about human relations. Born in Amiens on October 18, 1741, he was the second son of a minor official in Picardie and Artois, who had recently been granted a title. He was a soldier out of true vocation, and he chose the artillery, a technical branch well suited to his mathematical mind. He was admitted in 1760 to the predecessor of the École Polytechnique, given the rank of second lieutenant in 1761, and promoted to lieutenant in 1762. Pursuing a dream of conquest and glory, he had himself appointed to the colonial brigade stationed in La Rochelle. But the Treaty of Paris put an end to the Seven Years' War in 1763. With no war to be fought, the young lieutenant Laclos was forced to stifle his heroic ambitions and lead the dull life of a garrison: Toul in 1763, Strasbourg from 1765 to 1769, Grenoble from 1769 to 1775, and Besançon from 1775 to 1776. Promoted to captain on the basis of seniority in 1771, a rank he retained for 17 years until the eve of the Revolution, the cold and logical artillery man with a subtle mind grew bored among the coarse soldiers, and to pass the time he took up writing. His first efforts at light verse were published in *L'Almanach des Muses*. Taking his inspiration from a novel by Mme Riccoboni, he wrote a mediocre comic opera, *Ernestine*, that had only one—disastrous—performance, on July 19, 1777, with Marie Antoinette in the audience. Also in 1777, he was given the mission of setting up an artillery school in Valence, where Napoleon was later a student. Back in Besançon in 1778 he was appointed captain of engineers. During his extensive free time in the garrison, he wrote several works in which he appears as an ardent admirer of Jean-Jacques Rousseau, particularly of the novel *La Nouvelle Héloïse*, which he considered "the most beautiful work given the name novel."

He began to write *Les Liaisons dangereuses* in 1778. In 1779 he was sent on a mission to the Île d'Aix to assist the Marquis de Montalembert in overseeing the construction of fortifications against the British. In fact, he spent a great deal of time writing *Les Liaisons dangereuses* as well as an *Épître à Madame de Montalembert*. Promoted to captain in charge of artillery at the end of the year, he secured another leave of six months during which he finished his masterpiece, which went on sale on March 23, 1782. The success was immediate and dazzling; the first edition of two thousand copies was sold out in a month—extraordinary for the time—and the book was reprinted ten times in the course of the next two years. But the publication of this demonic book, seen as an attack against the aristocracy, was considered an error by his superiors. He was immediately ordered to return to his garrison in Brittany, and from there he was sent to La Rochelle in 1783 to help in the construction of a new arsenal. There he met Marie-Soulange Duperré, whom he seduced and soon made pregnant. He was forty-two and she only twenty-four, but he was really in love, married her in 1786, and recognized the child. She remained the love of his life, and they had two more children.

It would be a mistake to see Laclos as a counterpart to his character Valmont. He had none of the vices of the seducer, but rather was a faithful husband and an attentive father, whose sentimental life was limited to his beloved wife. He might even be considered a proto-feminist, showing how far ahead he was on the question of the equality of the sexes when he participated in an academic competition on the subject: "What would be the best way to improve the education of women?" It is amusing to note that the author of *Les Liaisons dangereuses* was that concerned with the proper education of young ladies. He left the army in 1788 and after a period of reflection about how to further his ambition and several approaches to great aristocrats, he entered the service of the Duke d'Orléans, whose ideas on the evolution of the monarchy he shared. It was there that he was able to display the full extent of his Machiavellianism. The private man who was above reproach saved all the turbulence of his feelings and the agility of his mind for the intrigues and machinations that he masterfully conducted as secretary to Philippe Égalité, the Duke d'Orléans. It was indeed when the Revolution broke out that Choderlos de Laclos began to live as he wished, intensely. The great days of his life were those days in Versailles, tragic days for the royal family. Early in the week, on October 5 and 6, Louis XVI had gone hunting in the forest of Meudon, Marie Antoinette was in the Trianon, and the royal children had gone for a walk. Late on the morning of the 5th, it was learned that the Paris guard and a large cohort of men, led by an advance guard of women, were marching toward Versailles. It is hard to tell what this intelligent, perceptive man was thinking of at the time. In 1787, he had issued a proposal for numbering the streets of Paris, but he was also the author of maxims worthy of La Rochefoucauld: "Hatred is always more clear-sighted and ingenious than friendship," or "I was surprised at the pleasure one feels when doing good." Sometimes his remarks sound more like Saint-Simon: "One always becomes more ridiculous by defending oneself against it," "For him, making himself liked is only a way to succeed, for her it is success itself," "For men, infidelity is not inconstancy," "In love, you should give way to excess only with people you are soon about to leave," "Nature granted to men only constancy, whereas it gave women obstinacy." Sometimes Laclos indulged in personal confession: "I love her too much to be jealous. I have decided to be proud of her." Sometimes his innate nature comes to the fore, and he reveals himself to be an instinctive strategist: "A missed opportunity returns, but you never recover from a premature demand," or "It is good to accustom someone destined for great adventures to great events." These were the explosive thoughts that maturity had inspired in the man who was now conducting ballistic experiments to develop a hollow bullet filled with powder. Laclos later met the young general Napoleon Bonaparte, another artilleryman. The newly named First Consul commissioned him as a general of artillery on January 16, 1800. He was assigned to the army of the Rhine and finally received his baptism of fire at the battle of Bilberach. His personal history was finally rather bizarre, and even his death did not match his wild hopes. He died on September 5, 1803, in Taranto, not gloriously in battle but from dysentery, and he was buried there.

Back in the summer of 1789, the march of the women on Versailles was destined to remain in the history of France as one of the unknown masterpieces of Choderlos de Laclos. Lafayette, head of the National Guard, arrived too late at the assembly point to disperse the gathering or prevent the departure. The demonstrators refused to listen and some members of the Guard joined them. The general decided to follow the long procession with his available forces; he could not discern their real intentions but thought he could channel them, prevent serious incidents, and calm passions. The Commune of

Paris thought it advisable to have two commissioners accompany him.

As he was hunting near Paris, the king was informed that a troop of women was marching toward Versailles, and he headed back to the palace. The queen was quietly walking around Trianon. Dressed very simply, she was daydreaming in front of the ornamental pools when an emissary from Court Minister Saint-Priest came to beg her to return instantly to the château. There she joined the assembled members of the government. While waiting for the king's arrival, Gouvernet, the son of the minister of war, assembled the forces present, but no one dared order that the Sèvres bridge be blocked.

The king reached the château at three in the afternoon. The procession of women was said to be only an hour away from Versailles, and it was suggested that the queen and the royal children leave immediately for Rambouillet. The queen refused to be separated from her husband. Mounier, president of the Assembly, appeared and urged Louis XVI to promulgate the laws that had been passed. The king said nothing, but he agreed to receive a delegation of women. He seemed to them to be touched, understanding, benevolent, and reassuring. They wanted bread? He promised to have flour distributed in the capital. He was applauded. When they returned to the body of the procession, the delegates were shouted down, and tension was at its height. It was now imperative that the entire royal family, including the king, leave for Rambouillet. He hesitated, as always. It was nearly six, and night was falling. But demonstrators who had seen the carriages readied for departure cut the harnesses. There was now no way to leave, and the palace was in a state of confusion with contradictory orders and counterorders. Lafayette was announced at nine, but he did not arrive until midnight, "ready," he said, "to die at the feet of His Majesty, rather than uselessly, in the place de Grève." Paying no attention to this declaration of loyalty, the king asked what the demonstrators wanted.

"They want bread and for the bodyguards replaced by the Flanders regiment to resume their posts."

"Have them do that," said Louis XVI.

He went off to bed, and advised his wife to do the same. She agreed, and her ladies-in-waiting spent the night keeping watch outside her door.

Lafayette made a tour of inspection. Convinced that everything was in order, and overcome with exhaustion, he, too, went to bed in the Noailles house in Versailles. It was 2:30 in the morning.

At sunrise, a drummer called the sleepers scattered in the neighborhood of the château to assemble. The crowd, again compact, approached the gates, which were locked, except that one near the entry to the chapel had been left half open—it was never learned why or by whom. Demonstrators, men and women, poured through the entry, overwhelming the bodyguards, one of the whom, named Miomandre de Saint-Marie, cried out: "Save the queen!" The cry was heard, repeated, echoed like a tocsin. The queen's ladies led her through a secret passage to the king's apartment. Miomandre was massacred.

The king took the Dauphin with him, and he was joined by Madame Royale and the cabinet ministers. Necker was silent. The rioters, armed with pikes and some with battleaxes, hunted down the bodyguards, two of whom were decapitated and dismembered. The assassins and their accomplices smeared their faces with the blood of their victims. In a fit of madness, the aggressors decided to go further into the château. One door gave way, then others. But there was one they could not get through, because they came up against the determined and effective resistance of a group of soldiers who had come from Paris, led by a twenty-one-year-old sergeant, a native of Versailles who had served as a groom in the stables of the château before enlisting in the army. A former soldier in the Garde Française, he had been transferred to the National Guard. Within three years he would reach the rank of brigadier general. This hero of the days of October 5 and 6, 1789, who was at heart a republican, although he faced down the rioters, was named Lazare Hoche. Thanks to him, and to the belated arrival of his leader General Lafayette, who had had trouble waking up, the most directly threatened bodyguards were saved, because Lafayette had at his command a company of grenadiers. Although he dispersed the assailants, he did not prevent the second part of the maneuver from being carried out as planned, even facilitating it unaware.

Since the crowd was demanding that the king take up residence in Paris, Lafayette advised the monarch to accept the demand in principle. When he appeared on a balcony, Louis XVI was acclaimed. But this did not indicate that Lafayette had as yet succeeded in lowering the tension. The crowd now demanded that the queen appear, and appear alone. What did that mean, considering that demonstrators had just been heard in the palace corridors saying "we want the queen's heart," "we'll fricassee her liver," "we'll make cockades with her guts"? Rifles seemed to be aimed at the spot where she had to stand to be seen from below. Would she be shot at? Lafayette begged her to follow him, and she finally resigned herself. But he did not, as Marie Antoinette probably supposed, intend to harangue the crowd. He knew that his voice would not be heard above the shouts. To disarm hatred, something more than words was required. He took the queen's hand and with calculated slowness, bowing very gracefully as though on stage, he kissed her hand with enormous respect. This unexpected show of elegance at a moment of intense excitement was exactly the right gesture. The crowd was hypnotized. For a few moments, the image of the young and innocent queen of the first years of the reign replaced that of the "Austrian" whom pamphleteers blamed for all the ills of the country. She seemed worthy of the deference shown her by the authentic friend of the people and fighter for freedom standing at her side. But the king had promised, and the entire royal family had to go to Paris. It had to be freed from the influence of the evil advisers who swarmed through the court and come closer to the people. The people had to be able to see the royal family walking in the Tuileries gardens so they could make of it their symbol, their possession.

It took many hours to form the procession that would march to the capital. The most rancorous of the demonstrators had not disarmed, and the heads of bodyguards on pikes accompanied the august sovereigns throughout the journey. In Paris, there had to be a detour to the Hôtel de Ville. The king and the mayor exchanged pleasantries, speaking of welcome, confidence, the fine weather, and no one felt like laughing or even smiling. It was again necessary to appear on the balcony, but this time, since night had fallen, by torchlight.

At nine that night, overwhelmed by fatigue, the royal family settled into a hastily improvised apartment in the empty Tuileries palace. The king had lost none of his calm. Once he was alone, he ordered that supper be served.

There is no doubt that, on October 6, Lafayette saved the lives of the royal couple, or at least the life of the queen, who was in greater danger than the king. Another officer with the feelings of a knight had rushed to the château of Versailles as soon as he had heard of the arrival of the demonstrators, ready to do anything to save Marie Antoinette. This was, of course, Axel de Fersen. His presence helped the queen's morale, but he had no opportunity to intervene actively. But his role as a protector was only beginning.

Although he could tell himself that he had helped reduce the loss of life and material damage that might have been significant and even irreparable, because the château was already a museum, the head of the National Guard was nonetheless aware that he had been subjected to severe humiliation.

He held Philippe Égalité to be the instigator of the disastrous march on Versailles. The man with whom Lafayette had shared the favors of the beautiful Aglaë de Hunolstein now, he felt, had to bend before him. His vengeance was neither base nor bloody. He merely let the duke understand that in his situation, the best thing to do was to leave France as soon as possible, to go, for example, to England, a country he knew well, on some vague diplomatic mission to enable him to save face. Philippe Égalité agreed, but in his entourage was a collaborator who, obligated by loyalty to follow his patron, cursed Lafayette, although he had sought the general's support in 1788 against the unjust treatment he was suffering in the army and had spoken of Lafayette's "characteristic affability." This man who crossed paths with Lafayette on several occasions was Choderlos de Laclos, who gave the Revolution his full support.

An unpublished letter from Philippe Égalité, written in 1793, the last year of his life, when he was imprisoned in Fort Saint-Jean in Marseille, sheds light on the private life of the great seducer in his last days: "You cannot imagine the calm that spreads through my soul when I read your words. I don't understand why you found no letters from me when you got to Paris; why would they keep you from the pleasure of reading me and hearing me tell you that nothing can compare to the tenderness I feel for you." The woman to whom this letter was addressed was his mistress: Fanny, Marguerite de la Motte Cepoy, daughter of the Marquis de Cepoy. She had married the son of the celebrated naturalist Buffon in 1784, whom Rivarol called "the worst chapter in his father's 'natural history.'" Soon after her marriage, she became the mistress of the Duke d'Orléans and exercised great influence over him. At the moment the duke wrote this letter, his châteaus had been put up for sale, but Philippe Égalité was in love, and the possession of the beloved replaced all earthly goods: "Wherever I may live, whatever my fortune may be, provided I am with you, dear beloved Fanny, and I do not suffer the pain of thinking that people who were attached to me and whom I love are in poverty and need . . . I ask nothing more from heaven, and it shall be granted to me: I will be reunited with my Fanny and my two children, and if I do not die from joy, I will spend the rest of my days, happy and tranquil, occupied solely with her happiness. Farewell, dear friend, how I love you. . . ." The dreams of a life together, of peaceful love, family serenity, and a happy future, were the prisoner's final illusion. Indeed, the man who had voted for the death of the king his cousin was to feel the cold steel of the guillotine on his own neck. The Convention found him guilty of having aspired to the crown. Sentenced to death, he was executed on April 6, 1793, and buried at Picpus cemetery, as Lafayette was later to be. After his execution, his mistress was faithful to him in a way, because she got a divorce in January 1794, and her ex-husband was executed in July of that year. The still beautiful Fanny remarried in 1799 and died in 1808, leaving two children from her second marriage. None of her contemporaries had forgotten her grace in misfortune, her pert nose, her admirable blond hair, or her divine figure, saluted by all connoisseurs.

CHAPTER TWENTY-NINE

THE LAST FESTIVAL

I N A ROOM IN A PRIVATE HOUSE AN ALTAR HAD BEEN SET UP in haste on top of a chest of drawers. The ciborium, the cruets, the sacred book, all the elements needed to celebrate a mass had been assembled. Significantly, a mirror had been set on the other side of the chest, facing the priest who was to officiate. He entered the room; he was a handsome young man of thirty-five, with fine features, a penetrating gaze, and carefully groomed long hair. He exuded a rather lofty grace that bore only a slender relation to the humility of a country priest. He was wearing the sacramental vestments, as for an ordinary mass. Two abbots wearing surplices accompanied him to serve as altar boys. A strange mass began. The young priest often stopped and looked at the abbots as though soliciting their opinion about the movement he had just made: is that what he was supposed to do and in that way? He wanted frank responses, but the abbots were rather hesitant. Sometimes, the celebrant slowly accomplished the ritual gestures while looking at himself in the mirror, and began again, improving his performance. Broken down into separate segments in this way, the mass clearly seemed to be a rehearsal, which is what it was, but not for the theater or the opera. The officiating priest was not an actor. He had indeed been ordained, and was rehearsing the motions of the mass because he was afraid he had forgotten them. This could happen in the eighteenth century. The oddest thing of all was that he was not an ordinary priest but the Bishop of Autun. He was a prince of the Church and was preparing to celebrate mass as part of a very important ceremony at which would be present the king, the queen, government ministers, hundreds of French and foreign dignitaries, and tens of thousands of spectators. It was therefore obvious that it would be better if he did not look awkward or hesitant. Everyone knew that he did not owe his position to his piety or his theological genius, but to his birth and family connections: for the last twenty years, the nobility had controlled the upper clergy as it controlled the army officer corps. On the surface, things should be done in the proper way. It didn't matter that the bishop concerned cared little about religion and preferred society life and the company of pretty women to spiritual retreats. He was also a deputy to the Constituent Assembly, briefly its president, and frequented the circle around the Duke d'Orléans and the club of the Constitutionnels. In short, he frequented "advanced" circles, was devoured by ambition, and was destined to play a great role in these troubled times.

This ambitious man in the violet cassock was Charles Maurice de Talleyrand-Périgord. No better choice could have been found to celebrate mass at the gigantic civic and patriotic demonstration scheduled for July 14, 1790, the first anniversary of the fall of the Bastille.

This ceremony, given the name *Fête de la Fédération*, had been decided on three months earlier to demonstrate in principle the definitive alliance of constitution, king, and nation. A movement that had begun in the provinces in the spring had shown that the population was growing increasingly aware of the need for a broad and solid union to confront the intrigues of the enemies of the Constitution and the threats from abroad stirred up by the émigrés.

Rising above local interests, the "patriots"—as citizens advocating reforms now called themselves—had decided to "federate" themselves, that is, they had promised to remain forever united, to ensure the provision of essential goods, and to support the laws passed by the Constituent Assembly. It was a movement that had sprung up almost spontaneously to prevent civil war and the destruction of what had been won in 1789 and, if necessary, to protect the borders. The *Fédérés* of Alsace, Lorraine, and Franche-Comté, meeting in Strasbourg in June, had put up a tricolor flag at the Kehl bridge on the Rhine, with this inscription: "Here begins the nation of freedom."

The *Fête de la Fédération*, with the king and queen present, would consecrate this patriotic movement. And since it was impossible in France to imagine a national ceremony without a religious component, the Bishop of Autun had been called on— even though he belonged to the upper nobility, he made great show of holding democratic ideas.

For this ceremony, which was intended to be grandiose— thousands of *Fédérés* were to collectively swear an oath—the organizers had carried out excavation and construction work of extraordinary magnitude and in record time between the École Militaire and the Seine. An amphitheater that could seat 200,000 spectators was built on the Champ de Mars, as well as a huge altar to the nation, the platform on which the mass would be

celebrated. The entire population cooperated in the work. Bourgeois and aristocrats took off their coats to push wheelbarrows.
Elegant ladies in long dresses and feathered hats lifted shovels
alongside professional gardeners. It was a privileged moment, an
unexpected interlude of calm in this troubled period.

Songs rang out all day from this mass of volunteers, men and
women of all ages and conditions. It was a surprising episode of
fraternization that came to an end when the last lights of the festival were extinguished.

On July 14, everything was in place by six in the morning. Tricolor flags had blossomed everywhere, transforming the appearance of the city. It was not just the glory of Paris, capital of
freedom, that was about to be celebrated but the glory of the
entire nation. The 83 flags of the 83 recently created French
departments fluttered in the breeze along with the tricolors.
Fourteen thousand armed *Fédérés* from all the provinces of
France, assembled between the Barrière du Trône and the Porte
Saint Martin, were preparing to march in procession to the
Champ de Mars. They would be joined at the Place Louis XV
(now the Place de la Concorde) by the members of the National
Assembly, which had been meeting at the Tuileries palace since
August 19, 1789.

A great parade of troops was included in the program. Only
the sun failed to appear, but rain and wind did not dampen the
enthusiasm and good humor of the participants. A pontoon
bridge had been set up for the procession to cross the Seine to
the Champ de Mars. The horsemen of the National Guard led the
parade, which passed under a triumphal arch. Large pots of
incense burned at the four corners of the altar of the nation. Two
hundred priests in white albs with tricolor sashes around their
waists awaited the Bishop of Autun. As the prince of the Church
mounted the steps in his splendid ceremonial costume, he

managed to wear a mask of seriousness, but he is reported to have whispered to Lafayette: "I beg you, don't make me laugh."

The arrival of the king and queen, announced by artillery salvoes, was saluted by huge acclaim. Tens of thousands of voices cried out "Vive le roi," "Vive la nation."

The monarch took his place on a throne of violet velvet decorated with golden fleurs de lis, with the president of the National Assembly at his side. One thousand eight hundred singers and instrumentalists performed religious hymns and marches. After the mass, the commander in chief of the National Guard, Lafayette, with his sword lowered, pronounced the oath, provoking thunderous applause: "We swear to be forever faithful to nation, law, and king, to uphold the Constitution promulgated by the National Assembly and accepted by the king, to protect, according to law, persons and property, the free circulation of goods in the interest of the kingdom, and the collection of public contributions in whatever form, and to remain united with all Frenchmen by the unbreakable bonds of brotherhood."

It would be hard not to subscribe to such a generous and reassuring statement, in which there was something for everyone, including the king, as long as he accepted the role that he had now been assigned.

The *Fédérés* collectively took the oath to be faithful to king and country. Louis XVI himself, with apparent good grace, said in a firm voice: "I, king of the French, swear to the nation to use the power given me by Constitutional Act of the State to uphold the Constitution promulgated by the National Assembly and accepted by me." This provoked delirious joy. The king was acclaimed as he had not been since his youth. The monarchists wanted to see in this success an expression of the deep attachment of the majority of the French people to the monarch. But wasn't the king being acclaimed because he had given the impression of having accepted everything that had been accomplished since the first session of the Estates General?

The military parade that followed helped maintain the day's euphoria. Among the delegations that passed before Louis XVI, Marie Antoinette, the royal family, and the government ministers was a small group of American patriots, valiant allies of France. At their head, carrying the flag with thirteen stars, was Thomas Paine, author of *Common Sense*, sworn enemy of all the kings of the earth, and admirer of the French Revolution that he was to defend against Edmund Burke and in whose struggles he became a direct participant. He was accompanied by John Paul Jones, the American navy privateer who had served France and been received by Louis XVI at Versailles.

The triumphant victor of the *Fête de la Fédération* was not, however, the king, who had been so loudly acclaimed and whose popularity on this day was based on a misunderstanding. It was the commander in chief of the National Guard, Lafayette, who was the object of the greatest attention and the most intense fervor. The crowd wanted to approach and touch him; some managed to kiss his boots or his spurs. He was the hero, the star, the demigod, and this festival was really his day. This spontaneous cult of personality was somehow irritating and intolerable to other political leaders. The king himself, relegated despite himself, and probably despite Lafayette, to the role of foil, was offended by this glory, and his treacherous advisers were able to make use of that feeling.

But on July 14, 1790, regardless of misunderstandings, ambiguities, and jealousy, the festival went on. At noon, the bells in all the churches of France rang out in unison so inhabitants of the provinces could commune with the Parisians in a single surge of fraternity. A tricolor bouquet was laid at the foot of the statue of Henri IV. Cabarets and dance halls were full to over-flowing. Street merchants sold patriotic souvenirs, flags, portraits of personalities, fans. One relic was especially popular: fragments of stone recovered from the fallen walls of the Bastille that had been polished by industrious merchants. Mme de Genlis, governess of the children of the Duke d'Orléans, wore a very beautiful one on a chain, encrusted with the word *Liberté* in diamonds. In the evening there was dancing in the streets, and toasts were drunk to the nation and the Constitution. The Champs Élysées were illuminated as never before, and the king felt compelled to go down them in an uncovered carriage. Fireworks exploded, wine flowed, and the Palais-Royal was full of excitement. Paris, thoughtlessly, was celebrating.

CHAPTER THIRTY

IMPOSSIBLE DUO

THE GENERAL COULD TELL HIMSELF THAT HE HAD FINALLY achieved the popularity he had dreamed so much about, his only goal. Had he wanted to take power in the fall of 1789, few institutions or political forces would have been able to stand in his way. He may well have sensed that this extraordinary situation would not last. He had reached it with some difficulty after returning from Versailles behind the rioters, bringing the king and the royal family to Paris safe and sound, but, despite appearances, as prisoners. The monarchs had thanked him more politely than warmly for having saved their lives, and now considered him rather as a superior jailer than a protector. Madame Royale, happily for him, was more grateful to him than her parents.

Troops under his command had refused to obey on several occasions; he had been ridiculed by royalists and satirized by alleged democrats. He had been called General Morpheus because, overcome with fatigue, he had been unable to keep from taking a few hours of sleep in Versailles. He had probably played into the hands of the Duke d'Orléans and his allies by bringing Louis XVI back to Paris, but he could hardly have done otherwise, and he had significantly limited the damage.

Lafayette, moreover, had enough influence to oblige the duke, who protested his innocence, to go to London for a while, along with his faithful adviser Choderlos de Laclos. The anger of the commander of the National Guard did not stop there. He had publication of *L'Ami du Peuple* suspended and its editor Marat arrested. The investigation went nowhere, however, and the journalist, who continued to urge his readers to violent action, was released. He resumed his campaigns of calumny and rumor mongering, with the irresponsibility shared by most papers of the time, and their number was increasing. The son of a Spanish Protestant doctor and a Frenchwoman exiled in Switzerland, Marat was born near Neuchâtel, educated in The Hague and in England, and held a degree in medicine. He spoke several languages, was a former admirer of Mesmer, interested in electricity and optics, and thought of himself as a scientist and a philosopher. Former doctor for the guards of the Count d'Artois, he had opened a shop for medical electricity before plunging headlong into politics and journalism. Founded in September 1789, his *Ami du Peuple* was one of the most violent press organs of the Revolution until Marat was assassinated by the young royalist Charlotte Corday in July 1793. By targeting this bitter and hateful psychopath, Lafayette had made a substantial and persistent enemy.

An instinctive republican, as he had admitted to the king

and queen, the commander of the National Guard nonetheless thought it was urgent to stabilize the situation and give the king a power that might balance that of the Assembly, in the framework of a constitutional monarchy more democratic than that of Great Britain. But for such a regime to be possible, the king would have to accept, clearly and without reservation, all of the basic reforms carried out since the Estates General had first met. Lafayette strove to persuade him. But even when the king acquiesced or made remarks tinged with a very liberal spirit, he was in fact pretending. He hoped in the future to recover all the prerogatives he had lost, and in the meantime he resisted day by day, although he was unable to prevent the gradual diminution of his real powers. He was playing a double game. On one side, he was trying to appease and reassure the revolutionaries; on the other, he fostered the hopes of supporters of the Ancien Régime through secret contacts with the émigrés and foreign monarchs. While waiting for a change in the balance of power, he tried to use Lafayette. He knew the general's political inclinations as well has his limits. The ideal solution would be to associate him with a politician of stature who was knowledgeable about the major problems and enjoyed a high reputation in the Assembly and some influence on public opinion. This miraculous man, whose deep agreement with the court would be suspected by no one, would be the brains behind a politics of transition that would be executed by Lafayette. The king and some of his advisers thought they had found this man in the person of Mirabeau, the most popular orator in the Assembly and the clubs, a depraved, dissolute, gambling, cynical, and wildly talented aristocrat, who had the huge advantage of being devoured by debt and was therefore open to schemes likely to provide him with funds. When he was sounded out, Mirabeau was ready to become the court's secret agent, but a substantial obstacle stood in the way. Cooperation between him and Lafayette was impossible. The general despised the orator, whom he considered a downright scoundrel, and Mirabeau in return thought Lafayette had a mediocre mind, that he was a naïve idealist lacking in political intelligence and incapable of mastering a complex situation.

The king might insist all he liked on the benefit to the nation of an understanding between the two men; friends in common might well intercede and propose forms of alliance; despite all, the orator and the general could never form a duo. Upright and disinterested, the general believed that democracy was linked to virtue and that nothing valuable could be constructed with men who were not honest. Nonetheless, he did not overestimate his own capacities, as indicated in a remark he made in a letter to his cousin the Marshal de Bouillé: "As to me, whom circumstances and the confidence of the people have placed in a scale of responsibility far superior to my talents, I think I have proved that I detest faction as well as I love liberty."

It has been suggested that Mirabeau and the Count de Provence considered having Lafayette assassinated in December 1789 in conjunction with the so-called Favras plot. But there is no evidence to support the assertion, since the naïve conspirator was hanged without confessing anything.

In any event, on February 11, 1790, the commander of the National Guard had enough authority to arrest 234 rioters after a street battle, which earned him congratulations from the Assembly. The episode fortified his optimism, which showed through in his correspondence with Washington. After regretting that he could no longer benefit from Washington's advice, Lafayette announced that "a new political edifice is erecting, far from perfection, but still sufficient to ensure freedom and prepare the nation for a convention in about two years, where the defects [of the Constitution] may be mended."

On February 22, 1790, the Assembly, which he had asked to provide more resources and a more active role for the police, awarded Lafayette an indemnity of 100,000 livres. Hewing to his line of conduct, he refused to accept it. He thought he was more popular and powerful than Mirabeau, who alternated between friendly approaches and calumnies. The king, despairing of ever being able to bring the two men together, decided simply to buy the orator and make him his secret agent inside the Assembly, without informing Lafayette. In return for considerable payments—6,000 livres a month as well as a million in four installments to wipe out his debts— Mirabeau, whom the Assembly rules barred from being a government minister, would defend positions which, despite their revolutionary appearance, would favor the interests of the monarch. The more the form seemed aggressive, the more the content would be moderate or conservative. In addition, the secret adviser would provide the king with analyses and suggestions through the intermediary of the Count de Lamarque. He was never to go to the palace. Mirabeau was only too well aware of the weaknesses of Louis XVI and his pathological indecisiveness, as well as of the inconsistencies of most of his ministers. The king had only one man close to him, Mirabeau said, and that was the queen. When Mirabeau wrote to the court, the queen was his intended audience. The libertine, who believed in his own charms, took it into his head to attempt to exert direct influence over this level-headed woman, to whom he incorrectly attributed political intelligence when she was merely cool and willful. To do this he had to meet her. Overcoming her hesitation—the amoral man repelled her—Marie

Antoinette agreed to a clandestine meeting in a grove in the park of the château of Saint Cloud at eight on a Sunday morning, when the guards would be dozing and no one would be stirring in the buildings. There would be no disguises and no substitution of persons, unlike the notorious meeting with the Cardinal de Rohan at Versailles in the course of the affair of the necklace.

At their meeting it was the charmer, intoxicated with what he thought was his power over women, who was seduced by the energy and dignity of the foreign princess who felt herself to be more aware of the interests of France than her royal husband. Nothing is known of their dialogue, but one thing seems certain: the queen secured a commitment from the secret adviser that he would serve the court to the best of his ability, even if he had to sacrifice his life. Mirabeau himself confided to his nephew that he would save the queen and to Lamarque that he would die rather than fail to honor his promises.

This was their only meeting, and he never received a message from her. Until he died, he attempted to manipulate the Assembly through his unparalleled eloquence, though he was never able to escape suspicions about his integrity nor to halt the course of the Revolution toward ever-increasing violence and arbitrariness. His sudden death in late March 1791 put an end to the hopes the court had placed in him. His funeral was grandiose: such a large crowd had never gathered in Paris for the death of a politician. He was the first hero to be buried in the Pantheon. When evidence of his collusion with Louis XVI was uncovered after August 10, 1792, his remains were removed from the monument and thrown into a mass grave.

It is legitimate to wonder whether, in the aftermath of the *Fête de la Fédération*, Lafayette might have been able to seize power and govern without the help of the brilliant orator who constantly set the king against him, although it is, of course, idle to try to rewrite history. It may simply be observed that in July 1790, apart from Marat and Mirabeau, the commander of the National Guard had few very powerful enemies.

Robespierre, who was thirty-two (one year younger than Lafayette), was still a timid and confused provincial lawyer who seemed untouched by the whirlwind of Paris life. Concerned with his physical appearance, almost manic in his attention to elegant dress—his apple green coats provoked smiles among his associates—he led the life of a petit bourgeois or a student. His speeches in the Assembly stirred no one. The spark that made this cold, meticulous man into a tiger had not yet been struck. For those close to him, such as Camille and Lucile Desmoulins, whose blood he would later shed, he was the most loyal, discreet, and devoted of friends.

Danton, who was thirty-one and overflowing with vitality, the vociferous Danton was still a lawyer in the king's Councils. He declared monarchist sympathies, astonished his hosts by his appetite at table and his natural generosity, and began his career as an orator at the Cordeliers club. An officer in the Paris National Guard, he associated with members of Philippe Égalité's circle, and he must have participated, as did Saint-Just, in inspections conducted by Lafayette. Saint-Just was still a young man of twenty-three, clerk to the prosecutor of Soissons and secretary in the mayor's office of Blérancourt. His name would have been unknown had he not drawn attention to himself at the age of twenty by publishing an erotic work in verse, *Organt*. He secured an appointment as an officer in the National Guard in his region, but he was too young to run for a seat in the legislative assembly. He had to wait for the Convention in September 1792 to make his entry onto the parliamentary stage.

Camille Desmoulins, who made a lot of noise and who was much talked about but was not a man of action, was thirty. He published vehement articles and pamphlets against the court, the émigrés, and the abuses of the Ancien Régime, but he devoted himself to his tender wife, who perished on the scaffold with him.

Billaud-Varennes, thirty-four, a lawyer in La Rochelle, an unsuccessful dramatist, published an essay on despotism in France in 1789, and was seeking a role to match his ambition. So was Collot d'Herbois, forty, a failed actor and writer. He concocted an *Almanach du Père Gérard*, his first success, and received the applause he had dreamed of on stage at the club of the Jacobins. The situation was not yet turbulent enough for men of this type.

Hérault de Séchelles was thirty-one. He was already a deputy in the legislature: brilliant, elegant, a man of the world, he had not yet made his mark. Barnave, twenty-nine, a lawyer at the Parlement of Grenoble, was well known despite his relative youth because of his service in the Estates General. His mastery of language was considered exceptional. Like Hérault, he admired good manners. His influence, however, was felt primarily on the left of the Assembly.

Talleyrand, the Bishop of Autun (not for long), continued to make cuckolds. The most amusing of his victims was the Duke de Luynes, celebrated for his obesity: his stomach was so enormous that a piece had to be cut out of the dinner table so he could fit. The Viscount de Barras, a noble from Provence, a brilliant officer in the army of the Indies, had been going through a phase of serious dissipation since his return and often went slumming in the most infamous areas of the capital.

General Lafayette, on whom many eyes in France and the rest of the world were fixed, took no spectacular initiatives and even lacked a real strategy. Although the king was prodigal in expressions of friendship to Lafayette after the death of Mirabeau, he no longer counted on anything but foreign help to restore his authority. Fersen and Breteuil were working out plans to get him out of Paris and into a safe place.

In Nancy, Lieutenant General de Bouillé, commander of forces in eastern France, could offer secure protection to Louis XVI and his family. His monarchist sympathies were above suspicion. As ill luck would have it, serious disturbances broke out among his troops, even though he ruled them with a firm hand. The repression was ferocious: several dozen mutineers were hanged, not to mention those who were killed while being arrested, and dozens of others died in prison. Some members of the Assembly were shocked by the harshness of the measures taken by Bouillé, and the press criticized him vehemently. Lafayette, however, succeeded in passing a motion supporting the way Bouillé had been able to maintain order and discipline. Marat went wild, accusing Lafayette of "petty ambition," and calling him an "avid courtier" and a "lackey of despots." *L'Ami du Peuple* was seized by order of the Assembly, but Camille Desmoulins took over from Marat in a speech accusing Lafayette of playing the role that Monk had played in England, first fighting the royalists under Cromwell and then restoring Charles II to the throne. The tide had begun to turn for the Hero of Two Worlds.

The king was playing him for a fool by negotiating with foreign courts. For their part, the aristocrats had not forgiven him for having forced the royal family to pledge allegiance to the Assembly. Lafayette himself, however, still thought it necessary to attempt the experiment of a constitutional monarchy, as he wrote to Washington in unequivocal terms, but he alienated the most revolutionary elements by his insistence on defending public order when the very notion of authority was looked at askance.

When he returned from London, Philippe Égalité resumed his intrigues, which did not make the task of the head of the National Guard any easier. In April 1791, a serious incident gave Lafayette the opportunity to assess once again the limits of his authority and his prestige.

Louis XVI, a sincerely devout man and a respectful son of the Church, had been unable to accept the obligation of priests to take the oath of allegiance to the Civil Constitution of the Clergy, which the pope, contrary to the hope of some in the clergy, had finally condemned. The priests who accepted the law, known as "jurors," were seen as schismatics and renegades by intransigent Catholics who tried to find "non-juror" or "refractory" priests to fulfill their religious duties.

The king decided to celebrate Easter, on April 18, 1791, at Saint Cloud, where a refractory priest officiated. Informed of his intentions, demonstrators rushed to the Tuileries and prevented his carriage from leaving. The National Guards on duty sided with the protesters. Summoned urgently, Lafayette could not persuade his men to allow the king freedom to travel. The queen, who was present, spoke with merciless irony about the inability of the hero of Yorktown to secure obedience. Appalled by this failure that had made him lose face, Lafayette offered his resignation on April 21. He once again reversed his decision under pressure from most of his officers and men, who did not want him to leave. For Lafayette, feeling triumphed by a large margin over political intelligence. It took a good deal of naïveté to write, as he did to Washington: "I brought my fellow citizens to obedience only by making them fear to lose the leader they honor with their affection."

The king, determined to flee from the Tuileries, although he had given Lafayette his word that he would not, created a smokescreen by attending a Constitutional mass and asserting before the Assembly that he was perfectly free in his movements, which, of course, no one believed. Even so, this smokescreen helped him to deceive many Frenchmen, beginning with the commander in chief of the National Guard.

CHAPTER THIRTY-ONE

A DRAMATIC TURN OF EVENTS

WHEREVER ELEGANT WOMEN COULD BE FOUND, A hairdresser was not far off, and the Tuileries palace was no exception to the rule. So the guards, officials, and remaining courtiers who lived in the immense building in the heart of Paris, or came there every day, were used to seeing a man who was still young—age thirty-three, dressed with slight eccentricity, and with affected manners—on his way to the royal apartments. He had a provincial accent and a confident way of speaking. Everyone recognized and greeted him, and he responded with varying degrees of condescension, in the manner of a great artist. This familiar figure in the palace was named Autié, but he went by the name of M. Léonard. Some at court, imitating the Count de Provence who admired his talent, even called him Marquis Léonard, which the hairdresser found too flattering to notice in it a hint of mockery.

He was very conscious of being, in his domain, a great creator, and worthy of respect for that reason. Following the inspiration of the moment, he created hair styles the like of which had never been seen before. Some of his creations were so tall he had to use a veritable metal architecture to hold them in place. Sometimes he set one or more fruits or vegetables in a lady's hair, and that was known as a coiffure *à la jardinière*. Great aristocrats found it amusing to wear in their hair, for an evening, carrots, a cabbage, or an artichoke. Léonard sometimes used a toy, around which he draped curls and tresses. He had even been so bold as to set a chemise in the center of one of his compositions, which Marie Antoinette considered a "charming folly." Pampered by his clients, the "marquis" played at treating them harshly, and they bore his feigned insolence with appropriate smiles.

For the moment, the hairdresser was living in the palace with the status of *valet de chambre*, a not insignificant position when in service to the royal family. Used to the caprices of great ones, he was not surprised when the queen summoned him to her apartment on June 20, 1791, at one in the afternoon. Marie Antoinette, to whom he was sincerely devoted, had a serious look. He guessed that she had not called him to do her hair. After she exacted a promise that he would be as silent as the tomb about what she was going to tell him, and to obey blindly, the queen entrusted him with a secret mission, whose meaning he did not grasp for a long time. In the account by Georges Lenôtre, which I have relied on in what follows, he was told to put on a frock coat and a round hat and to go as discreetly as possible to see M. de Choiseul. He would give Choiseul a letter and receive instructions from him which he was to obey strictly.

Cordially received by the duke, the hairdresser expressed some worry when he was asked to get into a carriage to go to an undisclosed location. It was no good his pleading that he had urgent appointments with friends of the queen whose hair he was to do; Choiseul reminded him of his vow of obedience and carried him off. The journey lasted all afternoon and part of the night. Choiseul said nothing to his passenger, who was beginning to feel more and more ill at ease. They had gone past Meaux, Montmirail, and then Châlons-sur-Marne. At Pont-de-Somme-Vesle, hussars surrounded the carriage. It was then that Léonard learned of the plan that was to make this June 21 a historic day: the king and his family had fled from the Tuileries, and would be there in two hours. A detachment of hussars would escort them as far as Sainte-Menehould, and at Clermont, troops commanded by Colonel de Damas would block the road behind them. Léonard was to go to the château of Thorelles near Montmédy, where everything had been prepared to receive the royal family, which would be safe under the protection of the troops of Marshal de Bouillé. As soon as he arrived, Léonard would have to do the queen's hair. As he got ready to set out alone, Choiseul gave him a casket containing jewels and the red-and-gold ceremonial costume of Louis XVI.

So the king had escaped, fooling Lafayette, to whom he had given his word that he would not try to leave Paris; he had also toyed with the Assembly and deceived a large part of the population. Traveling with him were the queen, his daughter Madame Royale, the Dauphin, the king's sister Madame Elizabeth, and the children's governess Mme de Tourzel. Axel Fersen had worked out the scheme for escaping from the palace and played the role of coachman in the last phase. He had had passports made in the names of a Swedish family he knew, of whom the king in disguise was supposed to be a servant. The large green berlin holding all the travelers had had no difficulty in getting out of Paris, but it was behind schedule. A bystander recognized the fugitives at Châlons. No one intervened, but news of the escape spread. A cavalry detachment sent by Bouillé as an escort came upon a crowd of inflamed peasants and thought it advisable to withdraw. At Pont-de-Somme-Vesle, the hussars were no longer present. Tired of waiting, the troops at Sainte-Menehould had drifted into the cabarets. The berlin continued on the way to Montmédy. As it was going through Varennes, divided by the Aire River, it was prevented from crossing the bridge by the son of the manager of the relay-post, Drouet, who had ridden in pursuit of the escapees when he heard the news. Louis XVI and his family were taken to the home of Sauce, the town grocer and *procureur*, who offered them hospitality while awaiting official instructions. When Choiseul and Damas arrived on the scene, they suggested that the king use force to get away. Louis refused, not wanting to shed blood whatever the cost. At Sainte-Menehould, Léonard seemed to be taking himself very seriously, and he advised an envoy from Bouillé to send his men back to barracks. When he got to Varennes before the king, Léonard met two officers who had come with fresh horses for the king's carriage. He told them that Louis XVI had been arrested at Châlons and that it would be better for them if they headed to Clermont. When Colonel de Damas reached Varennes, his men were no longer there. Léonard then took the wrong road, turned back, and found Bouillé in Stenay. The marshal understood nothing of his explanations, but accepted the casket containing jewelry and the king's ceremonial costume and handed it over to one of his subordinates. This man was killed the next day by a thief who ran off with the treasure.

Whether acting out of panic or with the deliberate intent to sabotage a very carefully worked out plan, Léonard played a rather murky role in the events of the day by taking initiatives that could only undermine the planned arrangements. He was not seen in Paris for three months, and it was rumored that he had gone abroad.

In Varennes, the king had managed to excite his hosts' pity. There was talk of letting him leave the next day, but Sauce the *procureur* wanted to wait for instructions from Paris. However, the situation was resolved even before Sauce's messenger reached the capital.

Very early on the morning of June 21, Lafayette was informed of the king's disappearance. Was he surprised? According to some accounts, he had encountered the queen the previous evening as she was leaving the palace and had not recognized her, or pretended not to see her.

When he grasped the seriousness of the situation, in any event, he was deeply disturbed. The first person in whom he confided was an American passing through Paris, his old friend Thomas Paine, who had been going back and forth between England and France, and was about to spend the next ten years in the capital.

"The birds have flown," said Lafayette as he came into Paine's room. His host greeted the news with as satisfied smile. For this passionate republican the event simplified matters. Since the king himself had decided to leave, France would show other countries that it could easily do without a monarch. There would be no need to drive him out or imprison him to change regimes. Above all, no attempt should be made to recapture him. Let him stay where he was or go where he wanted to. The Republic would be instituted spontaneously, naturally, without shedding a drop of blood.

Lafayette, however, was unable to share this optimistic view because he was in no position to exhibit the same detachment as his old comrade in arms. After all, he had sworn on his life that he would ensure the king's presence in Paris. As Danton, who was becoming a prominent agitator, said the same day, we must have either the king in Paris or the head of Lafayette. The dilemma inspired in Lafayette an ingenious idea. He invented the fable that the king had been kidnapped, that he had left against his will, carried off by conspirators under the orders of the émigrés. It is uncertain whether he convinced his listeners in the Assembly and at the Hôtel de Ville. He gave evidence of his good faith by issuing a general order to search for and seize the king throughout the country. If the king had not crossed the border, he would be retaken. To strengthen the argument, an associate suggested that Lafayette say that he knew as he spoke that the king had been arrested, or if he preferred, released. This was the truth, anticipated by only a few hours, because the representatives he had sent to eastern France (he guessed the itinerary the fugitive had taken), met the messenger Sauce had sent on the road, and he informed them about the situation.

At seven, the green berlin headed back toward Paris, carrying very downcast passengers. As they went through towns and villages, they were greeted with jeers and spitting. A resident of Châlons who greeted them with respect was lynched by the mob.

Three deputies were urgently dispatched to protect the monarchs on the return journey: a monarchist, Latour-Maubourg, a rather hard-line Jacobin, Pétion, and the handsome and brilliant Barnave, a rather moderate Constitutional. They ordered the National Guard to keep demonstrators at a distance, and this made the return a little less painful for the royal family. They rode in the carriage with the family, and relations were struck up during a journey that seemed to all of them agonizingly slow; from Meaux to Paris alone took thirteen hours. In the course of the long journey, Barnave was gradually won over by the charm of the queen, who in turn seemed taken with the elegant manners and the wit of this rising star of the Revolution.

Pétion, a very commonplace lawyer and an uncultivated man, grew a bit more human. He naïvely thought his strong personality had aroused admiration in Madame Royale. The worthy

Latour-Maubourg remained reserved, feeling humiliated to be a witness to the humiliation suffered by his king.

The entry into Paris was gloomy. A heavy silence had fallen on the neighborhoods they went through, and it became menacing as they approached the Tuileries. On the Champs Élysées, the National Guard presented arms reversed, stocks in the air, as though they were celebrating the funeral of the institution of the monarchy. When the monarchs got out of the carriage to enter the palace, the guards were overwhelmed. Lafayette and a few volunteers, with difficulty, established a line to protect the couple that was supposed to reign over France. Louis XVI walked forward impassively and in silence, followed by the queen, who managed to control her emotions. The only detail that brought a little relief was the fact that the Dauphin and his sister, Madame Royale, were applauded.

The next day, the rumor spread that when Marie Antoinette awoke in the palace she discovered that her hair had turned white. Perhaps she wondered what Léonard could do, considering this transformation. But her faithful hairdresser never returned to serve her or her friends. The days of great festivities and the queen's parties seemed far away. When he did return, believing that the storm had passed, Léonard set his great talent aside, thinking it wise to accept a modest position in a stable. But this discretion did not keep him from being arrested for complicity in a royal plot, being sentenced to death, and sent to the scaffold on 7 Thermidor, two days before the fall of Robespierre, at the same time as the poet André Chénier.

According to Lenôtre, the history of this shadowy hairdresser did not have the fall of the guillotine blade for an end point. Indeed, the victim of the Terror, whose death certificate was formally issued and whose body was thrown into the common grave at Picpus, reappeared after the Restoration. His family claimed that he had never left the Paris region. Former clients returning from emigration must have recognized him if he had ventured into the elegant neighborhoods of the capital, but, a fact as strange as his reappearance, he no longer practiced the profession that had won him fame. Giving up combs, rollers, and scissors that might have restored his luster, he was hired as the organizer of convoys for the burial service of the prefecture, and the man who used to delight duchesses preferred the company of corpses to that of the elegant ladies of Paris until the day he died.

Does this mean that another prisoner had been guillotined in his place by mistake, or that a bargain had been struck with the revolutionary Justice Ministry to allow him to escape at the last minute in reward for the role he played on June 21? The mystery remains.

While the king's return to Paris allowed Lafayette to sigh in relief, the exploit earned him a further degree of hatred from the aristocrats who would not forgive him for the determination he had displayed in recapturing the fugitives. Among the enemies of the monarchy, who had not swallowed the fable of the kidnapping, his star had seriously dimmed. Many suspected him of having closed his eyes to the preparations for escape.

Barnave and Lafayette nonetheless persuaded the Assembly not to put Louis XVI on trial, against the wishes of the Cordeliers club, to which many left-wing members of the Jacobins club belonged; this was a veritable parallel assembly whose increasingly boisterous activities were interfering with the operations of government institutions.

The two men joined others to establish a club for moderates, which attracted those concerned with public order, the Feuillants.

On July 17, 1791, one of the bloodiest demonstrations in the history of revolutionary Paris took place, costing the commander in chief of the National Guard a good deal of his remaining prestige. Extremist petitioners had deposited on the Altar of the Nation, still standing on the Champ de Mars, lists intended to collect signatures in favor of putting the king on trial. A crowd soon assembled. Two tramps hiding under the altar to ogle women mounting the steps were discovered. Taken for agents provocateurs, they were slaughtered, setting off a general battle. Stones were thrown and shots fired at a battalion of the Guard sent as reinforcements by Lafayette. The general himself intervened and they took aim at him. One of his nearby officers was wounded. Faced with the aggressiveness of a crowd that it might not be possible to contain for long on the Champ de Mars, Mayor Bailly declared martial law in the capital. This decision did not put an end to attacks on the National Guard, who first fired in the air, which provoked a salvo in response from the other side. When a bullet barely missed their general, the soldiers opened fire on the mass of people that nothing seemed to stop. Several dozen demonstrators fell. To stop the growing combat, Lafayette backed up his order to cease fire with a spectacular gesture: he deliberately set himself in front of the mouth of a cannon that his soldiers were preparing to fire.

There was a heavy toll: more than fifty dead and one thousand wounded. On that July 17, 1791, the commander of the National Guard had confirmed Mirabeau's prediction: "Some day he will fire on the people." This did not keep Lafayette from declaring a general amnesty on September 13.

Three days later, the king, to whom the Feuillants wanted to restore some authority, swore allegiance to the Constitution in a public ceremony. On October 1, a new assembly, the Legislative

Assembly, replaced the Constituent Assembly, whose members were not eligible for reelection.

On October 8, Lafayette resigned, putting all his powers at the disposal of the Commune of Paris, which, in recognition of his services, offered him the bust of Washington by Houdon. This time, he was not asked to reconsider his decision. At thirty-four he had again become a private citizen and headed back to his native province.

CHAPTER THIRTY-TWO

THE INTERRUPTED GAME

I N THE OLD CHÂTEAU DE CHAVANIAC IN AUVERGNE, WHICH
the great architect Vaudoyer was in the process of partially
renovating, he made haste to display in a large study toiles
de Jouy depicting scenes of American life.

On the nearby dependent farm, a British farmer named
Dyson, with an international reputation in animal breeding,
was in charge of the livestock. Everything had been cleaned
and freshened up so that the tired and disappointed hero could
find a peaceful refuge and grounds for some enjoyment after
all the emotions he had experienced over the preceding two
and a half years.

Surrounded by memories and pictures of what had been the
happiest time of his life, speaking English every day with his
animal expert, perhaps he felt he resembled Washington after
signing the peace treaty with Britain: a great warrior who, once

his duty had been done, left the struggle for power to others and retired to his land.

The Haute-Loire was his Virginia. He lived there but in his imagination was on the banks of the Potomac, amid maples, pines, and sassafras, hearing the chant of a black laborer from a nearby tobacco field.

The nobles of Auvergne, of course, gave him the cold shoulder, but ordinary citizens were prodigal in their gestures of recognition and affection; he was their protector and their great man. Through him, the region's sober and tenacious peasants, russet cows, and fields of rye had been put on the map of France and become known throughout the civilized world. This was his delight, to be loved by the mass of ordinary men and women.

His loyal supporters in the capital came up with the idea of nominating him as a candidate for mayor of Paris, to replace the exhausted Bailly. They thought the former commander of the National Guard could render countless services if he was in charge of the capital. Paradoxically, Marie Antoinette, who was insanely furious at Lafayette, derailed the plan by asking the royalists to throw their votes to Pétion, the candidate of the left, to prevent the election of the man whom she held responsible for the fate she and the king were suffering. Pétion won by 728 to 328, a humiliating result for Lafayette. On Pétion's coattails, another representative of the left, Manuel, was elected *procureur-syndic*. His deputy was Danton, who, like Mirabeau, received subsidies from the court to provide secret support for the monarchy, and who was now among Lafayette's enemies.

Lafayette's electoral defeat unfortunately did not permit him to prolong his peaceful stay in Chavaniac with his beloved family who would have liked to keep him there. Other Parisian friends, among them the Duke de la Rochefoucauld, had him elected head of the legion of the National Guard. And when

Louis XVI, under pressure from the Assembly dominated by the Girondins, mobilized three hundred fifty thousand men divided into three armies to deal with the intrigues of the Elector of Trier, who was playing host to a group of turbulent émigrés, War Minister Narbonne insisted that the king give Lafayette command of the Army of the East. The two other commands were given to Rochambeau and Marshal Luckner, a naturalized German officer who had long been fighting under the French flag. Lafayette's peaceful retirement had come to a rapid end.

On December 24, 1791, Lafayette, who had been given the rank of lieutenant-general, thanked the Assembly for its confidence in him and left for his headquarters in Metz. He found an army with not enough troops, who were badly equipped and undisciplined. It recalled to some degree the army over which he had taken command in Albany fourteen years earlier on a mission to liberate Canada; and, as he had done then, he began by calling for reinforcements. The Elector of Trier, perhaps frightened by the presence of Lafayette, ordered the émigrés to disperse. The emergency seemed to have passed, but in reality it had not. The Girondin ministers had decided to combat Austria, hoping to create real national unity through war and at the same time to export democratic ideology. The king went along, thoroughly convinced that setbacks suffered by the French army, which he considered inevitable, would force the Assembly to reinforce his personal power.

The generals leading the three armies were summoned to Paris to finalize operational plans. Rochambeau had fallen ill, and Lafayette took command of his army. This advancement, which he had not sought, subjected him to attacks that were so numerous they seemed concerted. To begin with, Lauzun, his old comrade in arms in the American Revolution, declared that it would have been better to appoint Luckner to head the two armies and that he did not wish to serve "either the glory or the stupidity" of the man with whom he had fought at Yorktown. Brissot, who had long been his political friend and whose talent he admired, made common cause against him with Robespierre and Danton's ally Collot d'Herbois. Even the gentle poet André Chénier joined the group of his enemies and wrote texts that are better forgotten.

Fortunately, in the field, the general under challenge was able to show that his troops followed him. On April 20, war was declared against Austria, or rather against "the King of Hungary and Bohemia." On April 30, Lafayette occupied Bouvines, in Belgian territory, while the soldiers of the unfortunate Dillon, another companion from America, were routed and ended up lynching their general.

In Paris, there was rapid turnover of war ministers: Narbonne was followed by de Grave, the energetic Servan, and then Dumouriez, who moved from the foreign ministry. But troop numbers and matériel remained inadequate. It seemed that the Elector of Trier had given way on the advice of the pacifist Emperor Leopold of Austria (soon to be succeeded by his absolutist and bellicose brother Francis II), and it was rumored that Lafayette was sounding out the enemy about a truce. The war, however, went on, and, though he was criticized in Paris, Lafayette drove back an Austrian attack at Glisvelle. He was grieved by the loss of his subordinate and friend, Gouvion, cut down by a bullet. Another veteran from America, the future Marshal Berthier, was for the time on his staff, and demonstrated both devotion and loyalty. He really needed the support in the face of the maneuvers against him. Interior Minister Roland, the strong man of the Girondin government, suspected that the general, despite his victories, was divided between his ambition to win glory against the enemy and his wish to save the king.

Roland wrote to him with remarkable frankness: "There is no middle way for you: you have to be one of the heroes of the Revolution or become the most infamous of the French; your name must be forever blessed or cursed."

Lafayette was pleased with the appointment of Dumouriez (even though the minister did not have much affection for him), because he had always thought of the Girondins as sectarian and dangerous. But for some reason, he felt it necessary to write to the Assembly to ask that rule by the clubs give way to the rule of law and to implore it to preserve royal power intact. Was it conceivable that a general, by definition subject to civil authority, and while the country was at war, could claim the right to intervene in political life? His message to the Assembly provoked a chorus of protest: Vergniaud denounced his attitude; Robespierre demande that he be put on trial; Danton called him the "leader of the united nobility"; Fabre d'Églantine and others followed Danton's lead.

Lafayette had dared to ask the Assembly to free itself from control by the clubs, using the plural to take aim at the Jacobins and the Cordeliers; he had dared to congratulate Louis XVI for having opposed the proscription of refractory priests who had refused to take the oath required by the Civil Constitution of the Clergy. It is arguable that, from the point of view of the preservation of democracy, the interest of the country, and civil peace, the public man without a mandate was right. But from a general who was supposed to be at the front, the step was an act of folly. Did the action not imply that he was setting himself up as the leader of an opposition? Had he not revealed himself to be a seditious general who was beginning to show his hand? From then on, Lafayette was unable to convince the men in power of his innocence and the complete purity of his intentions, and once he was back with his troops, he recognized that the atmosphere was not quite what it had been. The king's attitude, courageous as it may have been, did nothing to improve his own position. On June 20, 1792, an excited mob led by professional agitators, including a butcher, a brewer, and a former henchman of the Duke d'Orléans, demanded to be heard by the Legislative Assembly. Out of weakness, the presiding officer, Vergniaud, acquiesced. The goal of this "spontaneous" group was to call for the abolition of the executive power. Nothing less. The Girondins in control of the Assembly saw fit to direct the mob to the Tuileries, which was what it wanted in the first place. Backed by other demonstrators with cannons at their disposal, the mob marched on the palace, meeting little resistance, broke down fences and doors, and invaded the royal apartments. They insulted the king, called him "perfidious," demanded that he recall the "patriot" ministers that he had just dismissed, and demanded that he give up his veto power. Louis XVI calmly answered the invaders, who abused him for three hours, that he would act in accordance with the Constitution. To make up for this principled stance, he agreed to put on a Phrygian cap and to drink a toast with the rioters to the health of the people of Paris and the nation. The exhausted "visitors" finally left the palace. After the "audience" was over, Pétion, who had been elected mayor of Paris thanks to Marie Antoinette, and a representative of the Assembly came to offer an apology that fooled no one.

One witness to the June 20 riot was a young artillery lieutenant who was appalled at the weakness of the opposition offered to the attackers. He was twenty-three, thin, and lithe, his skin was olive, and his long brown hair came down to his shoulders. He had tightened his fists in rage when he saw the brutes rush into the palace, while the guards offered only symbolic resistance, as though they wanted primarily to avoid any personal risk, and he wrote that with a few cannons it would have been easy for him to mow down the first rank, forcing the rest to flee. When the young man, filled with disgust, returned to his room at the end of the day to seek some calm, he began to write a romance novel that he did not finish until 1795.

He wrote several more before moving on to more serious subjects. The paths of this lieutenant, who for now had literary ambitions, unknown to anyone in Paris and elsewhere, and Lafayette, famous around the world, would cross several times in the next twenty-three years. His name was Napoleon Bonaparte.

From the titles of his books, it would have been impossible to guess the identity of the author, and of course they pale in significance in comparison to his deeds on the battlefield. But they raise the question of the strange relationship men of power often have with the enterprise of writing. It is as though power fostered a taste for all kinds of power. Or perhaps the impulse to change reality overflows into the desire to become a master of the imagination. Caesar's *Gallic Wars* and the *Meditations of Marcus Aurelius* are two examples among countless others. The lucky ones, such as Charles d'Orléans, managed to achieve genuine stature as writers. Others, such as Frederick II seeking to emulate Voltaire, or Richelieu trying his hand at verse, were not so successful.

The relationship of writing to force, poetry to facts, literature to power, grows more complicated once one recalls that literature holds power equal to that of kings, because a piece of parchment or a book lasts much longer than a human life. As a result, men who have known the frenzy of renown often turn to writing to cement their reputations. As Vigny put it: "Kings are now writing books because they sense that that is where power lies."

As Chateaubriand judiciously remarked in the *Mémoires d'outre-tombe*, the jealousy the little world of letters feels for great writers is parallel to the attitude men of power adopt to censor geniuses: "Notwithstanding these examples and countless others, literary talent, clearly the highest of all because it excludes none of the faculties, will always be an obstacle to political success in this country: indeed, what good is high intelligence? It serves no purpose. The fools of France, a peculiar national species, grant nothing to the likes of Grotius, Frederick, or Bacon. . . . Our vanity will never acknowledge that a man, even a man of genius, has two aptitudes, and the ability to do ordinary things as well as an ordinary man." Despite his pompous style and emphatic tone, Bonaparte was not a bad writer. He liked melodramatic adventures, which he always set against an authentic historical background.

While the Tuileries riot of June 20, 1792, provoked contained and impotent indignation in the young Corsican officer, fortunately channeled into a powerful literary impulse, it inspired Lafayette to engage in a wild enterprise that would, within eight weeks, end his involvement in the history of the French Revolution.

Having informed Luckner and turned over his command to General d'Hangest, he returned to Paris on June 28, and, determined to dot the "i"s, he asked to be heard by the Assembly, which granted his request. From the podium, he unreservedly condemned the crime committed by the invaders of the Tuileries and demanded that the leaders be punished. The fact that he himself had not respected the Constitution by leaving his army in time of war, without having asked authorization from the government, did not keep the Assembly from voting in principle to prosecute by 334 to 234.

This success may have encouraged the imprudent man to believe that his personality alone had carried the day and that, in any event, audacity paid. But this was not 1777, when disobeying the king's will by going to America had earned him ten days of house arrest. This time, an extremely violent campaign was launched against him. Brissot, who had been a friend, who had fought by his side in the Société des Amis des Noirs for the abolition of slavery, and who was an admirer of the United States (he had visited the country and written a book about it), took the lead in attacking him at the Jacobins club. The future victim of the guillotine asserted that Lafayette had unmasked himself, and that his extreme boldness had already caused his downfall. The next day, when the former commander of the National Guard wanted to inspect it in company with the king, Pétion (who seems to have been informed by the queen) prevented the ceremony from taking place. Lafayette returned to his troops and, on July 6, went to meet Luckner at Valenciennes. After analyzing the situation and taking into account the balance of forces, the two generals advised the king to begin peace talks. The advice was ignored. The only reaction of the government was to have the two generals switch places, with Lafayette assuming command of the Army of the North. While provocateurs were dispatched to foment mutiny among his troops, the campaign against him continued with renewed force in Paris. It was said that, after having signed a peace treaty, he dreamed of marching on the capital to destroy the popular forces, and restore the power of the king, or take power as a dictator himself.

For Robespierre, who was haunted by a fear of seditious generals (in his view, all victorious generals were potentially seditious, prepared to seize power from its legitimate holders), Lafayette's position of responsibility was a source of anxiety. He declared to the Assembly: "As long as Lafayette is at the head of our army, liberty will be in danger." The real danger to liberty, however, did not come from the victor of Yorktown but from the one hundred seventy-five thousand enemy soldiers assembled on the Rhine under the command of the Duke of Brunswick. Badly advised by the émigrés, Brunswick launched a manifesto to the population of Paris bearing his name. It was a warning as inept as it was threatening, which Fersen had had a hand in drafting. The French capital was warned that it would be razed if the slightest harm came to the king. The manifesto was received in Paris as an intolerable challenge. Its publication by *Le Moniteur* on August 3, 1792, provoked the insurrection of August 10. That day, a mob of rioters marched on the Tuileries to show Brunswick what the people thought of his threats. Mandat, the commander of the National Guard, and Roederer, the *procureur-syndic*, half-heartedly organized the defense of the palace. An insurrectional commune was set up in the Hôtel de Ville, led by Danton, who drove out the hypocritical Pétion. The brewer Santerre who had led the *sans-culottes* on June 20 proclaimed himself head of the National Guard in place of Mandat, who was dismissed and murdered when he left the Hôtel de Ville.

Before the attackers launched their assault on the Tuileries, theoretically defended by four thousand men, Roederer advised the king to go with his family to ask for asylum from the National Assembly, which was in session, and that is what he did. Vergniaud, who was presiding, welcomed the king and his family and solemnly placed them under his protection. They stayed there throughout the day in most uncomfortable conditions, while the *sans-culottes* and Santerre's National Guard, joined by volunteers from Marseille, launched the attack. The king ordered the Swiss Guard to cease firing, and the assailants were soon masters of the palace, which was sacked. Six hundred Swiss Guards lost their lives, not to mention other victims, in their futile defense of the monarch. The Assembly could only register what had happened and dissolve itself, since, with the executive destroyed, the 1791 Constitution could no longer be applied. A new assembly, the Convention, would be elected by universal suffrage and would establish the structures of a new regime guaranteeing liberty and equality. While awaiting the Convention's decision on his fate, the king was provisionally suspended and interned with his family in the Luxembourg palace. The government was run by a provisional executive council of six ministers, led by Danton as Justice Minister, along with some of the Girondins from whom the king had distanced himself. On August 17, Lafayette reviewed his troops at Sedan and once again tried to have them swear allegiance to the nation, the law, and the king. Many refused to mention the king. The general understood that his initiative did not take account of the current situation, that he was no longer in tune with the times. The day before this review, the Jacobins club had proclaimed the necessity of arresting and condemning Lafayette and dismissing his staff, "so that the Austrians will no longer have intelligence sources inside the French army."

On the seventeenth, he was officially relieved of his command, which he had to turn over to Dumouriez. His arrest was decided on the nineteenth. He was left with a choice between an ignominious death if he stayed and desertion.

Never inclined toward suicide, he chose the second solution. But desertion did not mean, for him, joining the émigrés, whom he continued to despise, nor submission to the foreign enemy. He hoped that by crossing the lines unarmed, he could secure as a civilian, in the name of the law of nations, free passage to a neutral country. It was a desertion compelled by exceptional circumstances but carried out with honor.

On August 19, then, with twenty-two staff officers and his friend Lameth, also threatened with arrest, Lafayette entered Rochefort, a little town in the principality of Liège. An Austrian patrol arrested them. They were handed over to General Cleyfart, who treated them as prisoners of war in spite of their written protest.

They still hoped that, when informed of their case, the imperial government would allow them to go to a neutral country. Emperor Francis II of Austria, capable of any form of ignoble action, decided otherwise.

CHAPTER THIRTY-THREE

A VICTORY OR AN ENIGMA?

TOWARD THE MIDDLE OF SEPTEMBER 1792, ACCORDING TO Georges Lenôtre, Beaumarchais (who miraculously succeeded in surviving the terrorist madness of 1793–94) went to visit the actor Fleury, an admired performer of his plays, but was told that he had gone for a week to the east, near Verdun. This was an odd destination at a time when war was raging and it had just been learned that Verdun had fallen to the Prussians. When he returned to Paris, the actor refused to tell Beaumarchais anything about the reasons for his journey, and the playwright was adrift in conjectures about Fleury's mysterious "vacation."

Beaumarchais had died by the time an item appeared in the press forty-seven years later that enabled a friend of his who was still alive to piece together an explanation of the enigma that had tormented him. It may or may not hold up, but it cannot be dismissed out of hand.

After his troops entered the city in 1792, Frederick William of Prussia himself went to inspect Verdun, which already housed many royalist émigrés prepared to advance further into France. At a ball one evening an unknown man approached the victorious king, whispered what was no doubt the password of a theosophical sect, probably the Rosicrucians, of which Frederick William, obsessed with the occult, was a member. The unknown man led the king, alone and without his guards, to a cellar. There in the dark, the king saw a human form emerge from a kind of fog, surrounded by flames that cast a half light on the scene that was about to unfold. The king recognized the coat, hat, and stick of his uncle Frederick the Great. As the features of his face became clearer, he had no more doubt: he was in the presence of the ghost of the former king. Frozen in terror, he heard the voice of the dead man speak. It proclaimed that the nephew on the throne was indeed the heir of his uncle's glory and power, but because of his concern for the future of his country he ordered his nephew not to lead his troops further into France beyond Verdun, because a traitor in the ranks might lead him to disaster. Once the warning was delivered, the specter dissolved in the mist, and the flames were extinguished.

On September 20, 1792, after a few artillery rounds, the Prussian troops under the Duke of Brunswick unaccountably retreated in the face of the French army under Dumouriez stationed on the hills of Valmy. The first great military victory of the new Republic, and the most symbolic one, had just been won practically without a battle. Goethe, who witnessed the event, wrote that the events of that day "inaugurated the history of a new era of humanity."

When Beaumarchais's old friend Abbé Sabatier read the account of the Verdun apparition in 1839, he recalled that the author of *The Marriage of Figaro* had told him in 1792 about

Fleury's strange trip to Verdun in mid-September. Taking off from that, it was a short step for a dramatist as inventive as Beaumarchais to imagine that Fleury's resemblance to the late king of Prussia, whom he had played on stage, had been used in some shady manipulation. He had said as much to Sabatier, who now in 1839 found a plausible confirmation in the press, given the king's superstitious nature.

Whether or not it was the result of trickery, Napoleon, who knew something about military matters, said he saw no logical reason for its outcome. In any event, Lafayette later wrote that had he not been proscribed, he would have savored a victory over the Prussians much more than his defeat of Cornwallis at Yorktown.

On September 20, 1792, the former general of the Army of the East was a prisoner of war, and he learned of the victory of Dumouriez and his volunteers, stirred by Danton's speeches about the nation in danger, in his prison cell. France was about to change regimes, and he languished in irons, powerless.

CHAPTER THIRTY-FOUR

A RETURN TO FRANCE ON TIPTOES

T HE REPUBLIC WAS PROCLAIMED IN PARIS ON SEPTEMBER 21, 1792. Thomas Paine, who had been elected as a deputy to the Convention from Pas-de-Calais just a few days after having been made an honorary French citizen, applauded the institution of a regime similar in principle to the one he had helped to establish on the other side of the Atlantic. It was the second fall of a monarchy he had witnessed, and he had no doubt that the English people, followed by all the peoples of Europe, would follow the examples of Philadelphia and Paris. But Paine's deep joy on that triumphant day was not unmixed with melancholy, for he could not share his delight with a dear friend and companion in arms, who was as much a republican as he himself, although he was not persuaded that France was strong and united enough and its people virtuous enough to put a radical end to the Capetian monarchy.

If anyone deserved to be in Paris on that day, it was his friend General Lafayette. But while they were toasting the victory of the people on the banks of the Seine, the general was champing at the bit in prison. The illusion that he and his group could get to neutral territory had soon been shattered. While those of his companions who had not been members of the National Guard were sent back across the border, his aides de camp were locked up in a fortress, and the authorities determined that Lafayette, Alexandre de Lameth, Latour-Maubourg, and Bureau de Pusy, former members of a revolutionary assembly, would be treated as hostages until they could be subjected to the justice of Louis XVI, when he had been restored to the throne and recovered all his prerogatives.

In France, the new republican regime seized all Lafayette's possessions, and the public executioner defaced the medal that had been engraved in his honor. For their part, the monarchs allied against the Revolution and the French émigrés were jointly preparing to take revenge on the man whom they held responsible for the misfortunes of the royal family. When the conditions of imprisonment of the royal family grew worse so did those of Lafayette. The Austrians transferred him to Prussian custody (they would later send him back), and he was deprived of air and light, given revolting food, and subjected to unsanitary conditions and brutal and sadistic guards. He nonetheless managed to send out messages, some written with his own blood, and to get some news. The American government was later even able to send him funds that enabled him to get better food. The information that reached him—the execution of Louis XVI, the beginning of the Terror, the arrest of his wife—increased his torment; but his morale never faltered.

He contemptuously rejected the offer by the king of Prussia to soften the conditions of his imprisonment in return for revealing whatever he knew of French army plans.

Adrienne was no less courageous. She was arrested in Chavaniac, spent two months in Brioude, and was then transferred to Paris. She was supposed to have traveled in a cart, but her servants pooled their resources to hire a carriage for her. She remained imprisoned in Paris until January 1795. Her paternal grandparents, her mother, and her sister Louise de Noailles were not so fortunate; they all died on the scaffold. Gouverneur Morris, and his successor as American ambassador, James Monroe, provided material and moral support.

It seems that wherever a Lafayette might be America was always present. For example, in March 1794, after twenty-six months of imprisonment, Lafayette, now in the Austrian fortress at Olmütz, just missed escaping in an attempt organized with completely unexpected help. One of his German admirers who was a refugee in London, a Dr. Bollmann, took it into his head to liberate Lafayette. To succeed, he needed an accomplice in Austria in whom he could have complete confidence. The man he found who was ready to embark on the adventure with him was a young American medical student named Francis Huger, none other than the son of Major Huger, the patriot who had welcomed Lafayette and his friends in July 1777 on the South Carolina coast. The coincidence is worthy of a novel by Alexandre Dumas.

In October 1794, disguised as Englishmen, Bollmann and Huger managed to establish contact with the prisoner, who was ill. His jailers were providing care, because they wanted to keep him alive until he could be put on trial in Paris after the restoration of the monarchy. He was allowed to walk in the park once a day. Informed of the time of this walk, his would-be liberators managed to spirit him away from the guards, but the three men soon had to separate to escape pursuit. Lafayette went off on horseback with Bollmann, and then went his own way. Unfortunately he took the wrong road, was recaptured, and put in solitary confinement. Huger and Bollmann were also arrested and sentenced to six months at hard labor.

Adrienne, meanwhile, wrote to Washington to ask him to intervene. The president expressed the sorrow he felt at the treatment inflicted on his spiritual son, but as the leader of a neutral country, he judged that he was not in a position to take a step that might appear to be an interference in the internal affairs of another nation. But he did agree to accept into his family as a relative George-Washington Lafayette, who sailed for the United States under the name Motier in 1795. Made desperate by the continuation of Lafayette's imprisonment, Adrienne decided to share her husband's captivity, which she carried out to the end, at the expense of her own health.

It is now difficult to imagine the cruelty, duplicity, and meanness of Emperor Francis II, his right-hand man Chancellor Thugut, and the other Austrian grandees who decided on the conditions imposed on Adrienne. She and the two daughters who were with her had to suffer the caprices of pitiless masters. The prisoner whom they saw, reduced to a mere skeleton, seemed not to recognize them, but they soon realized that the one thing that had not changed was the strength of his liberal convictions.

Adrienne, Anastasie, and Virginie were placed in a single cell, near the guards' latrines, a dismal, unhealthy location that stank day and night. They had to share two beds. Their candles were extinguished at nine, and no light was available past that time. It is clear that the jailers used Adrienne and her daughters to further torment Lafayette. Feverish, her body covered with sores, suffering from painful migraines, Mme de Lafayette was authorized to consult a specialist in Vienna only if she promised not to return to Olmütz; she haughtily refused.

Despite the pain, exhaustion, complete uncertainty about what the next day would bring, the darkness that wore out their eyes, and the stench, the couple had to find the strength every day to smile for the two young daughters who shared their captivity. Badly fed, deprived of air, space, and light, and humiliated at every turn, they derived energy and optimism from the gentleness and patience of their parents. When the couple was alone, Lafayette learned more details about the terrible events that had occurred in France after his arrest by the Austrians. How many deaths—not to mention those in Adrienne's family that touched him directly. Men for whom he had little respect—Brissot, Desmoulins, Danton, Hérault de Séchelles, and many others— after playing important roles, had left their heads on the scaffold less than two years later. His sworn enemy Marat had been assassinated by a young woman from Caen, who had probably merely anticipated the guillotine. And then there was Robespierre, the mediocre orator, simultaneously timid and wrathful, who had demanded Lafayette's arrest. How could such a man have become a dictator and plunged the country into a river of blood until he suffered the same fate he had inflicted in his madness on colleagues and even on some he called friends? They talked of Condorcet, Bailly, Mme Roland, Lavoisier, all the admirable people who had been executed or driven to suicide.

No doubt they also talked of the royal family, despite the absurd suspicion and even the ingratitude that Louis XVI had harbored against the man who was now only the prisoner of Olmütz. They lamented the sad fate of the Dauphin, whom Lafayette remembered wearing the uniform of the National Guard at the *Fête de la Fédération*. And the poet André Chénier, who in a moment of folly had anticipated with pleasure the sight of Lafayette on the scaffold, had suffered that fate himself just before Thermidor. The misery of the couple in Olmütz was set against a backdrop of more widespread misery.

Too much was too much. Despite his concern not to allow his feelings as a private citizen to interfere with his conduct as head of state, Washington finally wrote to the emperor of Austria in May 1796, asking him to allow his prisoner to go to America, imposing whatever constraints he wished on the journey. Mme de Staël, with her customary energy, urged Gouverneur Morris to see Thugut to ask for Lafayette's release. Morris complied but achieved nothing. Mme de Staël put pressure on General Pichegru, but he was hesitant. Then she turned to Barras, who had become a member of the Directory.

Barras was a curious figure, refined and pitiless, and the complexity of his character sheds some light more generally on the figures of the Revolution who were divided between doctrinal rigor and the appetite for pleasure. After cruelly repressing the revolt in Toulon, where he had acquired the friendship of the young officer Bonaparte, Barras, with his thirst for power satisfied, wallowed in a baroque blend of luxury, debauchery, and anachronistic privilege. He invented a kind of left-wing fashionableness, and he fostered under the Directory the sudden return of hunting with hounds. The huntsmen and gamekeepers of the Ancien Régime were astonished to see him appear in a kind of Roman triumphal carriage decorated with red leather.

After Thermidor, the time had come when the certainty of survival provoked a frantic pursuit of pleasure. When life itself seemed to be a privilege, everything became folly. And the fashion for champagne that figures like Desmoulins and Danton had adopted spread throughout society. And since everything was excessive in this age of excess, Barras, the provocative dandy, one day took a bath in a tub filled with champagne.

In fact, the Thermidor reaction created new dandies. And curiously, Bonaparte's Egyptian campaign under the Directory, in addition to launching a fashion for antiquities, revived the taste for jewels and the craze for lucky scarabs, ornamental padlocks, and cameos. And rings were worn on every finger, including the thumb, and even the big toe.

This frenetic pursuit of luxury was only beginning under the Directory; it was dazzling by the time the Empire was proclaimed. It was as though the horrors of the Revolution could be forgotten through ornament and social order. When he promoted eighteen marshals, Napoleon, always a stickler for detail, established at the same time an arts and crafts school for deaf-mutes, who were expected to learn to work with gold and precious stones so that the marshals' wives would be suitably bedecked for their appearances at the court of the new Caesar.

Diamonds, rubies, and emeralds were the official precious stones. For his coronation diadem, Napoleon was content with gold leaf interspersed with cameos. During the glittering years of the Empire, two women set the fashion: Josephine and Pauline. When he divorced Josephine, Napoleon made it clear that he would retain possession of all the jewels purchased during their marriage. As for Pauline, she collected all of her jewels to help her brother when he was on the Isle of Elba—they were found in his carriage at Waterloo.

In the period before this grandeur and decadence, Barras thought only of enjoying the present and distracting himself from the responsibilities he found too burdensome by indulging in frivolous pleasures. He had not yet lost power, but he had already lost his head. When the issue of Lafayette's imprisonment was submitted to him, he saw fit to hand it over to General

Bonaparte. Napoleon had just badly shaken the Austrians on the field of battle, and when they made overtures for negotiations, he let them know that it would be in their interest to release Lafayette and his family. Francis II and his government complied. The prisoners left Olmütz on September 19, 1797, "in deference to the government of the United States that had called for their release," a formula that enabled Vienna more or less to save face. They were taken to Hamburg, where they were handed over to the American consul in accordance with the agreement that had been signed. Gouverneur Morris had been informed in time to come and greet them at the consulate.

Their American friends and German admirers celebrated the freed prisoners, but some among the French frowned on them. Many royalist émigrés were living in Hamburg, and their hatred for Lafayette remained intact. The former head of the National Guard wanted to avoid at any cost being identified with these counterrevolutionaries, and he conspicuously displayed a tricolor cockade on his hat. But returning to France was out of the question, even though his first act on being freed had been to address a message of thanks, along with Latour-Maubourg and Pusy, to Citizen-General Bonaparte, for his exercise on their behalf of his "irresistible military strength." Napoleon had no wish to see Lafayette beginning a new career on the banks of the Seine. His very presence in Paris would complicate Napoleon's own plans, so Lafayette should stay abroad, at least for the time being. Free, but banned from returning to his native country, Lafayette thought immediately of his spiritual home, the United States. When they had been imprisoned together in Olmütz, he and Adrienne dreamed of going to America together and establishing a model farm in Virginia, and it now seemed that fate had chosen this moment to make the dream a reality. But Washington made it clear to him that the deterioration of relations between the United States and the government of the Directory had created an atmosphere that Lafayette, with his memories of Franco-American friendship at the time of the Revolution and the following years, would find painful, indeed unbearable. Despite his instinctive Anglophobia, he thought he might have to go to England, where there had been men who were independent-minded enough to express their admiration for the victor of Yorktown and to call for his release. Fortunately, he was not obliged to request hospitality from his former enemies. When Adrienne's aunt, Mme de Tessé, a liberal and an admirer of Voltaire, had been forced to flee a Revolution gone mad, she had settled in the Duchy of Holstein, near Hamburg, with a largely Danish population. On her estate in Withold on the shores of Lake Ploën, Lafayette and Adrienne would be able to recover from their ordeal with their united family, because as soon as he had heard the first rumors about the possible release of his father, the young "George Motier" had immediately left Virginia to rejoin his family.

Adrienne agreed to allow her husband to invite Diane de Simiane to spend a few days with them at Withold. The suffering each of them had endured had created a situation in which ordinary feelings were out of place. In any event, Lafayette's political ideas had not been altered by what he had endured in captivity. He was as intransigent as he had been in the past whenever a question of principle arose. For example, the coup d'état of 18 Fructidor, carried out with the help of Bonaparte, by means of which the Directory dismissed newly elected members of the Councils reputed to be monarchists and arbitrarily replaced them with republican candidates who had not been elected, seemed to him to be a serious violation of the democratic rules to which the regime claimed to adhere. His protest did nothing to help his position.

Nor did he absolve the majority of the Convention for the execution of the king. "The unfortunate Louis XVI, whose alleged friends preferred his downfall over seeing him saved by me, was soon assassinated through the most monstrous procedure," he wrote in his memoirs. He never forgave Robespierre's supporters for the Terror and the ignoble murder of his friends Bailly, Barnave, and Dietrich. Nonetheless, he praised the bravery of the armies of the Republic, "whose magnificent victories preserved the independence of France." He also praised the armies' leaders, particularly Hoche, whom he had met and appreciated when he was a sergeant at Versailles during the episode of October 5 and 6, 1789. Now a victorious general, Hoche and his colleagues had exerted pressure to help secure the release of his former commander.

To avoid troubling Mme de Tessé with the many visitors he received, Lafayette himself rented an estate in Lemkühlen (incurring a large debt in the process), where, in May 1798, his daughter Anastasie was married to Charles de Latour-Maubourg, the younger brother of his fellow prisoner.

In late 1798, while Adrienne made multiple approaches to all her relations in France to secure authorization for Lafayette to return to the country, he moved the family to Vianen, near Utrecht in Holland, to be closer to home. He received many visitors there, including Rouget de Lisle, author of *La Marseillaise*. Adrienne tried to preserve what she could of the family fortune, but resources dwindled swiftly in Vianen. When they were approached, neither Sieyès nor Talleyrand showed much eagerness to prepare the ground for the return of their former friend and colleague. Lafayette's public position against 18 Fructidor had frightened them away. What new hotheaded steps could they expect from this devil of a man? Adrienne had even gone to see Bonaparte, who chose to remain enigmatic. When Napoleon returned from Egypt, Lafayette sent him a personal message, but there was no reply. He decided to force the issue and, armed with a passport under a false name, returned to Paris in early November 1799. When he found out, the new consul (18 Brumaire had happened) was furious. Talleyrand advised the "illegal entrant" to return immediately to Holland, which Lafayette, of course, refused to do. Bonaparte finally calmed down. He was willing to "ignore" the presence of Lafayette in France, provided he lead as discreet an existence as possible and "avoid any commotion." Lafayette complied. The new master of France thought Lafayette had been forgotten to such a degree that he did not consider it worthwhile to invite him to the memorial ceremony for Washington at the Invalides in February 1800. He even gave instructions to Fontanes (the future head of the Empire's university), who had been designated to deliver the eulogy, that he avoid pronouncing the name of Lafayette, an obvious travesty of history. The all-powerful man, however, could not prevent the son of the hero of Yorktown from slipping into the audience to mourn the man whose name he bore.

CHAPTER THIRTY-FIVE

THE PLEASURE OF SAYING NO

T MARENGO, IN THE PIEDMONT, ON JUNE 14, 1800, A hard-fought battle had been going on since the morning between the French army under First Consul Bonaparte and the Austrian army of Marshal Melas. After the resumption of hostilities earlier in the year, Moreau had succeeded in driving the enemy back beyond the Danube. Enemy forces in Germany were cut off from those in Italy.

With the army that he had assembled as discreetly as possible in Burgundy and the Lyon region, Bonaparte plunged into the space left empty between the two enemy formations. He led his troops through the Great Saint Bernard Pass, an extraordinary exploit considering road conditions at the time, and they streamed into the Po valley. Melas had concentrated his forces, fifty thousand well-rested men, at the Bormida river. Bonaparte's soldiers were not well rested. To confront the largest possible number of enemy forces, Napoleon had imprudently spread out his army. The range was so great that the troops who were the farthest from the point of contact with the enemy were in danger of not having the time to come up as reinforcements. This was the same mistake that would be fatal to Napoleon at Waterloo—General Emmanuel de Grouchy's distance from the battle was too great for him to be able to provide support forces in time.

At Marengo, Melas, thinking he had the upper hand, attacked the French, who sorely felt the effects of their numerical inferiority. By early afternoon, the Austrians clearly dominated the situation, and Bonaparte wondered whether his star had deserted him. He nevertheless continued to urge on his officers and soldiers and very rashly exposed himself to enemy fire. Roederer, the former *procureur-syndic* of Paris, who had rallied to the Consulate and become a loyal follower of Napoleon, advised him not to risk his life needlessly. Would the French soldiers still have the heart to fight if they knew that their general, to whom they attributed almost supernatural powers, had been killed?

The First Consul more or less followed this wise warning and spoke briefly about the political situation his death would create in France. He told Roederer that only two men would be capable of replacing him: Carnot and Lafayette.

Around three in the afternoon, the military situation was so dangerous that Bonaparte seriously considered ordering a retreat. But the troops still held on, and what would not happen at Waterloo did happen at Marengo. The general leading the large detachment Bonaparte had imprudently sent toward Genoa and the northern Po had been reached by a courier—according to some accounts, he heard the sound of cannon—and he arrived with a fresh division at five. This savior was General Louis Desaix de Veygoux, like Lafayette a native of

Auvergne. An officer at fifteen, a noble who rallied to the Revolution and won glory in the Army of the Rhine, he had followed Bonaparte to Egypt, where he had conducted himself with such generosity and understanding that he had been known as "the just Sultan." Desaix had, in fact, been back in France for only a few months. His arrival and his drive and vivacity changed the course of the battle. The Austrians sensed that the victory within their grasp was suddenly slipping away. At nine, they broke contact and crossed the Bormida. The next day they asked for a truce. Although Marengo was presented in official bulletins and published accounts as one of Bonaparte's victories, there is no doubt that the victory belonged to Desaix. The First Consul's ingratitude (not to mention that of his sycophants) toward his memory is particularly shocking in light of the fact that Desaix was killed in the course of the fighting; he was only thirty-two.

Nonetheless, the remarks made to Roederer on June 14, 1800, are of more political significance than determining the true causes of the victory. It seems curious that the only names Bonaparte mentioned to indicate men capable of replacing him were those of Carnot and Lafayette. The two were far from unconditional supporters of him personally and of his course of action. Carnot, known as the Organizer of Victory when the fourteen armies of the Republic that he established provoked admiration around the world, deserved the name. He had rallied to the new regime but had not given up his deep convictions as a friend of liberty. Bonaparte clearly sensed as much, but he appointed Carnot War Minister because of his competence. Carnot publicly protested when Napoleon set up his own dynasty, and he gave up politics in favor of scientific research.

As for Lafayette, the history of his relations with Bonaparte up to 1814 is a history of impossible friendship and growing misunderstanding. His gratitude to the man to whom he owed his release from Olmütz was constant. Nor did Lafayette conceal, when he wrote about Bonaparte, that he could not help feeling a certain attraction to the man; but, although he acknowledged, in a letter to the First Consul, that Brumaire had saved France, he made no concessions on underlying principles, and throughout the time Napoleon ruled the country, he behaved as an opposition figure who was tolerated because he engaged in no active opposition.

After a brief and very formal meeting at the Tuileries arranged by Lebrun, the first between Bonaparte and Lafayette, chance placed an important intermediary between the two men, Joseph Bonaparte, the oldest member of the family, future king of Naples and then of Spain, who then had a long and comfortable exile in the Unites States after the Restoration under the name of the Count de Survilliers. He was an intelligent, benevolent, and cultivated man who did not always approve the conduct of his brilliant brother but was weak enough to obey him most of the time. A spontaneous liking sprang up between Joseph and Lafayette when they met at Talleyrand's residence, and their friendly relations survived the vicissitudes of history.

It was Joseph who provided Lafayette with the opportunity to meet the First Consul by inviting him to the reception he himself was giving in his château of Mortefontaine on October 20, 1800, for the delegates from the United States, with which France had just signed a new treaty replacing the treaty of 1778. The gesture was particularly thoughtful, because Lafayette was now nothing but a private citizen whose presence had been tolerated in Paris for only a few months; but he continued to symbolize the friendship between the two republics of France and America.

In the course of the festivities, Lafayette had several long conversations with the new master of France. When Bonaparte spoke of the battles across the ocean in which Lafayette had won glory,

Lafayette replied with the celebrated phrase that corresponds more his desire not to boast than it does to historical truth: "The greatest interests in the universe were decided by encounters between patrols."

Bonaparte was in fact testing his interlocutor, whom he wanted to make an ally, or at least to establish a relation of complicity or obligation. While he had enough esteem for Lafayette to imagine him as a replacement one day, as long as Bonaparte was alive, Lafayette could live and prosper only in his entourage and at his service. Bonaparte wanted to make him acknowledge that, after everything they had experienced and suffered, the French no longer felt the same enthusiasm for freedom that they had at the beginning of the Revolution. Lafayette did not share that opinion. He came back to the subject, which remained a bone of contention between them. "I am not unaware," he said, "of the crimes and the follies that have profaned the name of freedom, but I repeat, the French are, more than ever perhaps, in a condition to receive it, and *it's up to you to provide it, it's from you that they expect it.*"

It was advice that Lafayette probably offered with little illusion. At every one of his meetings with Bonaparte until 1802 (he stopped seeing him after the proclamation of the Consulate for life), and in every one of his letters, he insisted on the freedom that France expected from Bonaparte and that Bonaparte refused to provide.

Relations between the two continued to deteriorate, especially after 1802, because their temperaments were too different from one another. Bonaparte knew very well that Lafayette was a man of honor; he never failed to point that out in front of witnesses. He wondered at the fact that Lafayette was the Revolutionary figure who was most hated by all the crowned heads of Europe. He told Lafayette how surprised he had been by the hatred of the

kings for the unfortunate prisoner of Olmütz when he negotiated his release after his victories over Austria. If it can be said
that Lafayette was throughout his life a man of a single idea, the
same cannot be said of Bonaparte. He claimed to be the heir of
the Revolution, the one who would accomplish its promises, and
perhaps he believed it when he said it, but he did not draw the
necessary conclusions from his affirmation, and he reconstructed
in his own way the tyranny that it had been the Revolution's mission to destroy. His skepticism about both principles and people,
his instinctive belief that anyone could be manipulated, either
through trickery or through flattery and corruption, were not
compatible with the true republican spirit, which contains an
element of optimism and implies confidence in all that is best in
humanity.

Bonaparte respected Lafayette, while at the same time mis-
trusting him, because he thought of him as a blend of courageous soldier and secular missionary, obstinate to the point of
losing touch with reality. He was not a politician, and Bonaparte
deplored that fact, because with a politician one could always
make an arrangement.

However passionate Lafayette may have been about action,
like his spiritual father and friend Washington, he was capable of
retiring to the country and waiting to be called upon when he
was needed. This way of taking things was foreign to Bonaparte,
who had an essentially domineering temperament and thought
of himself as the supreme savior. He nevertheless tried to hitch
Lafayette to his cart through favors and flattering advances. One
never knew.

It was, in fact, a waste of time. Lafayette was determined to
refuse everything offered him. He twice refused a seat in the
Senate. He refused a seat on the regional council of Haute-Loire,
even though he knew that the refusal would be painful for the

residents of the department, who remained devoted to him. He refused an appointment as ambassador to the United States (an idea suggested to Bonaparte by Talleyrand), on the pretext that as an American himself (he had been granted citizenship in return for services rendered), he could not serve as a diplomat to the authorities of his own country.

Moreover, he refused an offer from his old friend President Jefferson in 1803 to be appointed governor of Louisiana, which the United States had just purchased from France. He refused the grand cordon of the Légion d'Honneur when the master of France offered it, on the pretext that he was not in agreement with the spirit of the institution. He accepted only one intervention by the First Consul on his behalf, because he thought of it as a right and not a favor: the provision of his pension as a former lieutenant general in the French army.

All the other requests Lafayette addressed to Bonaparte or his associates were for the benefit of third parties who had been the victims of injustice. For example, he helped to have removed from the list of banned persons people of good faith such as his aunt the Countess de Tessé and her husband, and many others who had settled abroad to save their lives.

All these refusals irritated Bonaparte, as did remarks Lafayette made at dinner parties about Bonaparte's policies, complaining about what he had said in front of Lord Cornwallis at a dinner given by his brother Joseph. Bonaparte was naïve if he thought he was in a position to induce Lafayette to censor what he said in salons and among friends and family. Bonaparte wanted him to retire to the country and avoid any public fuss, which Lafayette did. But he indicated his compliance offhandedly: "The silence of my retreat is the maximum of my deference," further irritating the impatient Bonaparte. What was even worse was Lafayette's negative vote in the May 1802 referendum on the Consulate for life. There were only nine thousand no votes compared to more than three million in favor, but Lafayette's negative vote was accompanied in the municipal register with this comment: "I cannot vote in favor of this public office until public liberty is guaranteed. Then I will give my vote to Napoleon Bonaparte."

He also wrote a private and very explicit letter to the First Consul in which he exhorted him, since he wanted his office to be permanent, to "found it on bases that are worthy of the nation and himself." The advice says a good deal of what he thought of the regime.

Faced with this smiling, courteous, and never ungrateful rebel, who acknowledged his immense past contributions and sent him "sincere personal wishes," but who was incorruptible no matter how he was approached, Napoleon displayed his weakness by petty acts of revenge. Indeed, his reactions were sometimes incoherent.

There was, for example, the case of George-Washington Lafayette, the hero's son. Having joined his father in Vianen, the young man (he was born in 1779) fought with the Dutch patriots against the Anglo-Russian armies, who were defeated by those patriots and by forces under Marshal Brune. When he returned to France, he asked to be integrated into the French army to fight wherever he might be sent. Bonaparte was touched by the gesture and willingly gave him an appointment as second lieutenant.

In the tradition of his father and his forebears, the young officer fought valiantly at Ulm in 1805. He then had the rank of lieutenant and his conduct under fire was reason enough for a promotion to captain. The recommendation by his superiors came up against an incomprehensible veto from the Emperor, who kept an eye on the promotion of officers. Outraged by this injustice, while many less brilliant comrades had already become lieutenant-colonels, George-Washington nonetheless continued to do his duty with enthusiasm. In the course of the battle of Eylau against the Russians and Prussians on February 7 and 8, 1807, one of the bloodiest of Napoleon's victories, causing the death of forty thousand French troops, Lieutenant Lafayette saved the life of General de Grouchy, whom he served as aide de camp. Such an act of valor in the midst of the frightful butchery of Eylau was of a kind that should finally have earned him his captain's stripes. But that did not happen. Nor did his valiant conduct at the battle of Friedland in June of the same year win him the recompense he hoped for and deserved, despite the support of Murat himself, the Emperor's brother-in-law. It seemed that the name Lafayette had become unbearable to the tyrant.

The young Louis de Lasteyrie, who had married George-Washington's sister Virginie in 1803, and had volunteered for the dragoons after his marriage, was treated even worse. He was unable to advance beyond the rank of a noncommissioned officer, and he and his brother-in-law finally drew the only possible conclusion from the petty imperial vengeance and resigned from the army.

Having understood that Napoleon's megalomania had made any dialogue impossible, Lafayette, following the model of Washington, lived in retirement in the château of La Grange, a property that had belonged to Adrienne's family and that she had been able to recover. The family lived peacefully as provincial landowners, hosting family members, close friends, and foreign visitors, particularly British and Americans passing through France.

In 1803, Lafayette had a very bad fall on ice. Rather than agreeing to an amputation, he chose to go through a horribly painful treatment that lasted several weeks and caused a stiffness in the leg that lasted for the rest of his life. From that day on, Lafayette was forced to use a cane whenever he left home.

A gentleman farmer, like his great friends across the Atlantic between periods in office, the general took a passionate interest in agricultural questions. It was not for nothing that he had been raised in the country. He very skillfully diversified grain crops, growing rye, barley, wheat, and maize. He paid particular attention to livestock, raising a flock of merinos seven hundred strong.

The year 1807 was marked by a bereavement that affected him very deeply. Adrienne, traumatized by the death of family members during the Terror, prematurely aged by ill treatment in Olmütz that had seriously affected her health, and suffering from ulcers, died at her aunt's house in Paris on December 24.

Lafayette wrote an account of Adrienne's suffering (see appendix), during which she displayed exemplary courage, patience, and serenity, and it proves that if he was not a faithful husband, he nonetheless deeply loved his wife and that he was aware of the extraordinary value of her personality and of everything he owed to her since the day, at the age of fourteen and a half, she had married an awkward adolescent whose name was to become famous throughout the world.

CHAPTER THIRTY-SIX

THE INGLORIOUS RETURN
OF A DYNASTY

I N PARIS ON APRIL 12, 1814, THE SKY WAS BLUE, BLUER
than it usually is in early spring; the sun, too, was warm for
the season; but the atmosphere was not filled with gaiety. At
two in the morning on March 31, the army defending the capital
had capitulated. At 11, the allied monarchs and their troops, who
had entered the city through the Porte Saint-Denis, conducted a
victory parade on the boulevards. The Empire was finished. After
winning so much glory on all the battlefields of Europe from the
Tagus to the Moscow River, France in turn was experiencing the
humiliation and sorrow of foreign occupation. How could
Parisians be gay when they saw arrogant enemy soldiers camping
in the gardens of the Champs Élysées? Yet there were many
people on the streets on that April morning. Although the atmosphere was heavy, perhaps curiosity won out over other feelings.
Forgetting for a moment the occupation that they hoped would

be very brief, the crowd focused its attention on a question of domestic politics.

Six days earlier, early in the morning of April 6, Napoleon had taken note of his marshals' refusal to continue fighting and presented his unconditional abdication to Caulaincourt. At eight that evening, the Senate unanimously adopted a proposed constitutional charter that began:

1. The French government is a hereditary monarchy with succession in the male line by order of primogeniture;
2. The French people freely call to the throne of France Louis-Stanislas-Xavier de France, brother of the late king, and, after him, the other members of the house of Bourbon, in the old order.

While yesterday's idol, now a prisoner, gloomily rode under guard toward the Mediterranean coast where he would embark for exile on the Isle of Elba, the representative of the royal family made his entry into Paris after a quarter century of exile. This was not the king but the Count d'Artois, now known as Monsieur, whom the Senate appointed on April 14 lieutenant-general of the kingdom until Louis-Stanislas-Xavier, who had been called to the throne, accepted the constitutional charter. Artois, who was fifty-seven, had a fitting physique to represent a dynasty that the majority of the French had repudiated, and that those under forty had practically not known. He was slim and well built, with handsome silver hair and regular features; his bearing was elegant and he held himself in the saddle like a young cavalry officer. From his person there emanated a gracious, benevolent, and self-confident authority, the attitude one would expect from a monarch. He rode a white horse whose saddle was covered with a scarlet cloth decorated with fleurs de lys. In a clearly political choice, he wore the uniform of the National Guard: blue jacket with red facing, white culottes, and a two-cornered hat with a feather. The borrowing stopped there. A symbolic detail, but one that embodied all by itself what was probably the fundamental mistake of the Bourbons restored to the throne: the cockade on the hat was not a tricolor, it was white, as though nothing had happened since 1789. Monsieur was nonetheless applauded on his passage, from the barrier of Bondy to Notre Dame, where a Te Deum was sung. Even on the long rue Saint-Denis, a very lower-class street, many windows were decorated with flowers. But were they celebrating the return of the Bourbon monarchy or the return of peace after all the wars that had exhausted the country? Lafayette, who was in Paris on April 12, admitted that he was rather moved, as a fighter for freedom hated by the friends of princes, to see that Royal Highness, who was his age and reminded him of his beginnings at the court of Versailles, the masked balls of the Opera, and other nights of pleasure. He sent Artois a short message of welcome in which he said he was pleased to see in his return "a signal and a guarantee of happiness and public liberty." Artois did not reply in writing, but he sent his compliments through Lafayette's nephew, Alexis de Noailles.

When the king himself, Louis XVIII, entered Paris on May 3, not on a white horse but slumped inside a carriage, imperfectly concealing his obesity with a tight blue uniform, with his tired face beneath a huge two-cornered hat, he made less of an impression than his younger brother. By his side was his niece the Duchess d'Angoulême, the daughter of Louis XVI. She was overpowered by sadness and fainted when she entered the Tuileries palace that she had left on the day of the bloody riot of August 10, 1792. Her husband, the Duke d'Angoulême, son of

Monsieur, had not had time to exchange his British uniform for that of a French general.

Louis XVIII, hindered by his physical condition, had grown into a rather benevolent man as he aged. Forgetting that Lafayette had mocked him in Versailles before he sailed for America—not to mention everything else—he received him graciously. But the hostile attitude of the aristocrats of the new court toward Lafayette almost made him regret that he had taken the trouble to come. He did not soon return to the palace. On the other hand, he was welcomed at the Palais-Royal by the Duke d'Orléans, the son of Philippe Égalité, former general under the Convention like Lafayette, and who became king under the name of Louis-Philippe, thanks to Lafayette, sixteen years later.

The only encounter of interest to Lafayette in the course of the First Restoration was the one he had with Emperor Alexander of Russia, to whom he was introduced by his friend Mme de Staël. A lucid mind, liberal in his way, and mixing clear political analyses with mystical ramblings, the tsar seems to have appreciated Lafayette. The two men spoke very openly of the inability on the part of the Bourbons to institute a veritable constitutional monarchy answering to the democratic aspirations of the French after so many years of oppression under the imperial dictatorship.

To be sure, there was more freedom than there had been, but it was very inadequate in many areas, and the returning émigrés seemed determined to challenge the egalitarian social advances of the Revolution, which might pave the way for a new civil war. The former commander of the National Guard had to defend himself against a wave of calumnies propagated by the ultra-royalists on his role between 1789 and 1792. Napoleon's unexpected escape from Elba provisionally freed him from these attacks, although he was not delighted by the knowledge that his former liberator was about to remount the throne. Far from witnessing this reversal of the situation with indifference, during the period of extreme political confusion of the Hundred Days, he played, after a period of abstention, a decisive role.

CHAPTER THIRTY-SEVEN

WHEN WORDS GIVE WAY
TO SILENCE

W HEN NAPOLEON RETURNED TO THE TUILERIES THAT
Louis XVIII had just abandoned on March 20,
1815, he had two major projects: to drive the allies
beyond the borders, and to make the French despise forever the
Bourbon dynasty. The first objective depended on the recon-
struction, as quickly as possible, of a strong and well-com-
manded army; his energy and his military genius would do the
rest. The second objective depended on a psychological operation: he had to charm public opinion. He knew that he could not
return to the imperial administration as it had been before his
abdication in April 1814. To win the population to his side, he
had to project the image of a liberal sovereign, much more liberal than the one he had just driven out.

He didn't shrink from the most outrageous demagoguery. As
he went through Autun on the way to Paris, he spoke to the

inhabitants like a pure Jacobin: "You let yourself be led by priests and nobles who would like to restore the tithe and feudal dues. I will bring them to justice. I will string them up!"

But his violent speeches were not enough. To win over the middle classes and the intelligentsia, he needed an apparently solid political instrument, an institutional framework. The Emperor then thought of appealing to a man of unchallenged talent and intelligence who had shown himself particularly hostile to Napoleon's policies; the effect would be all the more spectacular. This versatile mind belonged to Benjamin Constant. After having made insulting remarks about Napoleon on the eve of his return to the throne, going so far as to compare him to Attila and Genghis Khan, only "more terrible and more hateful because the resources of civilization are at his disposal," he rallied to the Emperor's support in the following days. Received at the Tuileries on April 14, he drafted for his new master the *Acte additionnel aux constitutions de l'Empire* (Additional Act to the Constitutions of the Empire), Napoleon's liberal fig leaf. It was a copy of the charter granted to his subjects by Louis XVIII in 1814, with a more democratic appearance: a Chamber of Peers appointed by the Emperor, a Chamber of Deputies elected by the people, freedom of opinion, worship, and the press guaranteed.

Backing was needed for this idyllic program. Of all the desirable figures, Lafayette would be the most striking. Who symbolized freedom in France better than he? But he had not left his château of La Grange and did not believe in the sincerity of the Emperor's conversion. He wrote as much very clearly to Benjamin Constant, who had made overtures to him. He feared that the man "who has just satisfied so many personal vanities and special interests, and who has come in the wake of so much stupidity, will finally deceive, as he did fifteen years ago, the honest hope of patriots. There can be no freedom in a country unless there are representatives who are freely and broadly elected, with the power to raise and spend public funds, making all the laws, organizing the military forces and able to dissolve them, deliberating with open doors, with debates published in the press; unless there is freedom of the press backed by everything that guarantees individual freedom. . . ." Reading this definition of democracy that constitutes the basis of his political thought, it is easy to understand why, in considering its possible acceptance by Napoleon, Lafayette ended his letter with these words: "I offer you my incredulity and join to it all my friendship."

Benjamin Constant was not the only one to sound him out. Joseph Bonaparte did the same, and although Lafayette did not question his good faith, his skepticism was not shaken, even though the former king of Spain was appealing to his patriotism more than to his political convictions. Weren't the allies the enemies that France had to combat first of all? Lafayette, who had locked himself in his room for an entire day to weep when foreign troops had entered Paris in 1814, could not but agree, even though he did not think that Napoleon was in a position to defeat the coalition armies in 1815. But Joseph persisted, arguing that Lafayette should join the system to test its validity rather than adopting an a priori skepticism. The Chamber of Peers, Joseph said, was open to him. This was a surprising psychological error on the part of such an intelligent man. Lafayette a peer of France through Napoleon's will alone? The suggestion came close to being an insult. If he were to agree to play a role in an assembly, the former member of the Constituent Assembly would hold his seat only as the result of a popular vote. Moreover, he refused Joseph's invitation to come to the Élysée Palace, where Napoleon had taken up residence. Nevertheless, as though he were taking the regime at its word, he presented his candidacy for the Chamber of Representatives in Seine-et-Marne. He was elected in Melun on May 8, which did not keep him from expressing reservations with regard to the plebiscite on the *Acte additionnel* held the same day. His comments in the electoral register were co-signed by his son. "It [the *Acte additionnel*] contains articles that any friend of freedom must, in my opinion, support, and others that I reject for my part, although the way the vote has been imposed makes it impossible to distinguish between them, even less to discuss them here; but I reserve the right to do so elsewhere. I say yes, despite the illegalities and the reservations noted above, because I want to hasten by every means in my power the meeting of a representative assembly, the first step on the road to safety, defense, and amendment."

The new deputy was thus determined to act from inside the regime. His language was that of a member of the opposition in the Chamber, consistent with what he was already.

He still refused to go to the Élysée as an individual, agreeing to go there only for an official reception, because of his position as third vice president of the Assembly. His conversation with the Emperor on that occasion was icy in tone, and silence and what remained unspoken were more important than the words actually pronounced.

"It's been twelve years since I've had the pleasure of seeing you," said the Emperor.

"Yes, sire, it's been that long."

"You look younger; country air has done you good."

"Yes, it has done a good deal for me."

The Emperor moved on to his next guest. Eleven days later came Waterloo.

It is conceivable that when Napoleon returned to Paris on June 20, he thought that he had lost a battle but not the war, since he had the resources to reconstitute an army of a hundred fifty thousand men with which he hoped to drive the enemy across the borders. But that after Waterloo he was obsessed by domestic politics, that he wanted to retake the power the *Acte additionnel* had given to the Chambers and exercise a wide-ranging dictatorship smacked of pathology. Lafayette, who had been observing him since 1797 with the clarity provided by distance and his refusal to accept any office, understood him better than anyone. After having served this strange "convert to freedom," out of patriotism, by requesting the intervention of the American ambassador William Crawford with a view toward negotiating an honorable peace, he then became the defender of the freedom that a mad autocrat again wanted to crucify.

When he stepped up to the podium in the Assembly, his colleagues thought they heard the voice of what was great and pure in the Revolution of 1789. He presented a motion that struck the fatal blow to the man who was threatening to restore absolute power. He called on the Chamber to declare that the independence of the nation was threatened; that it declare itself in permanent session and that any attempt to dissolve it would be a crime of high treason; whoever might be guilty of such an attempt would be a traitor to the country and immediately judged as such; and the ministers of war, foreign relations, interior, and police were asked to join the Assembly immediately.

Hence, if Napoleon were to persist in his determination to take back what he had granted, he would expose himself to the charge of high treason. He spoke of dissolving the rebellious Chamber, to foment a new Brumaire. But they were words, verbal threats from a man who felt his nerves cracking. Although his brother Lucien urged him to be firm, when his rage gave way to a lucid phase he knew that he would have to abdicate if he wanted to avoid plunging Paris into a bloodbath, which would not strengthen him against the foreign enemy. His rancor against

Lafayette was deep, all the deeper because he had no doubt that Lafayette would be the victor in this final duel. He tried, however, to use delaying tactics, had Lucien ask the two Chambers to set up a twelve-member commission to advise on emergency measures to be adopted, including negotiations in view of his abdication and contacts with the allies for a peace treaty. But international negotiations, Lafayette asserted, were impossible to consider as long as Napoleon had not abdicated, and he proposed—because he wanted to spare the defeated man from pure and simple dethronement—to go with his colleagues to the Emperor to confront him with his responsibilities. The proposal was not adopted. As time passed and every maneuver came up short, the question of dethronement inevitably had to be raised. One deputy suggested that the Emperor be given a deadline of one hour to abdicate. Acknowledging his defeat, Napoleon conceded. On June 22, everything was consummated. A delegation from the Chamber went to thank Napoleon and render homage to him. Lafayette was a part of it. Despite the discretion Lafayette had shown in the last hours, which he maintained during the final protocol visit, Napoleon knew that it was Lafayette who was primarily responsible for his being forced to abdicate. He exchanged a few words only with the president of the Assembly, and in his exile, he long chewed over his rancor against Lafayette.

CHAPTER THIRTY-EIGHT

A REGICIDE AT THE SERVICE
OF THE KING

URING THE DRAMATIC DAYS BETWEEN THE DEFEAT AT Waterloo and the beginnings of the Second Restoration, a man who might have been thought to have gone abroad or to be hiding in an out-of-the-way farm, because of the intense resentment against him and the opprobrium his name provoked, was in fact pulling the strings behind the scenes. One might almost say that some civilian and military dignitaries relied on him precisely because of his reputation as a Machiavellian. It is worth noting that he looked the part. The ex-seminarian was lean and pale with thin lips and a narrow, angular face. His eyes were often compared to those of a dead fish, because they were cold, gray, and without sparkle. He looked exhausted, distracted, fragile, and seemed completely uninterested in what was going on around him. But in fact, he saw everything and knew everything. He had an unusual capacity for hard work, and his indifference to human suffering had enabled him to create character armor that almost nothing could penetrate. His name was Joseph Fouché, former executioner of Lyon, who had become Minister of Police, the Emperor's chief spy, and the man who did his dirty work, before breaking with Napoleon and then returning to political prominence. He won 293 votes in the Assembly, second only to Carnot's 324, for a seat on the provisional executive committee that operated as a temporary government.

Fouché did not like Lafayette, who was everything that he deplored: he was upright, sincere, disinterested, and intransigent on questions of principle. He was, moreover, popular, and that made him dangerous. In addition, Fouché thought Lafayette was muddled and unrealistic. To get rid of this man who might compromise his plans with bold actions or rash outbursts, the simplest thing, Fouché thought, was to appeal to his patriotism and to send him for discussions with the allied powers to try to keep their troops from advancing further. Lafayette agreed, after being assured that the provisional government would not take advantage of his absence to proclaim a regency for Napoleon II, as the still numerous Bonapartists wished.

He thus found himself on the road again in a delegation with a loyal follower of Napoleon, another representative of the Assembly, one from the Chamber of Peers, a career diplomat, and Benjamin Constant as secretary.

The delegation had some difficulty in establishing contact with the allies. Always optimistic, Lafayette imagined that the liking Alexander I had shown for him in 1814 would enable him to win some concessions. This hope did not take into account the capricious character of the tsar, who had an attractive personality but unpredictable conduct, and claimed that he was unable to receive Lafayette. The British and the Prussians did not seem interested in an armistice. They wanted Bonaparte to be handed over and intended to continue their march on Paris. When the British representative demanded that the delegation hand over the ex-emperor before opening negotiations, Lafayette saw red and said he was astonished that they would think the former prisoner of Olmütz could possibly propose such a cowardly act to the French people. Negotiations collapsed, and the delegation returned to Paris. By the time they arrived on July 4, the capitulation had already been signed; French troops not engaged in battle were to retreat toward the Loire. In these circumstances, why was the commission, with four additional members, sent back toward the allied lines with a declaration to the monarchs? This was probably a diversionary tactic dreamed up by Fouché to conceal his dealings with the enemy and the representatives of Louis XVIII. In any event, the delegation was unable to get through the barriers at the gates of Paris. The Prussian Marshal Blücher was in Paris and opposed to their passage. The provisional executive committee announced its resignation. On July 7, Prefect of Police Decazes, who supported the Bourbons, blocked the deputies from entering the Assembly. Louis XVIII, who considered that his reign had not been called into question but merely interrupted by the Hundred Days, prepared to make his second entry. Lafayette had been thoroughly duped. There was nothing for him to do but return to La Grange.

CHAPTER THIRTY-NINE

ON THE FRAGILITY
OF CONSPIRACIES

ON SEPTEMBER 21, 1822, THE PLACE DE GRÈVE IN Paris
was once again the scene of a sinister event. The scaffold had been set up, and several thousand people
were silently bending an ear to catch the sound of the wheels of
a cart on the paving stones. There was a large contingent of
troops on horseback and on foot on the street leading to the scaffold and in the surrounding area. There was a fear of disturbances. Men in plain clothes with anxious looks moved
ceaselessly through the crowd, scrutinizing faces, noting every
gesture of the spectators, looking at clothing and haircuts for a
detail that might indicate a disguise. One might have thought it
was a repetition of the great macabre spectacle, the bloody festivities that had so frequently happened here. But that was not
quite the case. It was no longer 1793, although the ritual that was
getting under way resembled the earlier one. But the vast

majority of the people present had not come to scream for death—quite the contrary. The huge crowd was impressively silent. Sadness could be read on their faces. When the wheels of the cart could be heard, many women's eyes filled with tears, and when everything was over, many men could no longer hold back their sobs. What was happening on the Place de Grève in the early autumn of 1822 was a legal assassination, like many others France had known over the last thirty years. And the four victims who were handed over to the executioner on that day deserved as much compassion as the most touching victims of the terrorist madness of the end of the preceding century.

The victims were young men, all under thirty. They came from humble backgrounds; all four were soldiers with not particularly distinguished careers, since none was above the rank of non-commissioned officer. Their names were Bories, Pommier, Raoulx, and Goubin, and they have come down to posterity, as they were tried collectively, under the name of the Four Sergeants of La Rochelle.

Their appointment with death in a public square on that September day was not because of any crime that could be imputed to them. They were about to die because they had conducted themselves like men of honor, by not revealing a clandestine action that they knew about and with which, to be sure, they wanted to be associated, but they had not had the opportunity to do so. So they had been convicted for their silence and for their intentions.

Since the assassination of the Duke de Berry, the son of the Count d'Artois, by a mentally disturbed man in 1820, France had been living under an oppressive regime, although the charter Louis XVIII had granted his subjects in 1814, which acknowledged certain freedoms, was still in force. After the assassination, the moderates, known as the *Constitutionnels*, whose principal representative was Decazes, had been forced to cede power to the ultra-royalists, the *Ultras*, who dreamed only of vengeance. They had overwhelmed the king, who had some political intelligence and wanted to unite as much of the French population as possible around the throne, and were attempting to destroy everything good or acceptable that had been accomplished between 1789 and 1814; in a word, their goal was counterrevolution. Since parliamentary activity was ineffective for the liberal opposition, secret societies seemed to be the only desirable recourse for anyone who wanted to change things. These societies became fashionable under the Second Restoration, on both the right and the left, because the supposedly democratic system was not functioning normally and individual freedom and freedom of the press were seriously threatened from 1820 on by the Villèle government that had succeeded the moderate and relatively open Martignac government. Resentments were piling up in the France of the time: the Bonapartists accused the Bourbons of having sacrificed the interests of the nation to those of their dynasty; the republicans saw the gains of the Revolution being lost one after the other, after a brief period of reconciliation between 1815 and 1820; and the former émigrés and the *Ultras* thought that repression had been insufficient and that the supporters of absolute monarchy had not recovered what had been taken away from them. In this climate, informing, calumny, intrigues, and conspiracies, small and large, proliferated. The Catholic Church itself, although it benefited from its alliance with the government, was not absent from the galaxy of secret associations. The devotees of the *Congrégation* often acted behind a mask. The *Chevaliers de la Foi*, in the service of Throne and Altar, had organized their association in imitation of the Freemasons, as had the *Francs-Régénérés*, who acted in the interests of the Count d'Artois, who was jealous of his brother and eager to succeed him. On the opposition side, the principal secret society was the *Charbonnerie*. Its origins are obscure, although it is known that it played an important role in the revolutionary movements of Spain and Italy. It had, in fact, been imported into France from Italy by two young French republicans, Joubert and Dougier, on their return from Naples, where they had been initiated by local *carbonari*.

The basic cell of the *Charbonnerie* was the "vente," generally consisting of twenty members. The "ordinary" vente received orders from a "central" vente, with which it had minimum contact and whose names were supposed to be unknown. Above the central vente, the "haute" vente held supreme authority over the organization throughout the national territory. Although Freemasons, as individuals, could be affiliated with the *Charbonnerie*, there were no links between the two organizations, since one of the essential rules of Freemasonry in all countries was respect for existing authority and non-involvement in politics. The goal of the *Charbonnerie* in nineteenth-century Europe was on the contrary to overthrow oppressive governments by violent means, preferably selective, that is, by conspiracies, coups, and assassinations of men in power. The rule of secrecy was absolute. Members, who were required always to carry a knife—a means for instant defense or attack and easy to conceal, as well as a symbol—owed each other help and assistance wherever they might be and whatever their social position. They called each other cousins or good cousins.

In 1821, the Bazar conspiracy, so called because the Bazar Français in Paris served as cover for the principal conspirators, came to light. At the center of this conspiracy, which does not appear to have been the work of the *Charbonnerie* as such, was a colonel by the name of Sauzet. The political goals seem to have been vague, because the Orleanists and Bonapartists who were involved in the operation had not agreed among themselves on the composition of the provisional government they intended to set up at Vincennes. They hoped they would easily be able to seize that fortress, where they had accomplices.

Indiscretions meant that the police got wind of the affair before it could be put into operation. Some of the conspirators were arrested; the others had the time to flee and hide. The government thought it wise not to try to seek out those behind the conspiracy or to take public action against them. Lafayette, a liberal deputy, was suspected, as he was whenever a conspiracy was discovered; but, although he had been informed by some conspirators, he refused to be associated with the operation, and there was no evidence against him.

Another affair in the following year caused much more of a stir. It was known as the Saumur and Belfort conspiracy, the names of the two cities where insurrections among the troops were to serve as a signal for others. Survivors of the Bazar conspiracy were involved in this new attempt at subversion, which was clearly the work of the *Charbonnerie*. The organization had many branches in eastern France, and significant resources were at its disposal, supplied by the haute vente. Among the dignitaries whom the vast majority of members did not suspect to be their leaders were Lafayette, who seems to have held the highest position, and a number of colleagues from the Assembly, including de Schonen, d'Argenson, Koechlin, and Manuel, in addition to such well-known Parisian figures as the artists Ary Scheffer and Horace Vernet.

The plan was to seize Vincennes and the Tuileries and then to establish a provisional government in Alsace under the leadership of Lafayette, d'Argenson, and Koechlin. The date fixed for the operation was December 24, 1821. Because this was the anniversary of Adrienne's death, and it was Lafayette's custom to spend the day in meditation and perhaps prayer in his late wife's room, he did not leave La Grange until December 25. He left the château with his son and a servant, who volunteered because he guessed that his master was about to undertake a dangerous and exciting mission.

The retired general and current deputy was supposed to go to Belfort, but things went wrong. An accidental explosion in the arsenal at Vincennes caused the summoning of reinforcements, and the plan to seize the fortress was cancelled. The commander of the forces in Belfort, an *Ultra* named Toustain, detected suspicious movements. He made preventive arrests and, after an incident during which he was fired on, he decided to close the gates of the city.

Informed on the road, Lafayette hid in the home of a friend in Haute-Saône and destroyed the documents he was carrying. The government expected further operations and kept watch.

The leader of the *Charbonnerie* in Saumur, General Berton, did not go into action until February 22, 1822. With troops he had assembled in the region, he marched on the city, but a large number of the men panicked and dispersed. Recognizing that he was powerless, Berton went to hide in La Rochelle, but he was betrayed and arrested with two other members of the conspiracy, one of whom, Dr. Coffié, committed suicide. Berton and the other man captured with him, Sauge, were sentenced to death and executed.

At the trial, with no supporting evidence, the prosecutor threw out the names of Lafayette, Benjamin Constant, and Manuel as those who were truly responsible for the conspiracy.

In early February 1822, the 45th infantry regiment had been transferred from Paris to La Rochelle because the colonel had heard that a military vente had been established in his unit. But he did not know who was involved. The Four Sergeants, the unfortunate heroes of this episode, belonged to this regiment and to the *Charbonnerie*. When they left Paris, they had been given halves of cards that had been cut in two; other affiliates would make themselves known along the way by presenting the other halves. Since they were heading toward the west of France, it is likely that they were to be called on to back up the movement unleashed in Saumur. When Berton, after his failure, took refuge in La Rochelle, he met Pommier and other members of the vente in the regiment. Bories, the most intelligent and responsible of the Four Sergeants had unfortunately been put under arrest for having responded to a provocation from foreign soldiers, an incident with no connection to the conspiracy. An affiliate named Goupillon, who knew that Berton was being hunted, denounced his comrades. Arrested along with 24 other soldiers after the suspects had been interrogated by General Despinois, Goupillon was acquitted at trial because of his role as an informer. Under pressure from Despinois, some of the accused revealed some information about the central vente, but they retracted that at trial and remained silent about everything else.

Marchangy, the violent and bitterly sarcastic prosecutor, called for the heads of twelve of the defendants. He was granted four, with the others being sentenced to prison terms. The lawyers for the defense all belonged to the *Charbonnerie*. Bories, who was born into a peasant family in Aveyron and had been introduced to Lafayette, dominated the trial with his serenity, eloquence, and self-denial. To the very end, while not revealing the names that the government was eager to learn, he tried to assign all responsibility to himself. He addressed the jury in these terms: "The prosecutor, by declaring that no oratorical power could possibly save me from public condemnation, has designated me as the principal guilty party. Well, I accept that position, happy that if I lay my head on the scaffold I may secure absolution for all my comrades." The jurors were not swayed. The four who had been sentenced to death were promised their lives if they revealed the names of the members of the haute vente. The sergeants responded with contemptuous silence. When they were taken to the Place de Grève on September 21, they stood tall. On the way, Bories managed to throw a bouquet to a girl who had approached the convoy. She imagined she was his fiancée, and the story is that she lay flowers on the hero's grave several times every year until 1864.

At the foot of the scaffold the four men embraced, and each of them found the strength to cry out "Vive la liberté!" before the blade fell. The crowd was appalled.

By choosing to sacrifice their lives the Four Sergeants of La Rochelle earned the status of martyrs. Beyond the cause they believed in, these simple noncommissioned officers provided a tremendous lesson in honor to all the ministers, glorious generals, diplomats, prefects, men of letters, and all the other dignitaries who, in the years following the fall of the Empire, had distinguished themselves by their betrayals and the repudiation of their past. During the trial, the prosecutor Marchangy had made it a point to stigmatize the "nobles of the haute vente" who urged unfortunate men to commit crimes and remained comfortably at home while subalterns alone faced the rigors of the law. The argument had no effect on the sergeants. After the execution, odious caricatures showed Lafayette, partly hidden and with a look of satisfaction, witnessing the ordeal of his young subordinates from a window facing the Place de Grève. The hatred of the former émigrés and the *Ultras* for the ex-commander of the National Guard fed on any circumstance that offered an opportunity to blacken his name.

But it is important to remember that the *Charbonnerie* had made every effort to save the condemned men. An attempted prison escape almost succeeded. An intermediary, the prison surgeon, had managed to bribe the director, who demanded 70,000 gold francs so he could flee abroad after opening the cells of the Four Sergeants. Lafayette had provided the bulk of the money, with the help of Ary Scheffer, Horace Vernet, and Colonel Fabvier. After making his decision, the director confided in his friend, the prison chaplain, so that he could share the burden of this secret with someone who was absolutely safe. But his trust was misplaced, and the clergyman made haste to reveal everything to the prefect of police. The director and the surgeon were arrested, and a sum of 10,000 francs was seized. The rest, saved by a medical student, was returned to the secret committee. Other plans were made to rescue the prisoners on the way between the prison and the place of execution. Determined men had been stationed at various spots. But the density of the crowd and the magnitude of military and police forces made it necessary to abort the operation, as a similar attempt to save Louis XVI had had to be aborted on January 21, 1793.

A few years earlier, having contributed to Napoleon's abdication, Lafayette returned to La Grange and to his trees, flowers, and well-tended stables filled with animals of high quality. He had many visitors. In the eyes of people who did not like the regime of Louis XVIII, he took on the figure of the patriarch of the opposition. The king detested him but let nothing of his aversion show directly. Decazes and the constitutional party were searching for a middle way between democratic monarchy and counterrevolution, but the path was narrow. In principle, the government had nothing against freedom, but it strongly feared possible excesses, particularly in the press. People came from all over France and from abroad to see Lafayette in La Grange. Some came to ask for advice, others were impelled by curiosity. During the day, his heavy boots tramped through the damp earth and the manure of the stables, but in the evening, he was an impeccably dressed and dazzling host, with a refined courtesy that had disappeared with the Ancien Régime and that the Restoration had been unable to bring back. His conversation, because of the wealth of his memories and his frankness, was treasured by all who listened to him.

It is not surprising that he was urged to again play a role in public life commensurate with his talent and experience. In 1817, he failed to win a seat in the Assembly, but a year later, he was offered a chance to run by three departments, Seine, Seine-et-Marne, and Sarthe. He chose Sarthe, and received 569 out of 1,055 votes.

On the opening day of the session, he maintained an icy silence when cries of "Vive le roi" rang out, and he did not take to the podium until March 22, 1819. The liberal opposition, which consisted of 28 deputies, some of whom were well known and courageous, such as Manuel, d'Argenson, de Schonen, and Perier, had found in Lafayette—a constant enemy of despotism, whether it came from the Bourbons or from Bonaparte—a spokesman who was already legendary.

He was involved in all the battles for freedom. He defended Abbé Grégoire, former constitutional bishop, who had been elected as a deputy from Isère, but whose mandate the reactionary majority succeeded in invalidating. He demanded the complete application of the 1814 Charter, which the government continually interpreted narrowly so that it gradually lost any content.

He opposed the manipulation of the poll tax to favor the wealthy, whereas he wanted to broaden suffrage and eventually make it universal. Each of his appearances set off sneers and insults from the conservative benches. Every position he took, every attitude he adopted was taken by the mass of his opponents as a provocation. Was he a statue looking for a pedestal, even if that turned out to be a scaffold, as Laffitte (who had nothing against him) said to him one day? Lafayette answered, "Perhaps"; and there is no reason, considering his past conduct, to question his sincerity.

Perhaps this dark vision of his fate is a reason explaining his affiliation to the *Charbonnerie* and his accession to the haute vente. But it was not the only one. Lafayette, with his optimistic, enthusiastic, and slightly naïve temperament, had not grown suspicious with age. He easily accepted arguments that went in the direction of what he hoped for. Associates had likely made him dream of a great coup whose success would be strongly consolidated if, by agreeing to give his public support on the day of victory, he revealed that he himself was in the front rank of conspirators. When the parliamentary path seemed blocked, he had agreed to join the struggle, and we know the results. The failure of the conspiracies of the Bazar, Saumur, and Belfort, and especially the tragic end of the Four Sergeants of La Rochelle made him recognize the vanity and danger of conspiracies, and he returned to open and public action to the extent permitted by the Charter and its partisan interpretation by the Villèle government.

In 1823, he opposed the policy of support for Ferdinand VII of Spain, who had been driven out by the Cortes, and whom France restored to the throne through military intervention.

In March, he defended with particular vigor his colleague the liberal deputy Manuel, who after having attacked the policy of intervention in Spain, refused to leave the podium when he was threatened with expulsion from the Chamber, and who allowed himself to be expelled by the gendarmes only after the National Guard had refused the order to arrest him.

The Chamber was dissolved on December 24, 1823. In the election of February 25, 1824, Lafayette was defeated, 184 to 152, in Meaux, the constituency including La Grange, by his conservative opponent, Baron Pinteville de Cernon.

More than rest, at sixty-seven, the former general and former deputy needed to change his ideas. To do this, he chose to return to the source.

CHAPTER FORTY

"WHAT BETTER PLACE TO BE THAN IN THE BOSOM OF ONE'S FAMILY"

O N AUGUST 15, 1824, THE PORT OF NEW YORK, WHICH was on the way to becoming the most important on the east coast, was the scene of unusual frenzy. More than thirty thousand people had gathered at the docks, and not to admire the steamboats, the invention of Robert Fulton, the imaginative American whose offers of service had been rejected by Napoleon.

Artillery salvos were fired at regular intervals, shattering the silence of the hot and humid summer day. All the ships in the harbor had raised their ensigns and signal flags. They created thousands of dots of color stirred by the gentle breeze over a distance of several miles. Uniformed soldiers and their officers, wearing their decorations, waited in impeccable order. Some of the soldiers were very old, and many of them could not walk without crutches or a cane; others wore a patch over a missing eye. They were veterans of a war that had ended more than forty years earlier.

What was the reason for this display of banners, richly colored uniforms, flower-covered barges, and warships with full crews? It looked as though they were there to greet a fleet returning from a victory over the navy of an enemy country or a foreign head of state. It was, in fact, an ordinary American merchant ship that entered the harbor, the *Cadmus*. To welcome it to the great harbor, the *Chancellor Livingston*, carrying the city authorities and some veterans like those on the docks, sailed to meet it. Three travelers in civilian clothes disembarked from the *Cadmus*, one of them a tall man of sixty-seven, leaning on a cane. He had abundant white hair combed upward in the style of the day. Next to him was a man who looked very young, although he was already forty-five; the older man sometimes held onto his arm to keep his balance or to control his feelings. The third man followed at a respectful distance.

When they set foot on land, tens of thousands of people applauded and cheered, almost overwhelming the music played by the orchestra, a French tune: *Où peut-on être mieux qu'au sein de sa famille?*

The three travelers so warmly greeted by the city of New York were an American ex-general, Gilbert de Motier de Lafayette, his son George-Washington de Lafayette, and his secretary M. Levasseur. The members of the detachment assigned to be his personal guard wore a badge on their uniforms with his portrait and the inscription "Lafayette's Guard."

He had crossed the Atlantic for the fourth time in his life. After an absence of forty years, he had returned, officially invited by his friend James Monroe, president of the United States, to the country where he had experienced the most exalted times of his youth.

The choice of music to greet him was much more than a gracious gesture. It was a symbol whose import could be grasped only by those who knew thoroughly the life of the hero of the day.

Indeed, what better place to be than in the bosom of one's family? For it was indeed his family that the passenger on the *Cadmus* had returned to, his spiritual family, just as important as his biological family, a family that would take him to its bosom for more than a year, among whom he would recover his strength, reconstitute his identity, and rediscover himself after so many painful ordeals.

What he could not suspect, although he had constantly maintained friendly relations with Americans, some of whom had visited him in France, was the extent of his popularity in the United States. He entered a jubilant city, and flowers were thrown from every window onto the triumphal chariot designed for him and pulled by four white horses. At crossroads, orchestras played *See, the Conquering Hero Comes*, an appropriate tune to greet him. The parade through New York, whose population had increased tenfold since his last visit, lasted for two hours. Greeting him in the name of the city and the entire country, the mayor expressed sentiments that overwhelmed Lafayette: "The people of the United States cherish you as a venerated father; the nation considers you its beloved son." The image of the family was a constant, one that historians later confirmed by numbering Lafayette among the Founding Fathers of the nation. The title of the song expressed a deep truth. Where better place could he be, at this point in his life, than in America, the cradle of his personality?

This upwelling of warmth and affection coming from all social classes and all ages of Americans made him forget the insults, calumnies, and underhanded maneuvers perpetrated against him in France. At bottom, the king and his ministers were not angry that the former commander of the National Guard had left France. Had they had enough evidence to arrest him, he would have energized the entire opposition with his new role as martyr. A vast movement might have coalesced around his name alone, attracting young people and the lower classes; and that the government did not want to see. Manipulating the electorate so that he could not recover his seat was for the government already a positive outcome.

Thousands of miles from his mediocre enemies, the hero of the Old and New worlds (especially of the New) was swept up into a whirlwind. Banquets followed balls, and speeches came after concerts. Six thousand people were invited to the ball given in his honor in Boston. Everywhere, he had to speak, recall memories, answer hundreds, thousands of questions. He was received officially by 132 municipalities, and on each occasion that he had to stop for a meal or spend the night in a village or town, the population came to see him, to shake his hand, touch his clothes, hear him speak.

If there were only the municipalities and the great national and local institutions! America was a religious country with churches of many denominations. Lafayette had to endure sermons and hymns in churches of every denomination: Episcopalian, Presbyterian, Methodist, Unitarian, in Catholic churches, synagogues, and more. He showed himself to be thoroughly ecumenical. But the real spiritual family of the former American general were the Freemasons.

Perhaps he found no welcome more moving, as a mason, than his solemn reception at the Great Lodge of Pennsylvania, in Philadelphia, where Benjamin Franklin and George Washington had been officers. There he rediscovered the purity and spirit of fraternity beyond political or religious splits that inspired the men who had laid the true foundations of the country, whose work and struggle he had had the honor to share as a brother from afar; and his memory had survived, since 37 Masonic lodges in the United States already bore his name.

Through Lafayette, who had left America in 1784, and had therefore not been worn down by subsequent political confrontations, whose image had remained intact while he was still alive, America recovered the spirit of 1776–1781 for the time of the visit of a sure and unshakably loyal friend; it was that vast movement of enthusiasm and optimism of men who, as Thomas Paine had said, had it in their power "to begin the world over again."

He visited his dear friend Jefferson twice in the course of his stay, and it was Jefferson who humorously pointed to the dangers that lay in store for Lafayette on his triumphal tour: "I'm afraid they will kill you with kindness. Do not lose, in the embraces of enthusiastic affection, a life that we dearly wish to preserve."

Lafayette wanted to revisit the battlefields where the fate of the country and probably the world had been decided. It was a devout pilgrimage, and on each occasion a reason to mourn dead friends. The visit contained as much piety, memory, nostalgia, and sorrow as it did joy. At Mount Vernon, where George Washington, the man who had counted the most in his life, had lived and died, he was overwhelmed by his feelings when he descended to the crypt where Washington was buried. When he came back up to rejoin Washington's nephew and Martha Washington's grandson, Jack Custis, Lafayette was unable to say a word for some time. He continued his stay in Virginia with a pilgrimage to Yorktown. A delegation from the French navy was present but showed itself as little as possible, as though it had received the order to do nothing that might contribute to the glory of the man who had done so much for the victory on that field. He also spent two weeks with an illustrious Virginian, one of the most francophile of former presidents, the gentle and cultivated James Madison who had retired to his property at Montpellier, as Jefferson had settled in his imposing estate at Monticello, where the guest of the American government spent several days in private before he left the United States.

On December 10, he discovered Washington, the federal capital that had been built from scratch since his last visit, following the design of Pierre Charles L'Enfant, a major in Rochambeau's expeditionary force. After visiting President Monroe, he was given an official reception by Congress. Twenty-four representatives escorted him from his residence to the Capitol, where he was welcomed by Speaker of the House Henry Clay. The reception, attended by the senators and the diplomatic corps, was conducted with great formality.

In his speech, Clay did not address only the veteran of the glorious years but also the man as fate had shaped him down to the present day through all of his actions: "Your constancy of character, your uniform devotion to regulated liberty, in all the vicissitudes of a long and arduous life . . . commands [our] admiration. . . . The vain wish has sometimes been indulged, that Providence would allow the patriot, after death, to return to his country, and to contemplate the intermediate changes which had taken place. . . . General, your present visit to the United States is a realization of the consoling object of that wish. You are in the midst of posterity." Lafayette replied with modesty: "I find myself greeted by a series of welcomes, one hour of which would more than compensate for the public exertions and sufferings of a whole life. . . . I have been allowed, forty years ago, before a committee of thirteen States, to express the fond wishes of an American heart." There is no doubt that his heart was and would remain American until the day he died. He was a rare example of a perfect representative of dual nationality.

On December 20, the House and Senate, "in consideration of the services and sacrifices of General Lafayette during the Revolutionary War," decided to award him the sum of $200,000 as well as a plot of unsold public land. Several states wanted to add individual gifts to this federal grant. Lafayette had to be insistent in order to refuse these generous gestures, which he considered excessive.

In January 1825, the celebrated hero boarded a steamboat for Louisiana, where a city had been named for him. The journey, which lasted for several months, enabled him to discover regions he had never seen before. But it was also a journey of memory in the South, where he lay the cornerstones for monuments to the memory of former companions, Baron Kalb and Nathanael Greene.

In North Carolina, he discovered Fayette County, and visited his old friend Huger, who had organized his failed escape from Olmütz thirty years earlier. Portraits and countless products bearing his image were sold everywhere.

In New York, where he returned after a tour in the north, he received such a flood of invitations that he could not possibly respond to them all, but there was one that he could not in conscience refuse. It came from Joseph Bonaparte, ex-king of Naples and Spain, who was living in the United States under the name of the Count de Survilliers. He had bought a beautiful estate at Point Breeze, near Bordentown, New Jersey, and that was where he welcomed the official guest of the United States, to whose friendship he had always remained faithful, despite the role Lafayette had played in 1815.

The welcome was more than cordial. Joseph lived in a great house, surrounded by a vast park, with his eldest daughter and her husband and the former lady in waiting of his younger daughter, who had left America. Joseph, who received crates of books from Europe and could pursue his interests in science and ornithology, was living an existence more in conformity with his deepest tastes than he had in the palaces of Naples and Madrid. It is likely that they spoke of Napoleon and the circumstances of his surrender to the British, as Joseph sailed alone for the United States. And although Napoleon, writing in Sainte-Hélène, had accused Lafayette of an act of betrayal, Joseph had never agreed with that assessment. Napoleon had died on Sainte-Hélène, Joseph was living in comfortable exile, and Lafayette, at the age of sixty-seven, was enjoying the rare condition of receiving the deep and lasting affection of an entire people although he possessed no power.

He had promised Jefferson that he would return to Monticello again before leaving America, and he kept his word in the summer of 1825. The visit was tinged with melancholy, because he would soon embark to return to France and his beloved family, but also an uncertain political situation and perhaps threats against his person. His youth was miraculously extended here in the United States by the power of friendship, but he was unsure about the conditions under which he would be able to resume the combat for freedom in France.

This second visit to Monticello was a celebration of memory. Madison and Monroe were invited, so the former volunteer for the rebel army found himself with three former presidents of the United States. The conversation had its share of nostalgia, but that was not all. These men now in their autumn years had built a solid and lasting edifice whose history was only beginning. Faithful to their youthful ideals, they could truly say that they had fought the good fight and kept the faith. They had the right to look to the future; the battle was not over, but they had already laid the foundation for an edifice whose construction would continue.

After this meeting with the Founding Fathers, Lafayette returned to Washington to say his farewells to the new president, John Quincy Adams, who delivered the final official speech, thanking Lafayette for his visit and expressing the good wishes of the nation: "If, in after days, a Frenchman shall be called to indicate the character of his nation by that one individual, during the age in which we live, the blood of lofty patriotism shall mantle in his cheek, the fire of conscious virtue shall sparkle in his eye, and he shall pronounce the name of Lafayette."

On September 7, the day after his sixty-eighth birthday, the visitor to his spiritual fatherland boarded the steamboat *Mount Vernon* that took him to Chesapeake Bay where the most recent ship built in American shipyards was waiting for him. In honor of its illustrious passenger, it had been christened *Brandywine*. In the hold was a vast chest containing soil that Lafayette himself had collected from the battlefield of Brandywine, with the intent of having it scattered on his coffin at his funeral. He would thus be buried in the soil of America that he had so loved.

Thirteen cannon salvos were fired when he boarded ship, one for each of the states that had been liberated at the time of the American Revolution by the rebel army in which he had served with glory and honor.

When he arrived at Le Havre, the ship's captain gave him in homage the star-spangled banner that had flown from the mast during the crossing. It is no exaggeration to say that a nation had never heaped so much honor on a foreign friend.

When he set foot again on his native land, the crowd wanted to come near and acclaim him. The king's officers charged the enthusiastic admirers, who were in danger of declaring too loudly their love of freedom.

CHAPTER FORTY-ONE

WHEN HISTORY REPEATS ITSELF

W
HEN FOUR THOUSAND PEOPLE ASSEMBLED IN A
small, usually quiet town in Seine-et-Marne, it was
noticed. This was especially true because on that
early October day in 1825 there was no religious festival, no particular ceremony to justify so many people coming together. And
it was even less likely to escape notice because it took place at the
château of La Grange, which the police and many informers had
for many years kept under discreet surveillance.

The telegraph and the telephone had not yet been invented,
but one can be certain that the prefect of the department in
Melun was informed several times every day of the comings and
goings at the gates of the château, and that the names of the visitors, even if they were simply local farmers, were scrupulously
reported to the representative of royal authority.

These thousands of French people, however, had no subversive intentions. They were carrying neither weapons nor signs and their presence posed no threat to public order. They had simply come to greet the lord of the manor, who had returned after an absence of more than a year. They knew that he had been welcomed in a distant country, which was a friend to France, more warmly than a head of state. How could they not be proud of their neighbor, whom they were used to seeing dressed in old wool trousers and mud-covered boots inspecting fields and stables, talking familiarly with peasants, and never hesitating to lend a hand to a herdsman rounding up his cattle or a cart driver pulling his hay wagon out of a ditch. He would have liked to answer everyone who had come to welcome him, who applauded him, told him he looked younger and had gained weight, but there were too many of them. He had to speak to them in groups to thank them and express his happiness at being again among his countrymen. It was as though the American celebration was continuing on the plains of Brie.

Or so it seemed. If the master of La Grange had fostered some illusions of that kind on the ship bringing him back, the French authorities had taken care of opening his eyes during the first hours of his return: sympathizers who had come to greet him when he disembarked at Le Havre were brutally driven back; a dawn serenade in his honor planned for Rouen was prevented by the police; and the newspapers close to the government had printed harsh commentaries.

Nonetheless, the former deputy, who had been defeated in the last elections and was suspected of being involved in anti-government plots, demonstrated his continuing and even stronger popularity. His triumphal tour of America had restored his militant spirit. He had seen firsthand what a democratic system could do for a nation. Why could France in turn not harvest the fruits of freedom? Hadn't it suffered and struggled enough;

hadn't it received solemn promises? The new king, who had acceded to the throne during his absence, was a man he had known for a long time: the former Count d'Artois, who had become Charles X on September 16, 1824. Lafayette was too well informed about what was happening at the Tuileries, he had too many friends and family close to the throne to be unaware that the king respected him. Charles X expressed this feeling in a formulation that he intended to be flattering to Lafayette but in fact reflected badly on himself: "There are only two men who have not at all changed their ideas since 1789, M. de Lafayette and I."

What the king thought should be to his credit in the name of constancy or fidelity was in fact his lack of perception, not to say blindness. In 1789, he had been so firmly committed to the principle of absolute monarchy by divine right and so opposed to any constitutional reform that he was the first prominent figure in the state to emigrate. Was this foresight, aside from the fact that by going into exile he probably saved his head? But in 1824, after everything that France had gone through, ten years after Louis XVIII had granted the charter that was intended to reconcile the French with the Bourbons, an attempt to restore absolute monarchy smacked of madness. Even so determined a counterrevolutionary as Metternich condemned this policy of "mad dictatorship" as contrary to reason.

In any event, Lafayette—of whom Metternich had no higher opinion than he did of Charles X—was determined to resume the fight against the *Ultras*, who had still "learned nothing and forgotten nothing," and he felt more enthusiastic than ever and convinced that history would vindicate his position.

During the Revolution his property had been seized and sold at auction, and although Adrienne had been able to restore some of her patrimony, Lafayette himself had never recovered his fortune that had made so many envious when he became a millionaire at the age of thirteen. That loss of property was the only thing he had in common with the aristocrats who hated him.

When Charles X, who, like Louis XVIII before him, had been constantly petitioned by those whose property had been seized, decided after many discussions to grant them an indemnity, the so-called "billion for the émigrés," Lafayette had no qualms about accepting the sum he was allocated, 325,767 francs for his land in Auvergne.

This attitude might seem surprising when one considers his great unselfishness during both the American and French Revolutions, but it was neither a gift nor a payment for services but the restitution of a modest portion of his family fortune, and he had no reason to surrender it to a government that he was combating. He also had obligations to his children, and his generosity could be relied on to use the money for the benefit of the persecuted whom he continued to support until he died.

In June 1827, he recovered his seat as a deputy that he had lost in 1824 to Baron Pinteville de Cernon, who had died in May. As soon as he returned to the Assembly, he showed that he had lost none of his spirit. In August, he delivered the funeral oration for Jacques-Antoine Manuel, his colleague and companion in the struggle, using terms that were a call to the spirit of resistance against authority. The journalist François Mignet published an admiring account, for which he was tried on criminal charges.

While Charles X gave some hope of an opening to the liberals when he intervened in favor of the Greeks against Turkey and relaxed some press restrictions, the way he reversed the latter step alienated from him anyone who believed compromise was possible. Since all measures taken by royal authority were subject to vigorous discussion, the king decided to take the easy way out by dissolving the Chamber, convinced that a larger number of deputies supporting him would be elected. The result was contrary to his expectations, and the monarch held Prime Minister Villèle, who was close to the *Ultras* but relatively moderate, responsible for this setback. He then decided to replace Villèle with Polignac, a committed *Ultra*, but this rankled even some at court; the king gave way and chose Martignac, a jovial southerner valued for his flexibility, who remained in office until August 1829.

During these two years, Lafayette was a powerful presence in the Chamber. It would be no exaggeration to say that he was the soul of the liberal opposition. As an example, he made an argument in favor of compulsory nationwide education. Education, he said, was the primary need of the French population, and the government's first duty to it. The government proposed a budget of fifty thousand francs for that department, and Lafayette's counterproposal was for one hundred times that. That was what "this great social duty" required. When it came to the University, this precursor of mass education denounced the invasion of the institution by the Jesuits, which was hardly to the liking of the very devout Charles X, nor did he appreciate Lafayette's attacks against the court's excessive expenditures and the enormous size of the civil list.

In 1829, Lafayette, who had tried to avoid breaking relations with Martignac, tried to secure a revision of the election law. A supporter of universal suffrage, he asked that at least all taxpayers (whatever the amount of the taxes they paid) be allowed to participate themselves or through their intermediaries in voting for candidates for public office.

The king did not understand that this broadening of the electorate would in the end be to his advantage, because it would make electors out of naturally conservative farmers. Badly advised and extremely stubborn, Charles X dismissed Martignac, whom he considered too flexible, and reverted to his initial choice, the Prince de Polignac, who, through his blind obedience, would lead the king to his defeat.

Lafayette was not in Paris when the government changed. He was traveling in the provinces, first to Chavaniac and then to Grenoble, where his son George-Washington's daughter Nathalie had married a brother of the liberal banker Perier. This tour could have been called triumphal; he used speeches at banquets to strengthen the opposition, which was growing more organized and effective, largely thanks to the mistakes of its opponents.

The mayor of Grenoble bestowed on him a crown of silver and laurel, to the applause of a large crowd. It was almost as though the American tour was beginning again. Lafayette hailed Grenoble as the city where "the first banner of freedom flew." He was welcomed with such enthusiasm by the mayor and citizens of Vizille that the government dismissed the mayor. In Voiron, Bourgoin, Vienne, and Lyon, he received the same enthusiastic welcome and, he and his friends addressed the same warnings to the government, suspected, with some justification, of intending to completely eliminate the Charter and establish rule by decree.

Lafayette sometimes adopted a threatening tone, as in Lyon, where he said he was heartened by "the calm and even disdainful firmness of a great people who knows its rights, feels its strength, and will faithfully do its duty." He suspected that the royal authority intended to take illegal actions and he said so loudly and clearly, but the measures had to be published before people responded.

If his purpose in undertaking this tour was to galvanize the energies of the liberal camp, Lafayette had succeeded. One hundred thousand copies of a pamphlet covering the triumphal journey and the public positions he expressed in the cities visited were published and distributed. Back at La Grange, he could wait for Charles X and his faithful servant Polignac to continue to accumulate political mistakes. In 1829, he promoted the candidacy of Guizot to the Chamber to replace Vauquelin. Although he did not consider Guizot sufficiently democratic, he admired his cultivation, talent, and probity.

To cover his attempt to restore complete control over institutions, the king needed some foreign success, and for that he needed an enemy. There was one who was really ideal, who could be fought effectively with a great likelihood of success and without taking the risk of setting all Europe ablaze: the dey of Algiers. The expedition was organized, and French forces began landing on June 13, 1830; by July 5, the city of Algiers had been taken.

In France, despite the fuss made by the *Ultra* newspapers that hailed the army's victory, the news was not greeted with great celebrations. The citizens were too absorbed by the elections, which ran from June 23 to July 19. The conquest of Algiers was of no benefit to the right; the opposition increased its numbers from 221 to 274 deputies. The king responded to these distressing results for the government in place with a challenge, which turned out to be suicidal. As Lafayette had foreseen, he set in motion a coup d'état which had all the appearances of legality. Four ordinances prepared in secret were published on July 26 in *Le Moniteur*. Their content can be summarized as follows:

1. suspension of freedom of the press, restoration of prior authorization;

2. eligibility for office and for voting rights based solely on property taxes;
3. dissolution of the newly elected Chamber; and
4. setting the date for new elections.

Thiers declared: "Legal rule has been suspended and the rule of force has begun. . . . Obedience is no longer a duty." Charles X in his blindness had himself set off the revolution. The newspapers, published without authorization in contravention of the ordinances, were the first to respond to the challenge by giving an example of "resistance to authority that has shed the aspect of legality" (*Le National*, an Orleanist paper).

For his part, the king left it to General Marmont, Duke de Raguse, to maintain order, with ten thousand men and inadequate reserves of supplies and arms, while Charles himself remained in his summer residence at Saint-Cloud devoting his days to hunting.

"It is up to France to determine how far its own resistance should go," Thiers had declared in his manifesto on the resistance of the press. On July 27, the deputies were not yet thinking of moving on to the insurrectional phase. Most of the liberals, following Casimir Perier and Guizot, wanted to stick for the moment to legal action and protest against the ordinances. But the situation swiftly escaped from their control. That evening soldiers fired on demonstrators at the stock exchange and the Palais-Royal. There were fatalities.

Lafayette hurried from La Grange to Paris. Polignac had signed an order for his arrest that Marmont did not dare execute. As soon as he returned to Paris, Lafayette's popularity grew even further, and his name spread like wildfire. He was the man on whom had devolved the task of bringing down the monarchy. He was aware of this, and he brushed aside his colleagues, including Guizot, who wanted to continue the dialogue with the king on legal grounds. In his view, the Charter had been well and truly violated, and the troops had dared to fire on innocent citizens. It was the king and his ministers who had taken the path of illegality, not the people. Insurrection, in an expression he had made famous in other circumstances, had become the "most sacred of duties." And the insurrection had begun, regardless of what the "legalist" deputies said, wished for, or did. Marmont grouped his men around the Louvre and the Tuileries and called for reinforcements from the provinces. While the members of parliament considered what measures they should take at their meeting on July 29—Lafayette had spoken of establishing a provisional government—the *charbonniers* set up insurrectional committees during the night in the twelve *arrondissements* that made up the Paris of the time. At the same time, citizen delegations went to Lafayette to ask him to take command of the National Guard, as in 1789. As soon as the deputies met under Laffitte as presiding officer, they ratified that nomination. In charge of the safety of the capital, the new head of the National Guard, at the age of seventy-three, hastened to put on the old uniform that had been made forty-one years earlier. The deputies created a five-member municipal commission, consisting of Laffitte, Perier, Lobau, de Schonen, and Audry de Puyraveau. A sixth member was chosen, a young revolutionary who had distinguished himself in street battles named Mauguin.

In the crowd of demonstrators was a young man of twenty who was following the events with enthusiasm and some degree of anxiety. For him, as for all young men, the revolution represented hope. But perhaps he already sensed that he would be disappointed by the results of the July Days. His name was Alfred de Musset. Four years later, in the course of the year in which the man most disappointed by July, old General Lafayette, was buried, the young writer put the finishing touches to his play *Lorenzaccio*. It contains these revealing lines: "The duke is dead; another must be chosen, and that as soon as possible. If we don't have a duke tonight or tomorrow, it's all over for us. The people are ready to boil over. . . ." It is impossible not to think that in dramatizing a political event in sixteenth-century Florence, he was recalling the exciting moment between two reigns that he had witnessed in Paris in 1830.

If one considers the fact that the insurrectional committees were controlled by *charbonniers*, that there were *charbonniers* on the municipal commission itself, and one also takes into account the growing popularity of Lafayette, who was solicited from all sides for orders and instructions, it can be asserted that, as at no other moment in his life, the Hero of Two Worlds was in a position to determine by himself the future of France. He had force and the confidence of the people at his disposal. Marmont was retreating to ever-shrinking positions. None of his colleagues was in a position to set himself up as a rival. From a public building of his choice, he could have proclaimed the Republic: he would have aroused popular enthusiasm and been begged to present himself as candidate for president in a contest he was guaranteed to win. This opportunity to become the leader of an authentic democracy, to raise himself to the rank of a French Washington, was in his hands during the *Trois Glorieuses* of 1830. Why did the dream not become a reality, when, as an added virtue, it could have happened without bloodshed?

Because, although he had once dreamed of becoming the French Washington, and others thought he still did, this was not what drove him in July 1830. Was the Republic the fitting regime for France? He was not sure. Demonstrators acclaimed him on his return to Paris, and the next day asked him when the Republic would be established. He did not answer. Some days earlier, on

July 21, he had asked the American ambassador, William Rives, what his American friends would say if the Republic was proclaimed in Paris, he was told: "They will say that forty years of experience have been lost to France." So his country was not yet ripe to institute the regime that was closest to his heart. But when would it be? The fact that a representative of free America had expressed this skepticism must have impressed Lafayette. His attitude in July 1830 also proves that this ambitious dreamer was not really seeking power, because in the course of those heady days he could have taken power with no difficulty. It is impossible to question his sincerity when he wrote that he was "ambitious for glory not for power."

During the *Trois Glorieuses*, he kept all this to himself, and concentrated on seriously organizing the defense of the Parisian people, of whom he said that their courage, devotion, and virtue (and this applied to "the lowest social classes," he added) had been admirable.

On July 29, when there were already eight hundred dead and five thousand wounded among the people of Paris, Charles X, understanding his mistake too late, withdrew the ordinances and appointed a prime minister he thought acceptable to the liberals, Mortemart, whom he dispatched to Paris to announce his decisions. The cautious newly appointed prime minister in Saint-Cloud sent a colleague, Colin de Sussy, to the Chamber to establish contact. The liberal deputy Benjamin Constant told Sussy that the government was no longer recognized.

While Lafayette was attempting to maintain courtesy in the break with Charles X and his ministers, an active group led by Adolphe Thiers was maneuvering to deprive the head of the National Guard of his position as arbiter and to block any personal ambitions for power in a republic that he might have. One never knew.

Thiers and his friends, who advocated a truly constitutional monarchy, which could only be Orleanist, started to cover the walls with posters appealing to the Duke d'Orléans, and Thiers himself persuaded Lafayette that the duke, a former general under the Convention, would protect freedom better than anyone if he was made to acknowledge that he held the throne only because of the will of the French people.

The pace of events accelerated, although the future Louis-Philippe, who concealed his cunning behind his apparent good nature, pretended to hesitate to ascend the throne held out to him, a throne he had long dreamed of. But the duke thought he was not popular enough. Lafayette replied in the negative to the friends who asked him if he wished to become president of the Republic and recommended that the Duke d'Orléans, "one of the patriots of 1789," be appointed lieutenant-general of the kingdom.

But a conflict broke out between the municipal commission and the Chamber of Deputies on the manner in which things should be presented to the nation and on the process of the duke's accession to the office of lieutenant general. It was once again up to Lafayette to arbitrate. Even the American ambassador urged him to accelerate the movement in favor of the Duke d'Orléans.

On July 31, at two in the afternoon, the son of Philippe Égalité, who knew that he could gain legitimacy only from the Hôtel de Ville, rode on horseback, wearing a general's uniform with a tricolor cockade, to the seat of Parisian power, followed by 89 deputies.

He was booed along the way but remained calm. He was playing a delicate game. He knew that he could be harassed and even molested by republican activists, of whom there were many at the Hôtel de Ville, and he also knew that he could receive the public approval he sought only through Lafayette. This was the man he had to please at any cost. Hence, on his arrival he presented himself as a veteran of the National Guard paying a visit to his former general. The gesture was clever. Lafayette, seated on the second floor, greeted him, and the duke respectfully reminded the general that he had fought at Valmy and Jemappes in the ranks of the republicans. Lafayette could no longer put off taking a definitive public position. The crowd waited in the square outside in anxious anticipation. Recovering his sense of public relations, Lafayette no longer hesitated. He took the duke by the arm, held a tricolor flag in his other hand, and headed toward the balcony. Thousands of eyes were fixed on the two men. Lafayette, an extraordinary communicator, sensing that the crowd was hanging on every one of his gestures, took the prince in his arms—with more resignation than enthusiasm in his heart—and wrapped the tricolor around him.

Whether or not he really said at that point "This is the best of Republics" in no way affects the powerful symbolism of the scene on the balcony on July 31, 1830, that put a definitive end to a dynastic branch and marked a step forward for freedom.

CHAPTER FORTY-TWO

THE SEASON OF FAREWELLS

O N THE EVENING OF DECEMBER 13, 1830, IN A COLD and damp Paris, a great man was buried, one of the men who had embodied liberalism since 1815. Less than five months earlier, on July 31, he had been carried in a chaise in the procession of his colleagues in the Chamber following the Duke d'Orléans from the Palais-Royal to the Hôtel de Ville, where the duke had come, according to Chateaubriand, "to beg for the crown." The deceased was Benjamin Constant. He had barely survived the establishment of the constitutional monarchy he had hoped and prayed for, although from the very beginning of the new regime he had joined the ranks of the opposition. The government nonetheless manifested its respect and recognition at his passing. Ministers, generals, peers of France, deputies, and all the dignitaries of the kingdom were there, along with the people of Paris, whose presence had an entirely different significance. Six legions of the National Guard preceded and six followed the coffin. A cavalry squadron headed the procession. The drums were muffled, and black ribbons fluttered in the breeze with the flags. The crowd following the procession was so dense that it moved more slowly than had been anticipated. Night had fallen when the hearse entered the cemetery, and the burial was conducted by torchlight.

Among the shadowy figures gathered around the open grave, one was taller than all the rest. As he approached the grave the others moved aside. He was heard to say a few words. The torches illuminated a very pale face that the others suddenly recognized: it was Lafayette, Constant's old friend, his companion in struggle in the Chamber, who said a few words of farewell to the man who had passed on. But his emotion and the cold sapped the energy of the old fighter. He suddenly felt faint, lost his balance, and almost fell into the hole into which the coffin had just been lowered. Louis Blanc, who witnessed the scene, wrote: "Everything had now been said, and the crowd melted into the shadows."

The death of Benjamin Constant in December 1830 had a symbolic value for Lafayette. He had only three years and five months left to live, and during this last period of his life, funerals of friends were to have consequences for his own fate. But in Constant's grave had been interred not just the body of a friend, ten years younger than he, but also the illusions they had shared in July.

It has been said that Lafayette the republican made a king. This was particularly true in the realm of public presentation. Louis-Philippe and his supporters needed Lafayette's blessing, a public gesture from him, the backing they would receive from his huge popularity. He had not dreamed up this solution in solitude and then tried to persuade others of its advantages.

The Duke d'Orléans was primarily the candidate of Thiers, the banker Laffitte, Odilon Barrot, and Armand Carrel. This group of men, who knew what they wanted, required Lafayette's agreement, and they got it. Without the weight he threw into the scale at the last moment, matters would not have been so simply resolved, because there were many republicans prepared to fight. Lafayette's intervention had made it possible to avoid a long and bloody revolution with an uncertain outcome. But unlike Thiers, he did not know what he wanted, except to have the hateful ordinances abrogated, get rid of the Polignac government that had passed them, and institute a real regime of freedom, faithful to the spirit of the Charter and going beyond it through measures of gradually increasing democratization. Because he would derive his power from the two Chambers, that is, theoretically from the people, because he accepted the tricolor flag and the title "King of the French," because he gave up the coronation at Reims, and because he was associated with the democratic "program of the Hôtel de Ville," the Duke d'Orléans appeared to be a crowned president of the Republic setting the country on that path. But only in appearance.

When he became king, Louis-Philippe told Lafayette that he agreed with him that what was suitable for the French people was "a popular throne surrounded by entirely republican institutions." Subsequent events justify casting doubt on his sincerity. At the outset, Charles X, who was still at Saint-Cloud pretending to believe and asserting that he still represented legitimate authority, had to be forced to abdicate. He would have to give up the idea of naming his grandson the Duke de Bordeaux as his successor, and go into exile with dignity. The next priority was to arrest and try Polignac and his ministers, responsible for having violated the Charter by promulgating the

July 26 ordinances and for having ordered that the people of Paris be fired on, although they had merely been demanding that their rights be respected. Polignac, Guernon-Ranville, Peyronnet, and Chantelauze were captured before they could flee abroad. They were tried by the Chamber of Peers and sentenced to long prison terms, after Lafayette, following an old habit of his, had saved them from an attempted lynching.

On August 9, following a decision by parliament, Louis-Philippe was proclaimed king at the Palais-Bourbon, where the peers had joined the deputies. The benches were festooned with tricolor flags. Four marshals of the Empire carried the insignia of this unprecedented kingship to the new monarch on velvet cushions. This was far from the pomp of Reims. No foreign state had yet recognized the new regime. But in the population's eyes, this historic event was the work of Lafayette. The Parisians presented him with two cannons intended to be set symbolically at the entrance to his château at La Grange. On August 15, the city of Paris gave a banquet in his honor with 350 guests, including the cabinet ministers of the new government.

A famous singer named Nourrit sang a hymn composed in his honor, and the guests stood to sing the chorus. The new Prefect of Seine, his friend Alexandre de Laborde, delivered a speech in his praise. The next day the king appointed him commander in chief of the National Guards of the entire country; until then, he had commanded these forces that had come out of the insurrection only in Paris. On that day he was indeed the rampart of freedom.

Was this finally the glory that he had pursued with varying results since the age of nineteen? It had all the appearances of being just that. It was not missing titles, honors, hymns, popular acclaim, praise in the press, or success in the salons, but the glory was ambiguous, not to say poisoned.

Lafayette was a symbol, an immense symbol, an admirable statue who occupied a considerable place in the new landscape of France, but the king and his most trusted ministers, formidable politicians, wanted him to be nothing but that. Louis-Philippe was in a hurry to pay off his debt of gratitude. He admitted that he owed Lafayette a good deal, but he did not want to have him as a mentor. The king might very well appear to be a simple bourgeois with manners as democratic as those of an American senator; he was hungry for power, had an elevated idea of his own abilities, a very cool head, and a good deal of stubbornness. In his view, Lafayette was simultaneously a figure from the past and a bothersome political ally. If he were given free rein, the regime, in which he considered himself a participant, would drift dangerously to the left, since the country had not yet recovered its stability.

Already on August 7, this "disciple of the American school," as Lafayette called himself, had asked for the abolition of the hereditary peerage. On August 17, he called for the abolition of the death penalty, a proposal he had already made to the Constituent Assembly forty years earlier.

The new regime was not yet fully in place when he called for the abolition of the slave trade, the erection of a monument to the memory of the Four Sergeants of La Rochelle and their transfer to the Pantheon, the presentation to the king of all political prisoners since 1815, the removal of the proscription that prevented members of the Bonaparte family from living in France, and the reduction of the king's civil list. How far would one go if one were to follow this terrible old man, more enthusiastic and agitated than when he had been thirty?

Perhaps the king had been too indulgent by appointing him commander of the National Guard, to which Lafayette dared to address an order of the day shortly before Christmas 1830 declaring: "Everything has been done for public order. Our reward is to think that everything will be done for freedom." What did he mean by that last sentence? Had the king not already done everything for freedom that could be expected from him; and what were the limits of this freedom in the mind of the man who seemed to utter nothing but that word? The time seemed to have come for Louis-Philippe, sooner than he had expected, to seriously rein in the man who thought he had made him king.

The procedure chosen was singularly lacking in elegance, but then, political struggle is seldom elegant. On December 24, 1830, the Chamber approved a bill organizing the National Guard. It provided that command would be exercised only at the local level. Lafayette was thus deprived by law of a tool that gave him real power in the country. From one day to the next, he was demoted to the rank of head of the National Guard in the city of Paris alone. He refused the title of honorary commander intended to appease him, and offered his resignation, which the king accepted with "deep regret," after trying to persuade him to reverse his decision by sending emissaries for whom Lafayette had some respect, such as his cousin General de Ségur.

Louis-Philippe may have acted too soon. By the end of the year, less than five months after the Revolution, Lafayette had resumed his role in the opposition, which seemed to be his natural place.

From then on, he would defend all the causes in France and around the world that he considered just, with no concern for immediate political circumstances, persuaded that the king would lose his throne in a few years if he did not frankly play the democratic card, just as Charles X had lost his. He no longer wanted to be merely a flag dividing his time between La Grange and the few salons he frequented in Paris.

He fought for the rights of Poland, appealing to Britain and Sweden, and urging the French government to act. He fought for the freedom of Ireland, and called for the independence of Belgium, where some patriots wanted to call on him not as the leader of insurrectionary forces, nor as president, but as king, a proposition that he found simultaneously touching and funny.

In the elections of June 1831 he was again elected deputy for Meaux and for Strasbourg, where admirers had voted for him as a write-in candidate. Out of loyalty, he chose to represent Meaux. He was also regional councilor for Seine-et-Marne, and mayor of Courpalay, the little town that was a dependency of his château.

He was recognized in the Chamber as the greatest opposition figure. He tried in vain to have the electoral law changed to bring it as close as possible to universal suffrage. He wanted to replace the Chamber of Peers with an elected Senate, and he failed to achieve this reform as well. The peers stayed in place, but he at least secured the end of hereditary transmission of seats. Armed with this success, he tried to reduce the length of their mandate to fifteen years. Casimir Perier, the hard-line prime minister who had replaced Laffitte, opposed his views, despite the esteem in which he held Lafayette's character.

In May 1832, Lafayette, who had lost all his illusions about the new regime, participated in a banquet at which toasts were drunk to the Republic, which gives an inkling as to his state of mind.

On June 5, he followed the funeral procession of his friend, the liberal General Lamarque, whose body was solemnly transported to the Pont d'Austerlitz, from which the coffin was to be taken to Mont-de-Marsan, his native town, for burial. As he had for Constant, Lafayette delivered a eulogy for Lamarque, exalting the great hopes of 1789 and of the end of the reign of Charles X, but he prevented excited supporters from seizing the body to take it to the Pantheon. This earned him widespread jeers, and he heard some activists talk of throwing him into the Seine in the hope of having the crime blamed on the government. He returned home in great disappointment. But the demonstration resumed and spread in a totally unforeseen way. Red flags appeared. A portion of the National Guard (now commanded by General Mouton de Lobau) refused to repress the disturbance in contravention of their orders.

The next day, the hard core of the insurgents, who had gathered near the Saint-Merri cloister, had to be defeated with cannon fire. The forces of order had prevailed, but the repression exacted a toll of eight hundred victims. Shocked by this ferocity, which he called "counterrevolutionary," Lafayette resigned his posts as mayor and regional councilor, offices that he held from a government that he reproached for having gone back on its commitments.

In his last two years, he was more than a member of His Majesty's opposition, critical but courteous and playing the institutional game: he was an open opponent of the regime of which he had been one of the principal "founding fathers." He attended political banquets where the toasts made left no doubt as to the sentiments of the participants toward the king and his government. And in the Chamber itself, in January 1834, on the occasion of the debate on the address to the king, he asserted that the country was being led down a retrograde path.

His voice was again heard raised to call for freedom of association and to protest against the abandonment of Poland. His last speech was in fact in support of a demand for aid to Polish refugees, some of whom he was sheltering in his château in La Grange.

On February 1, 1834, the burial of a third friend had a direct effect on his personal destiny. This time it was the liberal deputy from Eure, Dulong, killed in a duel with General Bugeaud. The distance from the home of the deceased, rue de Castiglione, to Père-Lachaise is significant. Lafayette nonetheless covered it on foot, in the bitter cold, despite the fact that he still had to use a cane. As at the funeral of Constant, from standing for so long he felt faint, but this time more seriously. He was carried home. After two months of care, he seemed to have recovered. He remained in his room but read and wrote a good deal. In April 1834, following Lyon, there were troubles in Paris. A mob took over the Marais neighborhood. Repression was even harsher than in 1832. Once again, Lafayette protested against the brutality of the government and its threats to limit freedom. Paradoxically, the only good political news came from England, where Parliament was discussing laws in favor of the emancipation of slaves. He could not help but applaud this positive move, even though it came from a country he had fought against. He occasionally went out for an evening. Stendhal observed him in a salon among friends: "M. de Lafayette, at the tender age of seventy-five, has the same defect as I do. He is fascinated by a young Portuguese woman of eighteen who has come into M. de Tracy's salon, where she is friends with his granddaughters. . . . He imagines that this young Portuguese woman, like any other young woman, is taken with him; he thinks only of her, and what's amusing it that he's often right to think the way he does. His European fame, the basic elegance of what he says, despite its apparent simplicity, his eyes that sparkle whenever he finds himself one foot away from a pretty breast, everything contributes to his spending his final years in gaiety, to the great scandal of the women of thirty-five who frequent this salon."

On May 9, 1834, he thought he was sufficiently recovered to go for a ride in his carriage. He was mistaken; the weather was still unsettled, and he had a relapse. This time medical treatment turned out to be futile.

On May 20, 1834, at four in the afternoon, the major-general of the American army, lieutenant-general of the French army, deputy from Seine-et-Marne, Gilbert du Motier, marquis de Lafayette, member of the Supreme Council of the Ancient and Accepted Scottish Rite, gave up the ghost after kissing a gold medallion containing the portrait of his wife, Adrienne.

The national funeral ceremony in Paris on May 22, 1834, proceeded in perfect order from his home to Picpus cemetery, where he was buried next to his wife in a coffin that was covered with the soil he had brought back from Brandywine in 1824.

The authorities had taken measures to make certain that popular excitement would not cause the slightest disturbances during the ceremony. The army was in charge of security and it had carefully surveyed the entire route. Deputies and peers of France, along with members of official bodies, and the highest civilian and military dignitaries followed the hearse under army supervision. Three thousand members of the National Guard, led by their commander, followed in uniform but without weapons.

The ceremony went on for six and a half hours. Only a few officials were allowed to approach the grave. The people of Paris had only their tears and their memories. Among the deputies following the procession was one who had only been sitting since 1833. His name was known for reasons that had nothing to do with politics. He was one of the most prominent of the Romantic poets, and young men and women frequently knew his *Méditations poétiques* by heart. He had given up a diplomatic career to join the liberal battle (without giving up poetry) and became an opposition deputy at the moment Lafayette left the scene. Fourteen years later, he was a minister in the Second

Republic, and then saw his hopes swept aside, as Lafayette had seen his defeated in after 1830. This new deputy—who when the decree instituting the Second Republic in 1848 was issued proclaimed: "We are going to make the most sublime poetry"—was named Alphonse de Lamartine.

The ceremony in France had all the trappings of reasonableness. The mourning in America, his spiritual home, was more heartfelt, even on the official level. On June 24, the House of Representatives and the Senate expressed their grief and declared a national period of mourning of thirty days. The eulogy delivered on December 31 by Speaker of the House John Quincy Adams was published, and sixty thousand copies were sold. All army and navy flags were flown at half-mast; countless services were held in churches of every denomination; funeral rites were organized in all Masonic lodges, which were draped in black with silver tears.

In Paris, an American flag was put up next to the grave, and it has been replaced annually since then every July 4 by the American embassy.

CHAPTER FORTY-THREE

LAFAYETTE,
EXEMPLARY FREEMASON

FREEMASONRY, AS WE HAVE SEEN, PLAYED A LARGE ROLE IN
Lafayette's life. He sought initiation in Paris at the age of
eighteen and remained faithful to that choice until he
died. Freemasonry was, of course, in fashion when he was
admitted, especially among the aristocrats who prided themselves on their liberal ideas, admired the Enlightenment
philosophes, and wanted to be in the vanguard in every area—
science, politics, art, and literature. But the lodges also accepted
commoners: lawyers, doctors, artists, and artisans. Many of the
upper nobility joined Freemasonry only out of snobbery, to have
it be known that they belonged, that they participated in "sublime labors," and also to bestow grandiose titles on themselves.
Membership for most of them was only fleeting.

"They're all in it," said Marie Antoinette about courtiers in a
letter to her brother. It is true that Masonic lodges had great

power under the monarchy and that the greatest names in France frequented lodges, although some of them were motivated by snobbery. This was not true of Lafayette, who took Masonic teaching very seriously and always tried to conduct himself in conformity to the ideal professed by the order.

He was introduced to a lodge in Paris by its former president, Adrienne's uncle Ségur. One of his fellow members there was his brother-in-law Louis de Noailles, to whom he remained very close until Noailles's premature death in 1804. His Masonic initiation coincided, unsurprisingly, with a period of intense intellectual curiosity. He read Rousseau, Montesquieu, and above all Abbé Raynal, who made him dream of America. At another lodge in Paris, he encountered Benjamin Franklin. In all of them, Lafayette discovered the importance and attractiveness of the notions, of freedom, virtue, and equality among men, the three pillars of his lifelong idealism.

When Lafayette, who was aide de camp to Washington, himself a noted Mason, revealed that he, too, was a Mason, their relations, as he wrote to Adrienne, greatly improved, and they gradually became truly fraternal. The young major general was able to frequent local lodges for American soldiers, as well as the one established by officers in Rochambeau's expeditionary force, where French and American Masons met together.

When he wrote to his wife that "America is going to become the sure and respectable haven of virtue, honesty, equality, and tranquil freedom," his words were close to the ideal of the Mason, who, by definition, according to the ritual of the time, was "friend to both rich and poor if they were virtuous." When he returned to France, he was delighted to meet again with his "brother" Benjamin Franklin. Adrienne herself embroidered the Masonic apron that Washington wore on the day he laid the cornerstone for the Capitol building in the city that became the capital of the new nation.

During the French Revolution, despite what has been said, Freemasonry split. Masons were found in opposing parties, and others emigrated. As early as October 1789, Lafayette was opposed for political reasons to Philippe Égalité, who was grand master of the Grand Orient de France, but a superficial Mason, who dishonored himself by accepting the banning of his order in 1793, on the pretext that Republics have no need of secret societies.

When Napoleon took control of the lodges, made up, during his reign, essentially of opportunists and social climbers, Lafayette generally abstained from Masonic activity until the Restoration.

His journey to America in 1824–25, in contrast, was a veritable Masonic festival. In Charlotte, he was elevated to the highest rank in the Scottish Rite. On his return to France, he was received in triumph in many lodges, particularly in the Lyon region.

It can be said the Freemasonry and Masonic music graced his final years as they had nourished the days of his youth in France and America. On October 30, 1830, the Duke de Choiseul, a high Masonic official, presided over the banquet given in his honor at the Hôtel de Ville. But the old fighter was no more intoxicated by Masonic honors than he was by any other kind. He was committed, whenever it was in his power, to defend his brothers who were persecuted around the world, and he modestly continued to assist in the work of a small lodge in Seine-et-Marne, whose members were essentially minor civil servants and farmers.

He proved by his actions that he was faithful to the principles of freedom, tolerance, equality, and fraternity, deeply convinced that the only source of real progress for society was the intellectual and moral improvement that each individual had to seek for himself. For this constancy, his memory is venerated throughout the Masonic world, on the same plane as other great Masons, such as Washington, Franklin, Bolivar, and Garibaldi. For this reason, many lodges in Europe and North and South America still bear his name today.

CONCLUSION

THE SPACE OF DESIRE

W HAT IMAGE OF LAFAYETTE CAN BE CHOSEN AT THE
end of this book that is not a betrayal of the truth—
either his own truth or that of history?

However agitated his life, one constant passion dominated it,
and that is perhaps the key to his paradoxical nature. It is easy to
find him hesitant, tortuous, unable to play the great roles fate
offered him more than once; commentators have pointed to his
naïveté, his illusions, his sudden retreats, and yet he was all of a
piece. In an era marked more than many others by spectacular
reversals of attitude—not to say simple betrayals—it is hard to
find a man who was less changeable than he. The child who
admired rebellious horses that could not be broken defended
freedom in arms at the age of nineteen on a terrain of his own
choosing. He continued this battle until his last breath, with the
sword when necessary, as with political speech and action, and

always with honor. The freedom that he cherished above all was a freedom that he wanted to be noble and pure. His version of freedom did not drift toward license, anarchy, or crime, even though he briefly believed that a conspiracy could replace a revolution to restore to the people an inalienable right that had been taken from them.

Unlike so many, who have "advanced" ideas in their youth, and grow moderate or conformist with age and experience—a classic itinerary in every country—Lafayette was a combatant for freedom and equality who was more determined and fervent on the eve of his death than at the age of twenty, because, in his old age, his ideal no longer had to coexist with other inclinations. For this fundamental optimist, who was never blasé, never overcome with skepticism or weariness, the fight could never stop. Life moved forward only with the vision of the space of desire.

There was no category of victim of oppression or injustice that he encountered along the way that he did not defend. He supported the American colonists in their rebellion against the British yoke, he spoke out against black slavery, and he treated Native Americans as brothers. Back in France, he defended Protestants and Jews, whose situation he found unacceptable. He defended the Irish against Britain, the South Americans against Spain, the Poles against Russia, the Greeks against Turkey, and the Belgians against Austria. Today he appears to have been a precursor of the idea of European union—when he was released from the prison of Olmütz, he intended to go to Holland and identified himself as a "Batavian patriot."

Had he known the terrible ordeal of power, his combat could not have but lost its purity, sunk from the realm of the mystical to the realm of politics. A paladin of freedom, a standard bearer, a Romantic hero—it is fortunate that Lafayette was just that, nothing more. His image has remained vital, and thanks to him, freedom has maintained all its freshness. To the number of titles posterity has granted him, I will simply add that of poet of action.

Throughout his life, Lafayette attempted to introduce probity into politics. While Barras declared that "times of civil war are not times for morality," Lafayette advocated the contrary, and he was always loyal to his ideal.

Jefferson had said of him: "His foible is a canine appetite for popularity and fame; but he will get above this." He anticipated in a sense the twenty-first century and the world of stars who govern us, people who seek love from the public rather than the control over decisions, beings who are more eager for popularity than power. Lafayette analyzed himself in a letter to Washington: "I do not say that I have merit but I say, I have its consequences—viz., enemies. My popularity is great throughout the kingdom and in this city; but among the great folks I have a large party against me, because they are jealous of my reputation: in a word, the pit, to a man is for me, and in the boxes there is a division." The perversion of Versailles had struck again, the sun of jealousy. And posterity long had the same capricious attitudes.

Indeed, a moment came when the success of his ideas became the source of great grief. Does this mean that the naïve marquis was stupefied that his beautiful American thoughts ended in the blood of the guillotine? Lafayette's crime, in everyone's eyes, was his naïveté. This cliché, however, needs to be rectified. A serious study of the facts reveals that this is a false account that amounts to accusing him of all the misdeeds of the Revolution. Lafayette in fact attempted to conduct a revolution of ideas that would have brought about a constitutional monarchy and freedom for French citizens equal to that enjoyed in the United States. It is inappropriate to hold him responsible before the tribunal of history for the excesses that no human force at the time was able to restrain in the name of justice. Lafayette many times did what was in his power to save the royal family, despite Marie Antoinette's unjustified mistrust. There was reciprocal misunderstanding between these two stars glittering in the firmament of their age. But, from the mouth of the Duchess d'Angoulême—the daughter of Louis XVI—after her release from prison, came these words that put a definitive end to the endless debate about Lafayette's responsibility for the tragic fate of the monarchs: "If they had trusted M. de Lafayette more, my parents would still be alive."

French opinion about Lafayette has remained divided. He has been scorned because of his naïveté, and criticized for his apparent thirst for fame above substance. But figures as varied as Stendhal and Guizot recognized his unfailing generosity and nobility of character, and his devotion to justice. As for the Americans, they would never forget him. As John Quincy Adams declared in 1824: "We will always look on you as belonging to us."

Perhaps the sharpest view of his nature was that presented in a letter Mme de Staël wrote to him in 1797: "You are, as a hero and a martyr, so identified with freedom, that I can pronounce your name and the name of freedom alike to express what I desire for the honor and prosperity of France." The Hero of Two Worlds and prophet of two revolutions, Lafayette cut from the fabric of time the new clothes of his perpetual presence.

APPENDICES

APPENDIX ONE

Letter from George Washington
To Lafayette
On His Departure
December 8, 1784

In the moment of our separation, on the road as I travelled, and every hour since, I felt all that love, respect, and attachment for you, which length of years, and close connexion of your merits, have inspired me with. I often asked myself, as our carriages distanced, whether it was the last sight I ever should have of you, and though I wished to say no, my fears answered yes. I called to mind the days of my youth, and found they had long since fled to return no more; that I was now descending the hill I had seen diminishing for fifty-two years, and though I was blessed with a good constitution, I was of a short-lived family, and might soon expect to be entombed in the dreary mansions of my fathers. These things darkened the horizon, and gave a gloom to the future, consequently to my prospects of seeing you again. . . . It is unnecessary, I persuade myself, to repeat to you, my dear marquis, the sincerity of my regard and friendship: nor have I words which could express my affection for you were I to attempt it.

⬥

APPENDIX TWO

Lafayette's Reply
On Board the *Nymphe*
December 21, 1784

No, my dear general, our late parting was not by any means a last interview. My whole soul revolts at the idea, and could I harbour it an instant, indeed, my dear general it would make me miserable. I well see you never will go to France: the inexpressible pleasure of embracing you in my own house, of welcoming you in a family where your name is adored, I do not much expect to experience; but to you I shall return, and within the walls of Mount Vernon we shall yet often speak of old times. My firm plan is to visit now and then my friends on this side of the Atlantic, and the most beloved of all friends I ever had or ever shall have anywhere, is too strong an inducement for me to return to him, not to think that whenever it is possible I shall renew my so pleasing visits to Mount Vernon. . . .

Adieu, adieu, my dear general: it is with inexpressible pain that I feel I am going to be severed from you by the Atlantic.

Everything that admiration, respect, gratitude, friendship, and filial love can inspire, is combined in my affectionate heart to devote me most tenderly to you. . . . Be attentive to your health. Let me hear from you every month. Adieu, adieu.

❦

APPENDIX THREE

Letter from Lafayette to Latour Maubourg
On Adrienne's Death
December 24, 1807

I have not yet written to you, my dear friend, from the abyss of misery into which I have been plunged. I had nearly reached bottom when I conveyed to you the last expressions of her friendship for you and her confidence in your feelings for her. My sorrow takes comfort from being confided to the most constant and dearest confidant of all my thoughts, in the midst of all the vicissitudes among which I have often felt unhappy; but until now you have found me stronger than circumstances. Today, the circumstances are stronger than I. I will never recover.

During the thirty-four years of a union in which her tenderness, her goodness, and the loftiness, delicacy, and generosity of her soul charmed, embellished, and honored my life; I grew so accustomed to everything she represented for me that I did not distinguish her from my own existence. She was fourteen and I sixteen when her heart attached her to everything that could interest me. I thought I loved and needed her, but it was only by losing her that I have been able to disentangle what remains of myself for the remainder of a life that had seemed to me given over to many distractions, but that now seems to have no possibility of happiness or well-being. . . .

When she received the sacraments, it was important to her that I was present. She then sank into uninterrupted delirium . . . and at the same time was constantly gentle and obliging, always trying to say something agreeable; she was grateful for the care she was given, afraid to tire others, needed to feel useful to them, feelings and expressions of goodness that she would have expressed were she in perfect health. There was also a clarity in her thoughts, a finesse in her definitions, an appropriateness and elegance in her expressions that astonished all who were present or who heard of the admirable or charming words that came out of that mind in delirium.

Do not think that the dear angel had any fears about the life to come; her religion was entirely one of love and confidence. . . .

The fear of hell had never touched her. She didn't even believe in it for good, sincere, and virtuous people who had no religious opinions. "I do not know what will happen at the moment of their death," she said, "but God will enlighten them and save them." . . . "How happy I have been!" she said the day she died; "what a role, to have been your wife!" And when I spoke to her of my tender feelings: "It's true," she replied in a very touching tone, "yes, it's true. How good you are! Say it again. It is so pleasing to hear. If you don't feel loved enough," she said, "take it up with God, he gave me no more capacity than that. I love you," she said, in the midst of her delirium, "in a Christian and a worldly way, passionately." . . .

She was only mistaken about me for a moment or two when she convinced herself that I had become an ardent Christian. "You're not a Christian?" she said to me one day. And when I didn't answer, "I know what you are, you're a Fayettist." "You think I'm very proud," I answered, "but aren't you a little proud too?" "Oh yes!" she exclaimed, "I feel I could give my life for that sect."

One day, I spoke to her of her angelic sweetness. "It's true," she said, "God made me gentle, but it's not like your sweetness; I don't have such high ambitions; you are so strong at the same time that you are sweet; you see things from such a height. But I agree that I am sweet and that you are very good to me." "You're the one who is good," I answered, "and extraordinarily generous. You remember the first time I went to America? Everybody was furious at me, and you hid your tears at Ségur's wedding. You did not want to appear afflicted, for fear they would hold it against me." "That's true," she said, "it was a rather nice thing for a mere child, but how wonderful that you remember what happened so long ago. . . ."

No doubt she knew death was near when, after saying to me in a touching way, as she often used to do, "Have you been happy with me? You really are so good as to love me? Well then, bless me." When I answered, "You love me too, you will bless me," she gave me her blessing for the first and last time, with the most solemn tenderness. Then each of her six children approached one by one and kissed her hands and her face. She looked at them with inexpressible affection. She was even more certain of her approaching death when, fearing a convulsion, she made a sign that I should go away; when I stayed, she took my hand, placed it on her eyes with a look of tender gratitude, thereby indicating the final duty that she expected me to perform. With no apparent suffering, with a smile of benevolence on her lips, and still holding my hand, that angel of tenderness and goodness ended her life. I fulfilled the duty she had indicated. . . .

You know as well as I do everything she was, everything she

did during the Revolution. I am not praising her for coming to Olmütz, but for having taken the time beforehand to do everything in her power to protect the well-being of my aunt and the rights of our creditors, and for having had the courage to send George to America.

What imprudent nobility of heart to remain the only woman in France compromised because of her name who never wanted to change it. Every one of her petitions or declarations always began with these words: the wife of Lafayette. Never did this woman, so indulgent toward party animosities, even when she was in the shadow of the scaffold, allow a remark to be made against me without rejecting it; never did she avoid an opportunity to stand up for my principles and be proud to say that she took them from me. . . .

My letter would never end, my dear friend, if I surrendered myself to the feelings that dictate it. I will repeat again that this angelic woman was surrounded by tender feelings of grief worthy of her. . . .

I embrace you in her name, in mine, in the name of everything you have been for me since we have known each other.

Adieu, my dear friend.

MAJOR DATES
IN THE LIFE OF LAFAYETTE

1757   Birth of Gilbert Marie Joseph Paul Yves Roch de
        Lafayette in Chavaniac, Haute-Loire.

1759   Death of his father at the battle of Minden in
        Germany during the Seven Years' War.

1768   Student at the Collège du Plessis in Paris.

1770   Death of his mother.

1774   Gilbert de Lafayette marries Adrienne, daughter
        of the Duke d'Ayen.

1775   Stationed in Metz as officer in the grenadiers.
        Initiated as a Freemason in Paris.

1777   First journey to America, first battles.

1781   Participates in the victory of Yorktown.

1783   Present at the signature of the Treaty of Paris rec-
        ognizing the independence of the United States
        of America.

1789	Elected commander in chief of the National Guard (July 15).
1790	Personal triumph at the Fête de la Fédération on the Champ de Mars.
1791	Appointed by Louis XVI commander of the Army of the East.
1792	Falls into the hands of Austrian troops (August 19). Remains imprisoned until 1797.
1797–1799	Exile in Germany and Holland.
1799	Return to France.
1807	Death of Adrienne.
1815	Secures Napoleon's abdication after Waterloo.
1818	Elected deputy from Sarthe.
1824	Defeated in elections at Meaux.
1824	Triumphal journey to America.
1827	Elected deputy from Meaux.
1830	Participates in the July Revolution. Helps Louis-Philippe accede to the throne.
1834	Death of Lafayette.

INDEX

INDEX

INDEX